Mozart in Revolt

*Strategies of Resistance,
Mischief and Deception*

David Schroeder

Yale University Press
New Haven and London

Set in Ehrhardt by Best-set Typesetter Ltd., Hong Kong
Printed in Great Britain by The Bath Press, Bath

Library of Congress Cataloging-in-Publication Data

Schroeder, David P., 1946–
    Mozart in revolt: strategies of resistance, mischief, and deception / David Schroeder.
    Includes bibliographical references and index.
    ISBN 0–300–07542–1 (cloth: alk. paper)
    1. Mozart, Wolfgang Amadeus, 1756–1791 – Correspondence.
2. Mozart, Leopold, 1719–1787 – Correspondence.   3. Fathers and Sons – Austria –
History – 18th century.   4. Composers – Austria – Correspondence.   I. Title.
ML410.M9S378   1999
780'.92 – dc21   98-45830
[B]   CIP

A catalogue record for this book is available from the British Library

10 9 8 7 6 5 4 3 2 1

For Daniel, Linda and Emily
with love

Contents

Illustrations

Preface

For anyone whose relationship with a parent has not been entirely straightforward, and to one degree or another that may include almost everyone, Mozart's exchange of letters with his father proves to be of great interest. Responding to that appeal, we tend to jump into these letters with enthusiasm, reading them in the same way that we understand letters from over two centuries later. Our relationship with Mozart at the end of the twentieth century has become nothing short of intimate: we have without question appropriated him as one of our own. In our eagerness to embrace Mozart, we sometimes ignore that these letters were written in the eighteenth century, and that that century had its own unique approaches to letter writing. If we look for biography in them, we may very well be entirely on the wrong track. While we may not find biography, it soon becomes apparent that what we do find proves to be even more interesting. In this book I wish to share the enjoyment of what these letters may reveal, as well as offer a map which allows them to be explored in an eighteenth-century spirit.

English-speaking readers familiar with the Mozart letters will undoubtedly know them from Emily Anderson's translation in *The Letters of Mozart and His Family*, originally issued in 1938, revised in 1966, and reissued with slight adjustments in 1985. This translation has served us very well in many ways, and in fact until the comprehensive *Mozart: Briefe und Aufzeichnungen* of the early 1960s, provided the most extensive collection of Mozart letters in any language. Considering how acquainted readers may be with Anderson's translation, in many ways it would have been desirable to use it here, but for a number of reasons that proved impossible. Most problematic for a book that explores among other things the subversive side of the letters is the sense of propriety that governed this translation. While Anderson was remarkably straightforward in her translations of scatological language, she seemed less prepared to reveal the double entendres in some of Mozart's more sexually suggestive passages. For that and various other reasons, including the substantial portions of letters she has excluded, all translations of the Mozart letters are mine unless otherwise cited.

To avoid the hundreds of endnotes for these translations, I use the abbreviation 'MBA' for *Mozart: Briefe und Aufzeichnungen* (Kassel, Basel, London, New York, 7 vols, 1962–75) following each quoted passage as a parenthetical citation. Since translations from Otto Erich Deutsch's *Mozart: A Documentary Biography*, translated by Eric Blom, Peter Branscombe and Jeremy Noble (London, 1965), are also used with some frequency, I treat them in the same way with the abbreviation 'MDB'.

A research grant from the Social Sciences and Humanities Research Council of Canada allowed me to acquire essential material and made my travel to various libraries in Europe and North America possible.

I would like to thank Josef Mančal for sending me copies of his articles which I would not have discovered otherwise, and for his comments on some of my preliminary thoughts. I am also grateful to Pat Rogers who forced me to think in a more focused way about some issues. My contact with Malcolm Gerratt at the London office of Yale University Press has been fortunate, since his interest and encouragement kept the project on track. I also happily acknowledge the support of Robert Baldock from the same office.

Writing a book for me is a genuinely pleasurable experience, and that enjoyment can be heightened if another person – through enthusiasm for the project, discussion of the ideas, reading and rereading – lives through it with me. I am privileged to have such a person, my wife Linda Schroeder, whom I cannot thank enough for her willingness to share and for all that she has to offer.

Introduction

Our fascination with Mozart, spanning over two centuries, remains in no danger of decline. In 1991, the two-hundredth anniversary of his death, literally hundreds of new books on Mozart appeared, offering a dizzying and often contradictory array of impressions. To some he stands as a champion of the secular Enlightenment, representing the highest achievements of truth and virtue. To certain notable German theologians he embodies the highest levels of spirituality, exuding Christian-Catholic devoutness, going beyond his father's dreams of morality and devotion to a pinnacle of mystical ecstasy in his works. At the same time we have Peter Shaffer's notion in *Amadeus*, embellished by Miloš Forman in the cinematic version, of Mozart as a kind of disrespectful, misbehaved, punk-*Musiker*, who, much to Salieri's annoyance and distress, also happened to be a genius. In Salzburg, where Mozart was completely ignored for about a century after his departure (Mozart probably would have thought of it more as an escape) until city fathers discovered that the city's economic stability could be linked with their recalcitrant expatriot, they continue to coat him in layers of sweet chocolate around a core of marzipan and export him to the rest of the world as Mozart-Kugeln.

These portrayals and representations happily suggest that Mozart can be all things to all people, but one would, of course, like to discover something closer to the real Mozart. One of the obvious places to look for the real Mozart is among those who knew him – or at least lived at the same time, people who wrote the earliest biographies of him or provided information to those who wrote these portrayals. As sound as that approach may seem, it turns out to be full of holes, since we now know that these biographers were also incorrigible myth-makers, determined to create a revisionist Mozart who bore little resemblance to the one that lived from 1756 to 1791; they purged him of warts (or pockmarks) and defects, making him vulnerable to the current readings of enlightened and spiritual essence or susceptible to a thick coating of chocolate.

As the veracity of much of the secondhand information crumbles, we have turned increasingly to the composer's own words – his correspondence first and foremost with his father, but also with other family members and a large group of friends. This correspondence for many has taken on an increased burden, standing as the only documents we can trust – coming from the horse's mouth – providing us with an intimate and reliable picture of the events of Mozart's life, his attitudes and opinions, and information about the circumstances surrounding his compositions. While this embrace of the letters may be tacit for some, others have expressed it more overtly, such as Robert L. Marshall in his book *Mozart Speaks*, where he pursues his goal of revealing Mozart through his letters with the guiding assumption that the letters will yield 'nothing less than Mozart's mind: that is to say, his opinions, perceptions, intentions, ambitions about a large variety of topics – music chief among them – but only to the extent, of course, that he (or others) took the trouble to write them down'.[1]

But will they? Mozart seems so relevant to us, so in tune with our twentieth-century consciousness – our foibles, ambitions, aspirations, phobias and complexes – that we have succeeded in forgetting one of the most basic facts about him (one of the few that we can state with absolute certainty): he lived over two centuries ago. Since his death in 1791 much has happened that we take as progress; we have developed, especially in our own century, some very sophisticated critical, analytical or psychological means for making sense of the world, approaches that seem to us not only useful but essential to our sense-making processes. The relationship of Mozart and his father looms as central to the correspondence, and to come to terms with this relationship, it seems entirely sensible to apply the tools we have devised for such purposes in this century, including those of psychoanalysis. Here Mozart's letters become the raw material for analysis; father and son are placed on a couch and their written words become the grist for a psychoanalytical mill. The letters, or the riddles penned by Mozart for the Carnival of 1786, may, according to Maynard Solomon in *Mozart: A Life* (1995), 'help us understand something about Mozart's personality – and even, perhaps, his creativity, for raw materials such as these are better suited for psychological analysis than are structured works of art'. The post-Freudian analyst may even find oedipal interpretations, 'the hieroglyphics of a secret discourse, a deadly play between a father and his son. But this is no abstract contest for supremacy. The surface is comic, the undercurrent is terror, the "answers" are mostly phallic, but the subject may well be Mozart's mother, Leopold's wife, as an emblem of the feminine. She is the prize for whom the contest is waged.'[2]

Is that how we should attempt to make sense of this extraordinary father-son relationship? As for Mozart himself, can it be possible to miss the mark further than Solomon has with his diagnostic fascination with mutilation, matricide, incest, or a 'quasi-infantile stage of development'? Indeed it is: Dr Benjamin Simkin succeeded with his diagnosis of Tourette's Syndrome (a mental disorder marked by twitching and uncontrollable cursing) for the playful scatology in Mozart's letters.[3] This appropriation of twentieth-century methodology to the Mozarts requires a blissful ignorance of eighteenth-century life and customs, especially of the extraordinarily rich tradition of letter writing from that century, and a substitution of our own relatively impoverished approaches – our age having virtually abandoned letter writing except for the recent electronic variety – which assumes that by and large letters can be taken literally.

Letters were at the heart of the most important advancements in writing in the eighteenth century, including the novel, journalistic correspondence, biography, memoirs and private or public correspondences, and both Mozart and his father recognized the full potential of letters.[4] Among their own friends, acquaintances and correspondents were three of the great *épistoliers* (or *épistolières*) of the century: Baron Melchior Grimm, Mme Louise d'Épinay and Christian Fürchtegott Gellert, and even among these three one discovers an extraordinary diversity in epistolary approaches and strategies. The list quickly multiplies when one takes into account that Grimm and d'Épinay counted all the great *philosophes*, including Voltaire, Diderot, Rousseau, d'Alembert, Galliani and Holbach, as their colleagues on the *Correspondance littéraire*, or that Gellert, the leading epistolary stylist in Germany, had himself learned from Gottsched, had read numerous of the great English writers, and taught no less a luminary than Goethe. Leopold and Wolfgang Mozart were supreme strategists as letter writers, each developing his approaches in relation to well-established traditions, and the collisions, sideswiping and ultimate breakdown in their correspondence relate directly to their chosen approaches. Leopold the moralist emulated Gellert, designing a correspondence intended for a larger reading public, one in which he would be recognized as a leading thinker, moralist and epistolary tactition. Wolfgang in his early twenties had no desire to be the subject of an epistolary moral biography, and devised an evasive mode of response which would have done credit to the most subtly dissimulating of the French letter-writing masters.

How useful are the Mozart letters to a biographer? If Leopold Mozart himself intended them as the basis for a biography, we have to admit they are much less useful for our purposes than we may have thought. This book is not a biography of Mozart; if anything, it will make a biography more difficult to write. The relationship between Leopold and Wolfgang Mozart has come down to us as an epistolary narrative, one of the most extraordinary from the eighteenth century, not as case studies for psycho-biography. The chapters which follow will attempt a reading of the correspondence as an epistolary narrative, invoking the rich letter-writing approaches from the eighteenth century which oblige that type of reading. As such, this cannot be a study of a life in the usual sense of biography. The life in this case, separated from us by two centuries of myth and obscurity, and cloaked in disguise and dissimulation by its own subject, is too ephemeral to take on the mantle of biography. We must accept what we have and explore the possibility that that may in fact be much more fascinating than biography. To be sure, there are implications for the works, but the correspondence will not necessarily show us the person behind the works. At the heart of Mozart's letters lies a strategy of resistance to the moralizing of his father and a defiance of the enlightened despotism of political authority. Mozart's revolt had nothing to do with the Jacobins or any other revolutionary movements; his was one of personal strategy, borrowing from the great French *épistoliers* as well as the spirit of Carnival, a strategy as evident in his works as in his letters.

EIGHTEENTH-CENTURY LETTERS

The writing of letters, of course, existed before the eighteenth century, but not with the same passion or frequency. With the enlightened inclination to develop refinement and improve taste, letter writing emerged as an ideal vehicle since any literate person could engage in it, and the number of literate people grew rapidly during the eighteenth century. Letter writing became an alternative to conversation, allowing not only communication with people at a distance but providing an alternate mode of discourse with those close at hand. Some things, it was soon discovered, could be said with greater ease in letters than face to face, as Mozart for example realized in his dealings with Michael Puchberg, a person with whom he dined regularly but to whom he made requests for money only in his letters. As the volume of mail grew, the quality of the postal service increased with it, allowing for more than one post per day within cities and faster service abroad as it became economically feasible to increase the frequency of mail coaches. Not unlike the telephone early in the twentieth century, reserved because of prohibitive costs for business or particularly important calls, letter writing before the eighteenth century remained restricted to the privileged. With a telephone in every home and affordable service, the nature of communication shifted dramatically, the telephone becoming a vehicle for personal and intimate discourse, facilitating a previously impossible and far-reaching network. The letter provided a similar possibility in the eighteenth century, and women carried on much of the new flood of intimate discourse. Letters also became accessible to social classes previously shut out by lack of education or financial resources.

With the new personal function of letters, distinctly different from business or diplomatic uses, styles in letter writing also went through profound changes, and in encouragement of this, master writers provided the general literate population with instructional treatises and volumes of model letters. The English and French led the way with these changes, and in part this reflected intellectual and creative activities in those countries. The style of writing for business and diplomatic purposes was excessively formal and pompous, embellished with turns of phrase that could easily yield a complete lack of intelligibility – not unlike some bureaucratic or legal language which still exists. Whether or not businessmen or diplomats actually understood this language is open to question since probably no one else did. The flood of treatises on letter writing with accompanying model letters counteracting the old style, produced by many of the leading writers in any given country, emphasized the efficacy of a simpler, more natural style. 'Natural' did not mean degeneration into colloquialisms, local dialects or crudity; good taste could not be sacrificed, as instilling refinement in the population continued to be the highest goal for the enlightened writers of treatises.

In German-speaking countries the formal approach of official letters was referred to as the chancery style, with its tortuous sentence structures, artificiality, obsequiousness and bewildering vocabulary.[5] Writers of treatises such as Gellert railed against its absurdities and excesses, and that attitude was emulated by Gellert's epistolary disciples, not the least of whom was Leopold Mozart. On 28 September 1777, Leopold copied out an example of the chancery style from a clerk of his disagreeable employer, Archbishop Colloredo, for his son to enjoy, an official reply to a petition Leopold had submitted, commenting that Wolfgang would 'see how hard they must have worked – if only to put it together':

Ex Decreto Cels^{mi}. Principis, 26 Sept., 1777.
To signify to the petitioner that His Grace desires that there should be real harmony amongst his musicians. In gracious confidence therefore that the petitioner will conduct himself calmly and peaceably with the Kapellmeister and other persons appointed to the court orchestra, His Grace retains him in his employment and graciously commands him to endeavour to render good service both to the Church and to His Grace's person.[6]

Leopold then asks rhetorically: 'Have you in your life ever read such gobbledegook? Whoever reads the petition and then the document cannot help but believe that the Chancery Clerk wrote this document to the wrong petitioner' (MBA ii 17–18). Both father and son could delight in ridiculing this type of writing, as well as using it to cast aspersions on the court of the Archbishop, whom they both disliked with a passion. Leopold clarified his own approach to language – not only epistolary but more generally, a style Gellert had surely influenced – in a letter to Lorenz Hagenauer concerning a translation (which never materialized) of his *Versuch einer gründlichen Violinschule* (*A Treatise on the Fundamental Principles of Violin Playing*) into Italian by their mutual friend Rochus Alterdinger: 'Only I would remind you that, since it is a manual of instruction in a style of writing lacking pretention, it should, on the contrary, be translated, as in the original German, into clear and intelligible language understandable to the ordinary person' (MBA i 266–7). Treatises had a higher purpose than the mere transmission of information: they must elevate the reader to higher degrees of refinement and taste, and Leopold Mozart thoroughly understood the nature of language required to accomplish this.

LETTERS AND OTHER WRITING

The letter became enormously important in the eighteenth century, allowing for the transformation of a language like German into a literary language, but its role went much beyond itself, influencing virtually every type of writing, providing a foundation for literary as well as non-fiction genres. The transmission of news frequently took an epistolary form, as correspondents in one locale wrote about their home venue for the benefit of readers at a distance. If that locale was a centre like Paris, the largest city in Europe with the most active intellectual and cultural life, there was great demand not only from the French provinces but from other major European centres to keep abreast of philosophical thought, legal developments, cultural activities and publications. This demand could be satisfied in various ways, such as through the *Correspondance littéraire*, a project coordinated by Leopold Mozart's dear friend Baron Grimm with the participation of Mme d'Épinay, Diderot and numerous others, consisting of letters on philosophy, economics and politics, or letters as reviews of books, plays and concerts, sent to various subscribing heads of state in other countries. Not only were letters of correspondents sent from Paris to the outside, but correspondents from the provinces or from abroad kept the *philosophes* informed of events or developments in their locales. It should be understood that these were not actual newspapers going in either direction but were letters to be read by individuals or to be circulated among friends and colleagues. Since the French government often considered the content of the correspondence seditious, circulation was tightly controlled, distributed so as not to fall into the wrong hands.

The eighteenth century saw a proliferation of various types of magazines, finding the light of day because of their subject matter – music being a particularly popular subject – or because of their audiences or clientele, including professional men, young people or women. Once again the mode of writing in the magazines often took an epistolary form, as the writer could in this way address the concerns of the reader in a manner that seemed more direct and even personal. Since magazines sought a wide circulation and therefore stood in the public domain, content had to conform to the scrutiny of censors. As a result, some magazines or journals developed a distinctly moral tone to make them suitable for public consumption, in some cases, especially if directed to young readers, serving an almost exclusively moral function. One of the most effective pieces to include in this type of publication was that of the letter (or letters) from a parent to a child, giving the child the benefit of the parent's wisdom and experience – providing instruction on every conceivable situation or moral consideration that the child may encounter – in a style of presentation distinctly recognizable as a particular genre of letter. Other types of letters or formats included the sketches of moral characters well known in the English *Tatler* and *Spectator* and emulated in German publications such as *Der Vernünfftler*, edited early in the century by Johann Mattheson, a writer better known towards the middle of the century for his musical treatises.

Important as these epistolary accomplishments were, nothing could match the achievement of the novel, originating and consisting in the early stages exclusively as collections of letters. Considering the new emphasis on sentimentality and intimacy in the letter as well as the new more natural approach, the letter became the ideal vehicle for the creation of the novel, allowing the reader an inside and intimate view of the characters and appealing to the reader on this level. Just as letters provided correspondents an opportunity to open their hearts to each other, the epistolary novel afforded readers the same opportunity to share the most intimate thoughts and experiences with the subjects of the novel – to fall in love when they did or experience the pain of rejection, the humiliation of seduction, the embarrassment of mistakes, or the triumphs of success. For Samuel Richardson, epistolary converse transcended real life in emotional satisfaction, seen in the words (although etymologically misguided) he allowed Lovelace to express in *Clarissa*: 'familiar letter writing was writing from the heart . . . as the very word "*Cor-respondence*" implied. . . . Not the heart only; the *soul* was in it'.[7]

Novelists appealed especially to the new reading public of women, most frequently focusing on women as the central characters, as in Richardson's *Pamela* and *Clarissa* or Gellert's *Schwedische Gräfin* (Swedish Countess) male novelists entering a female domain and creating feminine personas. Individual letters in a novel could serve a variety of functions, involving love, intrigue, description or moralizing – including letters from a parent to a child. Since any given novel assembled hundreds of letters, the correspondence generated a narrative over a span of time, a narrative that could be complicated by multiple correspondents whose epistolary interaction necessarily maintained a continuity. Novels might very well fulfill a moral purpose, serving as warnings to young women of the dangers that lurked in domestic service or unsuitable marriages, or a novel could, as with Laclos's *Les Liaisons dangereuses*, defy any attempt to find morality.

The list of other epistolary-based modes of writing could go on and on, including memoirs which might very well consist in large part of portions of one's correspondence, or biography, which could be based on the biographer's correspondence with the subject. In both of these cases an element of fame would be assumed, celebrity that would provide a publisher with the assurance that it would be worth taking the risk involved. Once again, the project might very well serve a moral purpose, particularly in the case of biography where the subject could stand as a moral exemplar and the biography itself as a type of extended sketch of a moral character. The moral content could also be generated from the biographer's stance, as his own correspondence with the subject yields a moral narrative which the biographer controls in a way best suited to his purposes. Leopold Mozart, a skilled epistoler – in fact, a genuine initiate into the Republic of Letters – and writer of a treatise with a deep sense of moral imperative, a man who loved writing and wished that to be an integral part of his career, found himself in a situation in the early 1760s where, because of the extraordinary fame of his children, he could contemplate such a biography – not just a work to describe the rarified world of himself and his children, but a work of the highest moral calibre in the refinement, pleasure and advice it could provide. A number of the chapters which follow will chronicle Leopold's epistolary project and the ultimate response of Wolfgang to it.

LETTERS PUBLIC AND PRIVATE

While letters may have served an intimate function in the eighteenth century, as a rule they were anything but private. If letters acted as a substitute for conversation, then they simply broadened discourse and more often than not were intended to be read or heard by others. In France letters often stretched the horizons of the salons, allowing absent members to keep in touch with the larger group. One of the foremost of the *salonnières*, Mme d'Épinay, kept up active correspondences with various absent members of her salon, and in maintaining his end a correspondent such as Galiani responded that 'you know that I would love my letters to be read and viewed by all my friends. This is not out of vanity: it is to preserve me in their memory; it is because I would love to talk to them, and I no longer can.'[8] Letters circulated among members and friends or were read aloud at salons, making them an integral part of the salon discourse. The public aspect of letters proved so pervasive, expected and understood that a correspondent had to specify explicitly to the addressee if privacy or confidentiality was in order.[9] The same can be said of Leopold Mozart, who intended that his letters written to Salzburg while he was travelling throughout Europe with his performing children should be read to or circulated among the larger group of friends at home. Occasionally he directed some matters of business or sensitivity to his addressee Lorenz Hagenauer only, and these portions Leopold set aside, possibly on the letter cover, with the label 'For you alone'.

The distance between public readings of letters or other manuscripts and publications could be fairly small if the writings were appealing and engaging. Readings could cause a stir, as Grimm reported to Jean-François de la Harpe had happened to one of his pieces: 'The commotion made in Paris by the readings from circle to circle, and the reputation that they have given the work, have caused it to sell 2,000 copies in three times twenty-four hours'.[10] Dena Goodman points out that the reading of letters or manuscripts could be an alternative to publication, or, if arousing sufficient interest, might lead to publication; in the case of La Harpe, both could be possible. Correspondents frequently entered into what the eighteenth century called 'epistolary commerce', involving formal agreements with mutual responsibilities.[11] Not the least of these involved the careful preservation of letters so that if the opportu-

nity for publication should arise, the complete correspondence in its full continuity could be presented. A similar agreement might hold in a one-way correspondence where the letter writer develops perhaps a travel narrative or where
a set of letters may serve as the basis for a biography.

The latter held true of Leopold Mozart's letters to Hagenauer, as Leopold
periodically reminded his addressee to save the letters and occasionally included
an inventory of the letters sent lest one might have been lost in the post.
Leopold, well aware of the biographical potential of this correspondence, had
little doubt that his epistolary narrative of his son and the vivid descriptions of
their exotic travels would be appealing to a wider audience than the circle of
Salzburg friends. From his home in Salzburg, Hagenauer, who facilitated the
Mozarts' finances for the early sojourns, also appears to have been in 'epistolary
commerce' with Leopold. Leopold's correspondence with Wolfgang in the
late 1770s was another instance of epistolary commerce, as Leopold frequently
reminded his son to preserve the letters carefully and to keep up his end of the
correspondence. Again he provided occasional inventories of letters already
sent. The implications of this epistolary commerce between father and son will
be discussed in subsequent chapters, but even after it had collapsed following
Wolfgang's complete subversion of it, Leopold, ever the epistolary dealer,
continued to save his son's letters. Wolfgang, who broke the commerce through
subtle dissimulation, saw his father's letters as a yoke preventing his own
independence, a burden to be shed with all the other baggage from the repressive years of Salzburg. From 1781 (the year Mozart settled in Vienna) until
Leopold's death in 1787, we have only the letters that Mozart sent to his father;
none of Leopold's letters to Wolfgang from that time survived. The editors of
the Mozart letters, *Mozart: Briefe und Aufzeichnungen*, speculate that these
disappeared because Mozart's widow destroyed them at a later date (MBA
vi 61), but the breakdown of the epistolary commerce suggests that Mozart
himself may have discarded them.

MOZART AND THE END OF THE ENLIGHTENMENT

Early in 1778, within a space of a few weeks, two notable Austrians arrived in
Paris, both intent on making their fame and fortune there. These two Austrians,
one aged forty-four, the other twenty-two, had known each other in Vienna a
decade earlier, and the elder had taken steps to assist his young compatriot's
budding career. Both left Austria under something of a cloud, the elder discred-
ited as a charlatan, the younger unable to find gainful employment. In Paris,
contrary to what one might expect, they met very different fates. For the elder,
aspersion in Vienna was transformed to extraordinary success in Paris, while the
younger, arguably the greatest genius of his age and perhaps of all time, met
with indifference and rejection. The elder, known to our century because
his last name, which combined with 'ize' has become a familiar word in our

vocabulary, was Franz Anton Mesmer; the younger, the best-known composer of all time, was Wolfgang Amade Mozart.

These two Austrians appear to have more in common than one may suspect. Both could cast spells over their audiences, although Mesmer's product, given the susceptibility of his audience and intervention of Parisian fashion, was clearly more saleable than Mozart's. Few medical experts dared to align themselves with Mesmer lest they should become the laughing-stock of the profession, but a malleable public conscious of fashion and eager to be free of physical ailments or discover the fountain of youth flocked to Mesmer, paying handsomely for the privilege. Both men had to endure the scrutiny of their peers, but Mesmer, with rare exceptions, was regarded as a quack. Scrutiny of Mozart's abilities universally resulted in awe and admiration, but such approbation held little sway with the public at large. The French public, as Baron Melchior Grimm rightly recognized in a letter to Leopold Mozart,

> knows nothing about music. Consequently everything depends on names, and the merit of a work can be judged by only a very small number. The public is at the moment ridiculously divided between Piccini and Gluck, and all the argument one hears about music is pitiable. It is thus very difficult for your son to succeed between these two parties. . . . You see, my dear *maître*, that in a country where so many mediocre and even detestable musicians have made immense fortunes, I very much fear that your son will not so much as make ends meet (MDB 177).

Grimm, according to Mozart, did little to help him, but his perception of the public and Mozart's chances of success nevertheless hit the mark. Taste in music could be easily manipulated, and at the moment it did not include the work of an upstart Austrian whom the French remembered from an earlier visit as a precocious but cute child.

But Mozart and Mesmer had a more fundamental destiny in common in that each would contribute in his own way to the demise of the Enlightenment. Mesmer's contribution may, however, have been somewhat more inadvertent than Mozart's. He came to Paris hoping to find patrons and clients (calling them patients would be going too far), and to be able to charge extravagantly for his services, which he succeeded in doing, but he did not anticipate that Mesmerism would become the hottest topic of conversation in salons or discussion in the press. It may also not have occurred to him that he almost single-handedly transformed France from a country bound by a sense of reason, order and morality to a land intoxicated with irrationality, mystery, secret solutions, dissymmetry and the occult.[12] Numerous shots had already been fired at the primacy of reason and order, entrenched in French thought since the seventeenth century, by the likes of Molière, Corneille, Holbach and Voltaire, but the fatal blow appears to have been struck by an Austrian charlatan, mystifying his public with exotic machinery, pseudo-science, and incantations in an unintelligible mixture of French mispronunciation and German doggerel. With such overwhelming displays of approval from the French public, authority conceded, granting Mesmer recognition and financial security that amounted to a fortune.

Mozart's rattling at the cage of the Enlightenment appears to have been more deliberate, although clearly less understood and appreciated. Subsequent chapters will itemize the extent of his achievement of this in both personal affairs and in some of his works, his skilful wearing of masks, his mastery of disguise, his ruses of symmetry, or his virtuosity of deception which leaves many of those committed to reason and enlightened morality unaware that they have been deceived. As with Mesmer, Paris played a key role in Mozart's direction, although in his case as a signpost rather than the absorbent sponge it was for the former. Mesmer succeeded in pushing the French over the precipice they had been lining, peering whimsically into the abyss, whereas for Mozart Paris allowed relatively safe discovery of the abyss with its dizzying and intoxicating depths. In Paris Mozart encountered over a century of French thought, unlike anything he had met in censor-restricted Austria, and persons who could tutor him sympathetically in it. Above all, this new way of thinking for him involved a subtlety of thought he was exceptionally well equipped to pursue, a mode of discourse in correspondence or musical works employing double entendres, dissimulation or masking.

THE PARIS SOJOURN OF 1778

Various phases of Mozart's life have proved attractive to biographers and critics, including recent examinations of his last year, his final decade, his years in Vienna, or older studies of his sojourns in Italy and England, his life in Salzburg, or his early years. His half-year stay in Paris in 1778 has evoked a somewhat mixed response as a period of both feast and famine. On the one hand this offers one of the richest sources of Mozart correspondence, the heart of the most active exchange of letters between father and son. On the other hand, this sojourn is customarily taken to be a time of abject failure and disappointment as his productivity as a composer fell to an all-time low, with virtually nothing of any significance written during this time. Further, he failed to secure employment, fell out with his father, and saw his mother die. The Paris episode belonged, of course, to a much larger foray into the outside world lasting from 23 September 1777 to mid-January 1779, almost a year and a half, during which time his separation from his father and Salzburg allowed him to experience an independence previously unavailable to him. This trip evoked an enormous correspondence between father and son, amounting to about one-half of all the letters they exchanged, a correspondence which demands to be considered in the light of the eighteenth-century passion for letter writing, including matters of style, purpose and intended audience. As with the months in Paris, Mozart's compositional output during this year and a half proved meagre in the extreme, amounting to little more than a few keyboard and violin sonatas, a symphony, some arias, and a few works for flute. If Mozart's life, instead of his mother's, had ended in Paris, we would no doubt lament the composer that might have been, given achievements like the Piano Concerto in E Flat, K. 271, but he would clearly not have the grip on our curiosity and affection he now has. Shortly after his return to Salzburg, the extraordinary works began to flow, including sonatas, chamber music, symphonies, and the operas *Idomeneo* and *Die Entführung aus dem Serail*.

This period of compositional inactivity, independence and new ways of thinking may have been a watershed for Mozart. He departed in 1777 as an overprotected young man, well beyond the age of consent but not allowed the freedom to choose his own clothes let alone make decisions about his life. Unable, in his father's view, to cope with even the smallest of financial or domestic responsibilities, he was accompanied by his mother. During this time, Mozart grew up. He tasted success, failure, bereavement, love, rejection, friendship, betrayal, independence and idleness, and the seeds were sown for a composer who could go beyond a wunderkind and phase of musical ingratiation to a genius who could bring to bear all his humanity and complexity on his works. Perhaps the most critical step in the entire process involved devising a way to deal with his father. The Archbishop refused Leopold permission to travel at this time, and now Mozart for the first time, relishing his freedom, emerged from under Leopold's thumb. Instead of constant advice and direction, the most Leopold could now do was send a letter every few days. Letters could be much more easily ignored than face-to-face lectures, and distorting the truth in letters proved much easier since Leopold had no reliable way of corroborating the stories reaching him. The regimen of composing now fell apart almost completely with Leopold no longer looking over his shoulder, but Mozart clearly preferred that Leopold should remain ignorant of this indolence. As Wolfgang travelled further from home, a pattern of lying to his father became more apparent. This involved numerous subjects, including his compositional activity; he happily wrote to Leopold about projects and specific works which did not exist.[13]

The vast correspondence between father and son during this time has generally been treated as a source of biographical information or verification of archival data. Its much more complex purpose will be the subject of chapters 3 and 5. The possibility that it should one day be published almost certainly permeated Leopold's thinking, and that had a strong bearing on his approach to the letters. Wolfgang's letters, on the other hand, reveal the essence of a generation gap, of a son on a very different wavelength from his father, and his artful technique of defusing the objectionable side of his father's influence.

THE GENERATION GAP

Virtually every generation experiences a gap similar to the one evident between the two Mozarts, but at this point in the eighteenth century the division became magnified as a result of other forces at work. The foundations for eighteenth-century attitudes towards morality had been laid and maintained by writers such as the Third Earl of Shaftesbury, J. J. Gottsched and Samuel Johnson. While their enlightened notion of morality appeared more secular than that of previous centuries, it was by no means entirely separated from the will of God. Moral truths could be passed on in a sermon-like manner, perhaps including some humour and entertainment to make the pill easier to swallow, but nevertheless by way of precepts which were rammed down the throats of young people. At the heart of this stood a notion of stability, one that could characterize other facets of thought and life as well, including the primacy of reason, order in social structures, and a belief in God as the architect of the universe. Evil may have had a place in this model, but only as a foil which would make the victory of good all the sweeter. For the younger generation, more compliance than thought was required.

For those wishing to stave off mental atrophy, of whom the eighteenth century saw many, compliance proved a very poor option. Scepticism festered among intellectuals as a societal sore, fed by the tedium of conventional moral codes as well as events that ripped at the fabric of society. These events included wars in which Christians obliviously slaughtered each other, where righteousness belonged to the victors, or so-called acts of God, such as the great earthquake of Lisbon, forced the question of how a caring, intervening god could allow such carnage, especially to the devout who perished while at worship. Voltaire's *Poème sur le désastre de Lisbonne* cracked the foundation of the conventional system of beliefs, and in *Candide* he forced that foundation to crumble. Disorder and evil were not to be taken lightly, nor to be absorbed as toothless villains into a system of theology that relegated them to the role of mere foils.

The challenge to enlightened morality hung in the air, although in the late eighteenth century it would have been folly to defy openly the order on which society was built. In France writers judged in the least way subversive would find themselves very quickly behind bars or enduring public floggings, forcing most of them to write anonymously. In Austria strict censorship laws, not only under the rule of Maria Theresa but Joseph II as well, prevented most subversive material from entering the country from the outside or coming into existence from within. Unlike their counterparts of the nineteenth century, writers of the late eighteenth century who wished to challenge the existing order did so with artfulness and subtlety, using satire and irony in ways that might cause doubt among their readers. Shaftesbury, in the first decade of the eighteenth century, had made this clear: 'if men are forbid to speak their minds seriously on certain subjects, they will do so ironically. If they are forbid to speak at all upon such subjects, or if they find it really dangerous to do so, they will then redouble their disguise, involve themselves in mysteriousness, and talk so as hardly to be understood.'[14] Doubt stood at the heart of much writing, doubt in a system of morals or reason that seemed no longer workable. Every person would be cast loose, forced to think about a thousand and one possibilities, compelled to make decisions in a complex world which had no straightforward alternatives to offer. Such thinking, of course, seemed dangerous, since it undermined authority at all levels from the heads of church and state to paternalism in families.

The generation gap between Leopold and Wolfgang Mozart ran parallel to the larger social transformation. As a creature of the Enlightenment, Leopold subscribed fully to the moral stance of Shaftesbury and Gellert, believing these principles should be disseminated to the next generation. Leopold's own formal education had been in moral philosophy, and throughout his life he cultivated friendships or correspondences with leaders in the field, including Baron Grimm and Gellert. His letters to his son beginning in September 1777, as chapter 3 will argue, were conceived as a more public correspondence, designed for the whole world to see, and in them he played the role of moral educator. To be sure, he wrote these letters specifically to his son, dealing at times with matters of a highly personal nature, but that did not prevent their accessibility to a larger public. As Leopold knew perfectly well, other published correspondences of his contemporaries did precisely that, and their authors did not find the personal content unsuitable for the larger readership. The literary format of letters from a father to his son was well established by this time, Leopold's correspondent Gellert having defined one of the clearest models for it. The father stood in a strong position of authority, giving advice to his son – advice that the son had no serious choice but to accept. Just as enlightened morality could tolerate some disorder and evil, just enough to enhance the victory of good, similarly this epistolary model could sustain some argument or disobedience from a son, just enough to show that the father was right and the son should regret not following the advice in the first place.

Wolfgang's initial letters of reply to Leopold seem to reveal a compliant son, dutifully playing the role that the son should follow in such an exchange. In fact, through much of the year and a half on the road, Wolfgang sustained the correct tone, although as time passed Leopold became increasingly aware that he was being told lies. In the end, Wolfgang played his hand much better than Leopold, writing letters with a virtuosity of deceit that ultimately rendered Leopold's moral discourse useless. If there had been outright rebellion, Leopold might have been able to manage it more easily and perhaps even score the victory for enlightened morality. But Wolfgang handled his side far too subtly, leading Leopold periodically to think that all was well, even though he knew at times that things had gone badly amiss; at no point could he be entirely certain what degree of the truth he was hearing. As a correspondent, Wolfgang discovered how to manage his father with consummate skill, how to secure his own independence, and live as he wished while appearing to subscribe to the old moral order.

The skill in deception Mozart acquired during this time played a role not only in his epistolary endeavours but in subsequent artistic efforts as well. This is not to say that his goal in later operas, symphonies or other types of composition was only to deceive, any more than the irony, satire or double meanings used by a large number of writers were intended only to delude. Mozart had a purpose in these later works, one which no longer coincided with the objectives of his father or even his friend Joseph Haydn, the leading composer of the time. Leopold incessantly advised on what and how to compose, but in response to the advice sent to him in Paris, Mozart produced all but nothing. Despite the idleness which may have set in at this time, other factors probably influenced this, especially concerning his own view of what types of work he deemed worthy of coming into existence. Writing for the sake of gaining approbation, it became increasingly clear to him, fared poorly as an objective. For the moralists of the past, approbation may have been a necessary first step before leading the audience in a desired direction, but Mozart avoided following that course. Henceforth, he and his father stood at cross-purposes on the matter.

THE 'AGE OF DECEPTION'

Chapters 1 and 7 will touch on some of Mozart's operas, showing how far removed from Leopold's principles Mozart had proceeded. Musical deception plays a major role in virtually all of Mozart's operas after 1779, and here Mozart found himself in very good company among his contemporaries, particularly those in the field of literature. In France one could look to writers much earlier, including some from the seventeenth century, to find such artfulness, and Mozart became very aware of these writers in 1778. The eighteenth century is often mistakenly labelled the 'Age of Reason', although this tagging much more appropriately describes the seventeenth century. Intellectually much more volatile, the eighteenth century degenerated into complete disorder in France by 1789, and would be more suitably called the 'Age of Disguise', as Maximillian E. Novak has titled it.[15] A gift Mozart received in Mannheim just before setting out for Paris, the comedies of Molière, from none other than Fridolin Weber (who would have been Mozart's father-in-law had he survived a few years longer, a man unlike his own father in spite of Mozart's claims), may very well have played an important role in Mozart's discovery of the possibilities of disguise in literature.

Masks, disguise, hypocrisy and deception present themselves in Molière's plays at every imaginable level, and Molière was but one source for Mozart from a very wide variety of writers from France, England and Germany. Writers with moral objectives could, of course, use deception as well, possibly as a means of projecting truth from dark shadows into the light. Deception had numerous possible benevolent purposes, although in the works of some writers, Molière among them, one searches in vain for virtue. These works may be presented as comedies, allowing laughter to obscure the darker implication of non-benevolent deception.

On his arrival in Paris, Mozart made contact with Baron Grimm and

Grimm's mistress, Mme Louise d'Épinay, and after the death of his mother lived in their household until his departure in September. Mozart's relationship with Grimm, who had so much in common with Leopold, fared worse the longer it continued, as Grimm found Mozart too indolent to pursue a career in Paris and Mozart accused Grimm of stinginess and doing nothing to help his career, with the result that Grimm sent Mozart packing out of Paris. In spite of his sour dealings with Grimm, he remained on the best of terms with Louise d'Épinay, regarded by some as the most exceptional woman in all of France. Considering the amount of time Mozart appears to have spent with Mme d'Épinay, taking meals with her and enjoying other types of social interaction, it does not seem unreasonable to assume that their conversations would have touched on the great French thinkers with whom she was so intimate, including Voltaire, Diderot and d'Holbach. The diverse range of thought, epistolary techniques and strategies of writing that Mozart may have discovered from Mme d'Épinary about these *philosophes* can only be speculated on, but may have included Voltaire's scepticism, deism and wearing of masks in his letters, Diderot's questioning of world order and uses of literary disguise, and Holbach's outright savaging of Christian tenets, distressing even Voltaire with his relegation of God to the junk pile of superstition and idolatry.

What Mozart encountered in France was, of course, an international phenomenon. In England, Henry Fielding described his own times as 'a vast masquerade, where the greatest part appear disguised under false vizors and habits'. In the preface to *Miscellanies*, he countered the common view of Newgate prison as 'no other than Human Nature with its Mask off' with the view that 'the splendid Palaces of the Great are no other than Newgate with the Mask on'. Like Fielding, Daniel Defoe characterized the times as 'an Age of Plot and Deceit, of Contradiction and Paradox. . . . It is very hard under all these Masks, to see the true Countenance of any Man.'[16] If these comments seem like complaints, they do not prevent the writers in question from using dissimulation in their works. Fielding's first play, *Love in Several Masques*, pairs two letter writers who simultaneously project and disguise their affection by means of dramatic impersonation. Horace Walpole takes epistolary masking even further, altering his identity from correspondence to correspondence so that he becomes a type of literary chameleon.[17]

MASQUERADES AND CARNIVAL

The fascination with masks, disguise, masquerades and deception in literature in many respects reflected behaviour in social settings. Masquerades became the rage across Europe in the eighteenth century, associated with pre-Lent Carnivals in some countries and held year-round in others. In London, the weekly revels at the Haymarket attracted thousands at three or five shillings a ticket, apparelled in exotic costumes ranging from chimney sweeps to harlequins, all with vizors and intent on intrigues, assignations and promiscuity.[18] Vienna too had its masquerades and Carnival balls, and according to Johann Pezzl they were just as dangerous as those of England or elsewhere. Behaviour otherwise reprehensible became acceptable behind masks: sexual suggestiveness ranging from speech to touching could be initiated by either men or women, ample displays of flesh generated neither shame nor shock, and cross-dressing with sexual role-playing obscured the gender of the individuals making contact. In a society otherwise suffering from repressiveness and censorship, from conformity and ostracization or punishment for nonconformity, the masquerade became a type of safe haven for illicit behaviour.[19] Risks for women at these revels, especially young unattached women, were high, as the sexual encounters could easily go beyond the suggestive stage, and this led some to equate the masquerade with the sexual act itself. Women received warnings in the moral weeklies to reject tickets from lascivious men, while men could attend but should not bring sisters or wives lest their mistresses should be present.[20]

The lasciviousness and deceptiveness of masquerades and Carnival attracted Mozart enormously throughout his short adult life; here he was in his true element. In Austria, Carnival could be indulged in by all upright people, dressing in *commedia dell'arte* costumes and enjoying a certain amount of harmless merrymaking before Lent. Even Leopold enjoyed this, and his son could write to him about such matters without fear of chastisement. As behaviour at the more sophisticated private balls may have been less licentious than the earthier public ones, Leopold would not be disturbed by the activities described by Mozart in various letters. These descriptions were undoubtedly abridged, and Mozart and his in-laws probably caroused in a variety of ways best left out of letters to Leopold.

We know of Mozart's inclination to the pleasures of masquerading which may have exceeded good taste from a letter during the Carnival season of 1778, written shortly before his departure for Paris. His correspondent in this case, his cousin Maria Anna Thekla Mozart (the 'Bäsle'), shared his more sexually illicit inclinations and with her he could discuss the possibilities of Carnival in a way entirely impossible with his father. The fascinating relationship between these cousins developed in the autumn of 1777 while Mozart and his mother were in Augsburg, and the delightfully scatological correspondence resulting from this relationship in itself has a Carnival-like aura. Now in Mannheim during Carnival and wishing he could have been with her to enjoy an improper intimacy that would probably not otherwise be possible, he speculated on the good time they might have had together in Augsburg. Since he never actually visited Augsburg during Carnival, one can only assume his impression of more fun there related to being with her. For believers in an enlightened or religious Mozart, the language of these letters remains troubling. Something certainly did go on between Mozart and the 'Bäsle', and for him the language as well as the sexual activity can be seen as an extension of Carnival or the masquerade, suggesting an element of protest against refinement, morality and authority. In

much of his correspondence Mozart plays the role of a masquerader, an epistolary harlequin as diverse as his number of correspondents. Few of these would
even recognize him if by chance they read his letters to someone else. This
diversity, of course, should not incline us to imagine a problem with multiple
personalities; as one who wore masks as a letter writer, Mozart stood in the
company of the most virtuosic epistolary practitioners from the eighteenth
century.

Chapter 1
The Battle between Carnival and Lent

The well-known painting by Pieter Bruegel the Elder, *The Battle between Carnival and Lent* of 1559, portrays a striking division not only among different groups of people in sixteenth-century Europe but within individuals themselves, and in varying degrees this opposition continued at least until the end of the eighteenth century. In proportion to the authoritarian rule of the state or the strict control of the church there existed an opportunity for release, a time to flaunt authority and mock the church, to drop good behaviour and indulge in the most lascivious activities, to hurl insults and curse as much as one liked – in short, to be everything that one was not in the normal course of life. Not only were most state and church authorities prepared to tolerate these periods of lapsed morality but to a degree some joined in themselves, recognizing that absolute power was much easier to maintain if tempered by an opportunity for protest or release. The duelling forces involved here elicit a large series of opposites, and by the eighteenth century the list had grown considerably to include Christianity and paganism, morality and immorality, order and disorder, refinement and coarseness or obscenity, moderation and overindulgence, spiritual and physical, seriousness and laughter, beauty and grotesqueness, gentility and violence, soberness and drunkenness, autocracy and equality, and others too numerous to mention. During the eighteenth century a new element entered the equation which, because of the passion with which some heads of state embraced it, particularly in the Habsburg territories, threatened to break down the existing balance of polarities, and, in the name of reform, to create an oppressiveness worse than the previous autocracy. This new force, reaching towards an uniformly higher type of culture, was the peculiar Habsburg version of the Enlightenment, which, according to those who attempted to implement it, removed the need for bawdy or unbridled forms of release since it was couched in what appeared to be a greater sense of freedom.

If the traditional forms of release or protest were removed, as in many respects happened in eighteenth-century Austria, in all likelihood they would be replaced by outright revolution, as occurred in France, or by more subtle means of revolt, incorporating aspects of the previous modes of dissent into accepted presentations of high culture. This did not necessarily mean political revolution, as it could be of a personal or social nature, and in the hands of the most skilled practitioner could be so subtle that few would even recognize the element of protest. Unlike France, where authority did not sympathize with the Enlightenment and the nature of the political oppression could generate a brutal revolt, Austria went through a steady process of reform during the 1760s and onwards; the Habsburgs lost nothing of their absolute power, but with their changes took the wind out of the sails of any potential movement towards political subversion. The reforms, however, did little to change the political order or the lives of people, in some cases actually making matters worse, and clearly called for response from those who could see what was happening. This response would have to come in a mode that could remain compatible with censorship; in short, it would have to be subtle in the extreme to get by the censors, but would run the risk, if designed to elude the most critical minds, of being grasped by no one. The highest achievement in this respect in Austria came from Mozart, although that is not to imply that he wrote his works to fulfill some quasi-political function. The element of protest in Mozart's works is every bit as personal as it is political or social, although considering the nature of the Enlightenment in Austria and its pervasiveness in political, social, family and interpersonal affairs, a response to it of necessity was multidimensional, touching the essence of the person it came from as well as addressing the nature of the society to which that person was expected to conform.

A DESPOTIC ENLIGHTENMENT

At the time of Mozart's birth the Enlightenment held Europe very much in its grip, with little intellectual thought and artistic activity untouched by its pervasive influence. This, of course, does not imply that the Enlightenment took the same form throughout Europe or that its thrust was necessarily welcomed by those in power. In the great centres of intellectual ferment, including Paris, northern Germany and Britain, the attitude to enlightened thought ranged from it being regarded as a wellspring of political stability to subversion punishable by imprisonment or public flogging. Britain had provided the foundation for modern democracy, and throughout the eighteenth century moved more rapidly than any other country towards achieving it. In France, on the other hand, the *philosophes* remained at odds with those in authority, publishing their works anonymously or secretly to avoid punishment. One of the most notable of those secret publications, the *Correspondance littéraire*, found its way to a select number of heads of state in other countries who paid handsomely to be *au courant* with the latest in political philosophy, ethics and artistic criticism from the best minds of France. One such subscriber, Frederick the Great of Prussia, responded by providing a sympathetic environment in Berlin for the flourishing of enlightened philosophy, literature and music; unfortunately for the *philosophes*, flirtation with enlightened despots like Frederick weakened their own credibility at home. Frederick relinquished nothing of his absolute authority, but that did not prevent him from expressing his political views in terms of a contract between himself and his subjects, in which, he claimed, he was not above the state but held the ultimate responsibility to apply the rule of law, maintain the economy in the interests of all, and allow freedom of conscience. In his own words, 'it is the first duty of the citizen to serve his country; it is an obligation which I have attempted to fulfil during all the various stages of my life. Charged as I am with the first magistracy, I have had the opportunity and the means of making myself useful to my fellow-citizens.'[1]

We may be tempted to assume that the young Mozart, well travelled throughout the continent and England, grew up with an awareness of the breadth and scope of the international Enlightenment, somehow absorbing its essence at each port of call. That anything of the sort happened is unlikely in the extreme; Mozart, along with his sister Maria Anna (Nannerl), performed for heads of state, aristocrats and others who could be of financial advantage, and one suspects little of an enlightened nature went on in these encounters. Further, virtually everything reaching the young Mozart's ears was filtered through his father Leopold, and Leopold's distinctive interpretations provided the basis for his son's education. While travel played a disproportionate role for the youthful Mozart, Salzburg remained his home during his formative years and early adulthood, and here the Enlightenment, while not unnoticed, took a form quite unlike any in most other parts of Europe. The Enlightenment of Mozart's early experience was the distinctive one of Salzburg and his father, and its inseparability from authority figures made it fairly unappealing to the boy with one of the most fertile minds of his generation.

Unlike northern Germany with its secularization in matters of state and higher education, the Habsburg empire remained solidly Roman Catholic and immune to many of the forces of tolerance or equality characteristic of the Enlightenment. During the first half of the century, non-Catholics were barely or not tolerated at all, and in the archdiocese of Salzburg this was pushed to the extreme with the expulsion of Protestants in 1731–2. Maria Theresa, after the death of her husband, relinquished much of her power to her son Joseph and other ministers of state, allowing for much more liberal policies. The most notable of these ministers, including Joseph von Sonnenfels, Gottfried van Swieten and Prince Wenzel Kaunitz, facilitated reforms in education, the distribution of land, and the justice system. Joseph himself, while still the co-regent, issued the *Tolerenzpatent* (declaration of tolerance) of 1777, ending the persecution of non-Catholics, although still not giving them the full rights of Catholic citizens. During his sole reign from 1780 to 1790 he initiated numerous other reforms, especially before the backlash accompanying the French Revolution.

Reform came in Salzburg as well, under Mozart's patron Archbishop Hieronymus von Colloredo, much maligned in musical circles because of his

Christoph Gottsched and Christian Fürchtegott Gellert for direction, writers whose moral outlook did not clash with that of established religion. A German observer such as Nicolai, who advised Lessing against accepting the position of director of the new court theatre in Vienna in 1769, in coming to Vienna as late as 1781 discovered attitudes typical of those in Germany from the 1740s, attitudes so outdated and thoroughly ridiculed in Germany that in his mind they no longer rated consideration as enlightened. For the Austrians, previously mired in feudalism, intolerance and religious dogma, these were important first steps, leading them towards the modern age before once again retrenching in the *ancien régime* in the late 1780s.

Mozart's encounters with notable persons of the Enlightenment happened during three fairly distinct phases of his life. The first encompasses the years from his birth to the age of twenty-one, a phase spent primarily in Salzburg where his father mentored his development and the Archbishop employed him. The second stage, while the shortest, appears to have had the greatest impact; this was the journey to Munich, Augsburg, Mannheim and Paris from September 1777 to January 1779, a time of freedom from his father except for their extensive correspondence. In Paris, especially after the death of his mother, Mozart spent much of his time in close contact with two of the notable figures of the century, Baron Melchior Grimm and Grimm's mistress Mme Louise d'Épinay, and each exercised a distinctly different influence on him. During this journey Mozart's desire to avoid returning to Salzburg became acute, and he almost entirely succeeded in that, spending the last decade of his life in Vienna. During this third and final phase he came into contact with all the best minds of the Habsburg capital, and here too he found two distinctly different approaches to the Enlightenment, one which appealed to him no more than the authoritarian approach he had so deeply resented in Salzburg.

Mozart's attitude towards Archbishop Colloredo seems fairly clear, and if he had any admiration for his patron's reforms, that has been lost in a sea of invective in which both son and father could indulge towards the autocratic and mean-spirited prelate. If Colloredo's manner in dealing with the Mozarts indicates anything of his *modus operandi*, one should not be surprised that his reforms failed to win the hearts of the Salzburg citizenry. This surely revealed the Enlightenment at its worst, an official, high culture forced on people from above, a cold, ordered, repressive culture impossible to disentangle from its authoritarian source. Mozart responded no more favourably to this type of Enlightenment than he did to remaining in the service of the Archbishop.

In Paris – in the person of Baron Grimm – Mozart discovered the same disagreeableness and high-mindedness he had found in advocates of the Enlightenment before 1778, and this will be discussed in chapter 4. While Mozart felt little appreciation for the official, high Enlightenment of the Habsburg territories, he appears to have found other enlightened activities more attractive, both in Vienna and Paris. By the time he made his permanent move to Vienna in 1781, a move involving a final rupture with the Archbishop and very much against Leopold's will, Leopold exerted very little influence over his son in career or personal matters. Mozart now chose his friends and associates to suit his own inclinations, and in the process met virtually every leading figure of the Austrian Enlightenment. These included the poets Aloys Blumauer, Johann Baptist von Alxinger, Michel Denis and Lorenz Leopold Haschka, the mineralogist and masonic leader Ignaz von Born, the President of the Court Commission on Education Gottfried van Swieten, Court War Secretary Franz Sales von Greiner, the senior government official Tobias Philipp Gebler, and, perhaps the most influential of all, the political, cultural and masonic leader Joseph von Sonnenfels.

FREEMASONRY

Vienna possessed its share – if somewhat smaller than other major centres – of intellectuals, people who, while supporting Joseph's paternalistic reforms, preferred something more independent of his interfering reach for themselves. Lacking the infrastructure for this type of intellectual forum either in the university (where politically or religiously driven appointments prevented the more intellectually vibrant atmosphere of northern German universities) or in an academy of arts and sciences (which Joseph, the economizer, had no intention of creating), the best minds of Vienna found themselves congregating in masonic lodges, and one lodge in particular: 'Zur wahren Eintract' (True Concord). Unlike the other seven lodges in Vienna before 1785, 'Zur wahren Eintracht', under the direction of Born and Sonnenfels, emerged more as an academy of arts and sciences than a typical masonic lodge, opening its door to leading representatives of all fields of endeavour. Its members included Blumauer, Alxinger, Haschka, Gottlieb Leon, Gebler, Franz Kratter, Joseph Mayer and Karl Haidinger, as well as Joseph Haydn, whose invitation to join came in 1784.

While most lodges preferred anonymity and secrecy, this one, with its numerous literati and scientists, took on an educational, literary and moral role with official publications such as the *Journal für Freymaurer*. Blumauer, in the preface of the first issue, articulated the altruistic purpose of the *Journal* as being 'to provide masonry with genuine workers devoted to its purpose and through them to give humanity just as many benefactors'.[5] The lodge gave the appearance of being at odds with Joseph's version of the Enlightenment, especially concerning the Catholic church, although individual members including Blumauer tolerated other religions much less than their professed ideology might suggest. Nevertheless, this appearance, along with other factors, provided enough ill will to prompt a restructuring of all the lodges in Austria from Joseph under his *Freimaurerpatent* of 1785, reducing the eight lodges of Vienna to two and eliminating 'Zur wahren Eintracht'. Most members of that lodge belonged because of the distinctive nature of their lodge, and few continued to hold masonic membership after 1785.

Mozart never held official membership in 'Zur wahren Eintracht', as he belonged to 'Zur Wohlthätigkeit' (Charity), but he attended frequently as a guest, and unlike many, continued as an active mason after 1785. While his involvement with freemasonry appears to have been genuine, one sees even here an element of irony in his attitude towards it, perhaps related to hypocrisy within the order itself concerning religious intolerance, racial prejudice and gender inequality. The most public manifestation of this, the opera *Die Zauberflöte*, treats masonry and the Enlightenment in a very peculiar manner. Most of what has been written about this opera emphasizes various aspects of masonic symbolism, and it appears that writers have hoped the frolicking side of it might vanish if ignored.

The instinctive high-mindedness of critics who insist on serious interpretations of *Die Zauberflöte* stands very much at odds with what the librettist Emanuel Schikaneder and Mozart gave us. On a simple proportional level, Tamino, the focus of the mythical and symbolic studies, sings a part roughly two-thirds the size of Papageno's. Serious critics will readily come to Tamino's defence: not only did Schikaneder write this part for himself (so of course it would be longer) but Tamino has learned his lessons from the trial of silence well, conveying a depth with fewer words (and notes) than would ever be possible for the mindlessly loquacious chatterbox Papageno. But where, one must ask, is the depth? We hear much from Tamino in Act 1, but Mozart increasingly marginalizes him in Act 2, giving him relatively small ensemble parts. His only aria occurs as the third number of the work, just after Papageno's song 'Der Vogelfänger'; Papageno sings the final aria of the opera. Most telling, though, is the finale to Act 2, the conclusion of the work, where Papageno sings four times as much as Tamino and shares his substantial section with Papagena long after we have heard the last of Tamino.

A number of fairly sensitive social issues arise in this opera, including slavery, the use of torture, and misogyny, and they cannot be made to disappear by suggesting that the eighteenth-century outlook on these was more accommodating than our own. Those who ardently profess causes, as freemasons did concerning social justice and reform, simply set themselves up for satire when in the end they turn out to be inconsistent, ambivalent or even hypocritical. The treatment of slavery, torture and misogyny in this opera may very well have more to do with the mismatching of theory and practice among freemasons than anything else, and Mozart does not let them off the hook. Slavery may not have been of great concern in the Habsburg empire, but it had become a hot topic of debate in England and France. The *philosophes*, as Mozart undoubtedly knew, had argued vigorously against slavery, and the debate in Britain led to the passage of a bill in the House of Commons against the slave trade in 1807. The position of freemasons in general, the protectors of the most fundamental attitudes towards human dignity, differed little from that expressed in the Illuminati Dirigentes: 'Fortune's favourites, kings and princes, are supposed to possess by right of birth qualities which they do not have to prove, and they retain a power which neither virtue nor intelligence can make up for among those condemned to slavery.'[6] That Sarastro's temple should have slaves may seem incongruous, but in reality it was no more so than the fact that the great enlightened American, Thomas Jefferson, an outspoken advocate of human rights, apparently had no qualms about owning slaves his entire life.

If slavery escaped the agenda for discussion in Vienna, torture most certainly did not. Sonnenfels had put it there in the 1760s with his efforts to persuade Maria Theresa to abolish it, and in the process he made enemies of Vice-Chancellor Kolowrat, Court Chancellor Chotek, and Cardinal Migazzi, all of whom accused him of being a radical. They won the first round, but in response to their attacks he published his views on punishment in a treatise in 1775 and succeeded in 1776 with the support of Joseph in persuading the Empress to order the elimination of torture.[7] Technically, of course, the seventy-seven lashes on the toes ordered by Sarastro for Monostatos in the opera are not torture since no one attempts to extract information or a confession from him. This is punishment for his mistreatment of Pamina, a penalty not out of line with what might have been demanded by Joseph II, who saw fit to balance the restriction on capital punishment with an increase in public whippings, chaining and hard labour. On this matter Maria Theresa took a more lenient position than her son as these punishments were not put into force until after her death.[8] In Joseph's view, offenders should suffer, although the hard labour came from a pragmatic stance that a working convict served the state more usefully than an executed one. Mozart undoubtedly sided with the elderly Empress, knowing full well that these punishments were unjust and arbitrary, resulting from a manipulation or misappropriation of power. This happened in 1781 to an acquaintance of Mozart from Munich, one Herr von Wiedmer, who, after responding in kind to a box on the ears from a certain Baron Buffa in Innsbruck, instead of receiving satisfaction, got fifty crippling lashes himself at the local prison. According to Mozart he needed to be avenged but in fact he could never receive adequate compensation (MBA iii 145–6).

Mozart had addressed the issue of women in previous operas, but never as clearly as in *Die Zauberflöte*. Mozart, the friend of Mme d'Épinay, could not have possibly tolerated the blatant misogyny of freemasons. No confusion with twentieth-century feminism exists here; the eighteenth century itself debated the subject vigorously, with the likes of Rousseau and the freemasons on one side and the *salonnières* on the other. Here Mozart and Schikaneder place the issue in focus, allowing the narrow-minded Sarastro and his priests to represent the conventional authoritarian position. Sarastro tells Pamina, who has learned at the feet of his great predecessor (her own father), that 'by man your course must be decided, for by herself a woman steps beyond her sphere and is misguided'.[9] Before Tamino and Papageno set out on their first trials, they are warned by two priests to 'beware of woman's crafty scheming: this is the Order's first command! Many a man, of wiles not dreaming, was tempted and could not withstand.' Unlike Sarastro's words in recitative, the priests sing theirs in a duet, and Mozart, unable to resist making them sound a little foolish, sets their final *sotto voce* words 'Tod und Verzweiflung war sein Lohn' (Death and damnation was his fate) to staccato bassoons, trombones and low strings in a jaunty little march rhythm.

Sarastro intends that Tamino should take the two final and most dangerous trials by himself, and brings Pamina forward to bid him farewell. Following this she despairs, but the Three Spirits rescue her and lead her to Tamino before he begins. He (now permitted to speak to her) and his attendants are delightfully surprised to see her, and in the face of her fearlessness do not object to her presence. Jacques Chailley argues the right of women to masonic membership at this point,[10] but Mozart's position about women here probably extended much further. Tamino seems unfit to pass these last trials on his own, but with Pamina guiding him he succeeds. Contrary to Chailley, who imagines that her prowess results from having 'been embraced by Tamino, who thus has communicated the influx of his masculine nature',[11] she brings to bear a force that he seems entirely unable to grasp. The magic flute, which she now hands him to protect them during their passage, symbolizes this force, and Mozart leads them on by the magical tones of the solo flute. Through magic they triumph, but this is no simple equating of magic and irrationality as one might imagine it in relation to some sort of feminine stereotype. This magic counteracts cold reason; there may be more than a touch of superstition here, and in one respect Sarastro was right when he warned of the Queen's superstition. More to the point, Pamina has brought together the most fundamental opposites – superstition and reason, woman and man, darkness and light – in fact, Carnival and Lent, reinstating the balance that despotic enlightened reformers had tried to eradicate. It should come as no surprise then that the next and final substantial scene in the work belongs to Papageno, the magical Three Spirits and Papagena. In that delightful scene, Papageno contemplates ending his life on the count of three if Papagena does not reappear; his stuttering count with various fractions added on serves as a cheeky parody of the more solemn three counts associated with freemasonry. Sarastro, who had sung in 'In diesen heil'gen Hallen' of the absence of revenge in his domain, had prefaced his song with the remark 'you shall see how I take revenge upon your mother'. If that sort of hypocrisy does not pull us into siding with the Queen, Mozart's musical representation of these two characters surely does, as the Queen with her spectacular coloratura has it all over the hymn-singing basso Sarastro.

At least one modern director, David Radok, working at the Stavovské Theatre in Prague (the same theatre where *Don Giovanni* received its première), has picked up the possibility that the work, like virtually all of Mozart's mature operas, may have an ironic ending. In Radok's production Tamino and Pamina seem somewhat ill at ease during the final chorus singing the triumph of virtue and wisdom, and the instant the chorus ends they run as fast as they can away from the sterile, conformist order of the temple to join Papageno and the rest of the ordinary people. Here, as Mozart seems to indicate with the perky twelve-measure orchestral conclusion after the stuffy hymn by the chorus, Carnival gets the last laugh.

CARNIVAL

In the Habsburg empire it would perhaps not be entirely unfair to equate the Enlightenment with Lent, considering the sense of austerity and deprivation in the definition given by Joseph and Colloredo. The opposite force in Bruegel's equation, Carnival, remained very active in Europe, especially in Catholic territories, attracting the notice of a number of prominent writers. Mozart leaves no question of his own enormous appetite for Carnival in various of his letters at different times of his life, not only to people like his fun-loving cousin Maria Anna Thekla but even to his father. His descriptions of his Carnival activities give only hints of what he may actually have done. At this time Carnival had by no means entirely lost the vibrancy or significance it held for the Renaissance as exemplified in the works of Rabelais or Hans Sachs, a point verified by numerous eighteenth-century descriptions.

During Carnival (the pre-Lent celebrations starting as early as November in some locales), normal life gave way to rowdiness, foolishness, licentiousness, cross-dressing (gender as well as class) and every imaginable overindulgence, allowing not only a time of merriment before the severity of Lent but also a protected form of revolt against those in authority. People ignored class and gender differences, and both civil and religious authority figures found them-selves open to ridicule by means that could be either crude or subtle. While Bruegel's painting represents an apparent battle, it marginalizes Lent to cloaked figures at the side and in the background; the activities of Carnival, including dancing, a game involving the throwing and breaking of pots, children's games, and eating and drinking in excess, take centre stage. Near the centre at the front sits the rotund figure of Carnival's exemplar, riding a massive wine barrel (instead of a horse) and contemptuously pointing his huge spit with a now mostly consumed pig in the direction of Lent. At the centre of the painting one finds an aging couple led by a fool, she with an unlit lantern; this unenlightened couple seems to sum up the entire spirit: all are fools, being happily led about in the upside-down world of Carnival.[12]

Goethe's 'The Roman Carnival', an entry in his *Italian Journey* from 1788, may very well be the best-known description of Carnival from the eighteenth century. Here he captures the flavour (although in a somewhat detached manner as if to avoid being drawn in himself) of Carnival time in Rome with vivid descriptions of the people, their activities and the settings.[13] A few extracts will give the spirit:

2   *Battle between Carnival and Lent*: painting by Pieter Bruegel
the Elder, 1559.

Unlike the religious festivals in Rome, the Carnival does not dazzle the eye: there
are no fireworks, no illuminations, no brilliant processions. All that happens is
that, at a given signal, everyone has leave to be as mad and foolish as he likes, and
almost everything, except fisticuffs and stabbing, is permissible.

The difference between the social orders seems to be abolished for the
time being; everyone accosts everyone else, all good-naturedly accept whatever
happens to them, and the insolence and licence of the feast is balanced only by
the universal good humour.

Shortly after noon the bell of the Capitol tolls, and from that moment on, the
most serious-minded Roman, who has so carefully watched his step all year,
throws dignity and prudence to the winds.

The number of people in fancy dress begins to increase. Young men disguised
as women of the lower classes in low-necked dresses are usually the first to
appear. They embrace the men, they take intimate liberties with the women, as
being of their own sex, and indulge in any behaviour which their mood, wit or
impertinence suggests.

One young man stands out in my memory. He played the part of a passionate,
quarrelsome woman perfectly. 'She' went along the whole length of the Corso,
picking quarrels with everyone and insulting them, while her companions pre-
tended to be doing their best to calm her down.

The workaday clothes of all classes can also serve as fancy dress. Persons appear dressed up as stableboys with great brushes, with which they rub the back of anyone whom they care to pick on. Others put on more handsome fancy dress and appear as peasant girls, women from Frascati, fishermen, Neapolitan boatmen and *sbirri*, or as Greeks.

The German baker-apprentices have a reputation in Rome for often getting drunk, so figures may be seen, dressed up in their ordinary or slightly decorated costume, staggering about with flasks of wine. I can remember seeing only one obscene mask.

During the first days the carriages one sees are mostly ordinary ones, for those who have any more elegant and sumptuous vehicles to display are reserving them for the days to follow. But presently open carriages begin to appear, some of which can seat six; two ladies facing each other on raised seats, so that one can see their whole figure, and four gentlemen in the corner seats. Coachmen and footmen are always masked and the horses decorated with gauze and flowers. As one might expect, only beautiful women have the courage to expose themselves so conspicuously to the gaze of the whole population.

Most of the coachmen choose to dress up as women, so that, in the final days, the job of driving horses seems to be reserved for women only. When a coachman spots women in the crowd whom he knows, it is customary for him to lift them up on to his box. They are usually dressed up as men.

The Romans have a passion for the stage, and in the old days were all the more ardent theatre-goers during Carnival because this was the only season at which they could satisfy it. Nowadays, at least one playhouse is also open during the summer and autumn.

Just as in other languages curses and obscene words are often used as expressions of joy or admiration, so, on this evening [Shrove Tuesday], the true meaning or *Sia ammazzato* ['death to you' or 'to hell with you'] is completely forgotten, and it becomes a password, a cry of joy, a refrain added to all jokes and compliments. Someone jeers: '*Sia ammazzato il Signore Abbate che fa l'amore*'.

All ages and all classes contend furiously with each other. Carriage steps are climbed; no chandelier and scarcely a paper lantern is safe. A boy blows out his father's candle, shouting: '*Sia ammazzato il Signore Padre!*' In vain the old man scolds him for this outrageous behaviour; the boy claims the freedom of the evening and curses his father all the more vehemently.

Bringing the descriptions of Carnival closer to home for Mozart (who had enjoyed it in Italy as well), Johann Pezzl, a leading late eighteenth-century Viennese writer, included commentary on the Carnival of Vienna in his *Sketch of Vienna* of 1786–90. In Vienna, Carnival lasted from 7 January to Ash Wednesday, and an irrepressible urge to dance fuelled almost all the activities: 'On every street corner there are invitations in white, or red, blue and yellow, announcing in the largest type: "Today there is music in the such and such rooms", "music with trumpets and drums", "music by candlelight", etc. The

most distinguished place of entertainment is the Redoutensaal.'[14] Michael
Kelly, the noted tenor who doubled in the roles of Don Basilio and Don Curzio
in the first performance of *Le nozze di Figaro*, underscored in his memoirs the
passion of the Viennese for dancing:

> The people of Vienna were in my time dancing mad; as the Carnival approached,
> gaiety began to display itself on all sides . . . the propensity of the Vienna
> ladies for dancing and going to carnival masquerades was so determined, that
> nothing was permitted to interfere with their enjoyment of their favourite
> amusement. . . . For my own part, I thought waltzing from ten at night until
> seven in the morning, a continual whirligig.[15]

While Carnival may be a time of nonsense and innocent fun, it could, Pezzl
warned, be much more than that:

> Carnival is a dangerous time. Many a virgin has lost her innocence and many a
> matron her virtue at this time. How could it be otherwise when, in those lovers'
> hours, flushed with wine and dancing, a couple find themselves alone in a closed
> carriage going home and, having arrived there, the cavalier escorts his lady to
> her bedchamber . . . while her strict father, her vigilant mother or her jealous
> husband . . . is otherwise engaged in pleasure.[16]

During Carnival falling in love could happen quickly, as happened to Mozart's
friend Karl Ditters von Ditterdorf, who fell in love with 'a nice graceful girl' at
a Carnival ball where 'I did not come away from this ball the same man that
I went to it. . . . So out I came with my confession, and she made hers at
the second ball, the day afterwards. Nothing in the world could have been
quicker.'[17] Dittersdorf fell in love often, although this one resulted in a proposal
of marriage which the girl's father rejected.

Carnival amours usually did not last long, and, as Pezzl cautioned, could
be perilous for women of all ages. Casanova's litany of seductions, no doubt
often embellished by boastfulness or touches of fantasy, occurred with considerable frequency during Carnival, and whether real or fictitious, could alert
eighteenth-century male readers to the possibilities awaiting their daughters or
wives during Carnival. In one of his more ingenious – if unfulfilled – stories,
Casanova begins by observing that 'during the Carnival in Venice nuns are
allowed to have this innocent pleasure. There is dancing in the visiting room,
and they remain inside, watching the festivities from behind their wide
gratings.' He claimed he loved two of the female observers, and after putting on
a spectacle in a Pierrot disguise, waited for the one he preferred at the moment
to join him in his bed. To his considerable disappointment the other one came,
who revealed that the two women, themselves in love, had a pact which allowed
her to come with the other's approval. But for Casanova, 'it would have been an
outright denial of love, which could not but rouse my reason to indignation. It

seemed to me that if I settled for doing the honors to C. C. I should be contemptible.'[18] They discussed their predicament all night, she eager to get into his bed, but he unprepared to concede the point on the distinction between love and sex. This 'love' applied to Carnival time only, and the argument seemed curiously abstruse under the circumstances. During Carnival the game of love appeared to hold more importance than the pleasure of conquest.

HANSWURST

Of the various festivities and indulgences of Carnival, few loomed as important as those belonging to the theatre. In fact, in some locales at certain points in time, theatre productions were allowed during Carnival season only. While the eighteenth century generally did not restrict theatre schedules that severely, Carnival nevertheless remained the most important occasion for new productions, commissions often timed to be premiered at Carnival, as happened with Mozart's *Idomeneo* in Munich. A couple of centuries earlier, specific types of plays or theatrical events became associated with Carnival, focusing on Carnival situations such as adultery, using scatological language, being of an improvisatory nature, and dropping the barrier of the proscenium – incorporating the audience into the work. In Germany the plays of this type by Hans Sachs stand out especially, while in Italy the improvisatory *commedia dell'arte* with its stock characters, slapstick action, abusive and scatological language, ridicule of respectability, lovemaking, dancing and games, emerged entirely from this spirit. Of the various *commedia dell'arte* characters, Harlequin most nimbly represents this spirit, with his abusiveness, his enjoyment of trickery, his manner of dress, his acrobatic skill, and his insatiable desire for Colombine.

Italian troupes performing *commedia dell'arte* generated an avid audience in Austria, but a challenge to their popularity eventually came from a German variety early in the eighteenth century, introduced by the Prinzipal (director, chief playwright and actor) of the new theatre near the Kärntnertor, Joseph Anton Stranitzky. In his satires on *opera seria* and other improvisatory pieces in the manner of the *commedia dell'arte*, he introduced a Harlequin-like character with distinctive German features – Hanswurst – a character who would dominate the Viennese stage for much of the century and eventually arouse a trenchant attack from the highest Habsburg authorities. In Stranitzky's conception Hanswurst came from peasant stock, derived in part from Shakespeare's clowns, with an engaging and disarming earthiness that he used to deflate the pretentions of the upper classes. His insolence, though, was not revolutionary; instead, he embodied a sense of unbroken spirit, a sharp tongue to sting attempts at suppression of the voice of the underclasses. His appeal reached well beyond these classes to include much of the Viennese nobility.[19] As Hanswurst went through successive realizations at the hands of Friedrich Wilhelm Weiskern, Gottfried Prehauser and Johann Joseph Felix von Kurz-Bernardon, his character became more grotesquely pot-bellied and foul-mouthed, although Stranitzky, who himself had a prominent pot belly and dressed the character in the costume of a Salzburg peasant – the ultimate country bumpkin in the eyes of the Viennese[20] – had already taken him far down the path of cultural vulgarity.

SONNENFELS'S ATTACK ON HANSWURST

By the time of Mozart's birth in 1756, Hanswurst had become a thorn in the side of some of Austria's enlightened reformers, who saw him as the greatest single threat to raising the level of taste and bringing refinement. The Empress had no interest in the matter, regarding those of the theatre as rabble who did not deserve her attention, but at least one of her ministers, Joseph von Sonnenfels, somewhat to her annoyance, turned the matter into a crusade that consumed much of his energy over a period of a few years, energy that should, Maria Theresa believed, have been directed towards more constructive matters. But for Sonnenfels, himself a writer with literary aspirations, the theatre provided one of the most effective instruments of the Enlightenment, and he wholeheartedly agreed with Lessing that the theatre had a significant educational and moral role to play. Like others in Austria at this time, his own views owed much to the thinking of Gottsched, who had made enormous strides earlier in the century in raising the level of German to the point where it could become a language sufficiently refined to sustain literary usage.[21] Unlike the ex-Jesuits who flooded to Vienna after the dissolution of the monasteries, bringing a vision of the Enlightenment shaped by a life of Jesuit training, Sonnenfels was Jewish by birth and rose to a position of remarkable height in Maria Theresa's administration, considering her prejudice against non-Catholics.

Maria Theresa's lack of interest in the popular theatre placed her with the old school that saw no great harm in these entertainments, perhaps even conceding that they offered a healthy counterbalance or useful outlet for disaffection with the policies of the regime. Sonnenfels, on the other hand, represented the new breed of enlightened bureaucrats, convinced that he knew what was best for the population and unable to allow any room for the common sense of the people. Lessing had already succeeded to a large extent in ridding Germany of its crude and vulgar entertainments, and Vienna's continued indulgence in these remained a source of considerable embarrassment. Unlike others who had waged this battle at the level of literary refinement or had attacked the actors themselves, Sonnenfels turned it into a social issue, arguing that the fundamental problem lay with the low level of the public taste. With improvements in the taste and standards of the audience through the correct approach to education, the quality of the drama and activities of the actors would naturally rise.[22] His distaste for comedy did not stop with *commedia dell'arte*, but also included

Goldoni and the whole range of comedy for the theatre. Concerning opera, he held all comic types up to comparison with Gluck's serious operas, and against that standard, in his opinion, they all fared badly.

As a literary reformer Sonnenfels sometimes went to absurd lengths, but in spite of this he came fairly close to achieving in Austria what Lessing had accomplished in Germany. While Joseph did not particularly like him, and Sonnenfels's star fell quickly during the new sovereign's sole regency after 1780, on this matter Sonnenfels received Joseph's support in spite of his high-handed and disagreeable manner in dealing with it.[23] His insistence on propriety in drama went much further than that of most writers; any force opposing morality in a dramatic work must be soundly defeated – there should be no unresolved issues at the end. Evil in its various manifestations could be present as a foil allowing virtue to be highlighted, but this clear weighting in favour of good all but eliminates the possibility of real conflict or drama from occurring. The mission of the theatre, then, was 'to defend the good, to fight evil, to uphold authority, to obviate subversion'.[24] Joseph may not have liked Sonnenfels, but their views on the theatre had much in common. Both of them disapproved of not only *commedia dell'arte*, but most of the foreign-language drama performed in Vienna. Joseph believed it important to have a national theatre, which he established modestly, but this ultimately led to the Burgtheater. Unlike his mother, Joseph took the theatre seriously, agreeing with Sonnenfels on its didactic and moral value, and the puritanical streak in Joseph that drove much of his own reform had much in common with Sonnenfels's motivation.[25]

Sonnenfels's request to Joseph, supported by Gebler, to ban improvised comedy from the Austrian stage (if words were not written down they could not be censored, and enlightened reform in this case depended entirely on censorship) was granted in 1770. Needless to say, this did not sit well with much of the audience, now deprived of its favourite entertainment, or with the actors and directors. The Enlightenment had been rammed down their throats, and it was lean and distasteful. Sonnenfels and Joseph had broken the balance between Carnival and Lent, turning it into a genuine battle in which Lent, with all the oppressive force of authority, attempted to destroy the spirit of Carnival, leaving people with nothing but virtue, refinement, good taste and high standards. The chances of success were no higher than Joseph's other reforms (although for different reasons), and likenesses of Hanswurst continued to pop up in various guises, none more subtle and engaging than the creations of Mozart. Mozart's colleague for *Die Zauberflöte*, Emanuel Schikaneder, perhaps summed it up best when he retorted that he would not trade all of Lessing's collected works for the first act of the slapstick comedy *Tirolerwastl*.[26]

Unlike Mozart's working relationships with some of his librettists earlier in his career, we know little of the nature of the collaboration with Schikaneder. In the absence of details, we have developed a fairly sober picture of the two of

them poring over various literary sources to construct the libretto and having
elevated discussions about the presentation and triumph of the higher values
of society in general and freemasonry in particular. More than likely it took a
very different form. Mozart had known Schikaneder for a long time, since
Schikaneder had been stationed with his troupe in Salzburg in 1780, and
the two of them had often enjoyed indulgences in questionable activities.
Schikaneder's sexual exploits will be noted in chapter 8; little appears to have
changed late in the decade as he occasionally found himself at odds with
respectable society. That included his attempt to join the masonic lodge 'Zu den
drei Schlüssln' (The Three Keys) in Regensburg; in May 1789 the lodge asked
him to avoid meetings for six months because of reports about his private life as
well as his 'self-aggrandizement'.[27] When he turned up in Vienna in July 1789
as director of the Freihaus-Theater, both he and Mozart no doubt were
delighted that they could pick up where they had left off almost a decade
earlier, encouraging each other's roguish inclinations.

Their collaboration is much more likely to have taken place in a tavern than
a library, fuelled by an abundance of wine, and one can easily imagine
them howling with laughter as the work took shape. Mozart clearly shared
Schikaneder's enthusiasm for Hanswurst, and here lay his opportunity to make
him a flesh-and-blood character and coat him in bird feathers, a real Hanswurst
this time and not just an Osmin or a Leporello with a mask. For the court
theatre such a character would not fly, but at the Freihaus-Theater with its
receptive audience it could. If anyone thought that the Catholic church, freemasonry, the nobility, the monarchy, the Enlightenment, or the values of any of
the above were not going to get a rough satirical ride at the Freihaus-Theater,
they were sadly mistaken. But this was not Punch and Judy: one did not hit the
sovereign (or any other figure of authority) over the head with an enormous
sausage; instead, one made the person with power look somewhat inviting and
made his objectives seem almost appealing, singing praises to him as well as his
higher purpose at the end, but all the while letting Hanswurst steal the show.
Further, one designed a suitably elaborate mythical web which would throw any
serious-minded censor or critic off the track.

Of Papageno's carnivalesque Hanswurst characteristics there can be no
doubt. He shuns enlightened attitudes, just like the old couple at the centre of
Bruegel's painting, and his real pleasures are all physical indulgences. He has an
insatiable appetite for food and wine, and an even stronger urge for his female
counterpart with whom he can make lots of little Papageno/as. Very simply,
when not eating and drinking, he can think of no better way to spend his time
than in endless love-making. If we attempt to write him off as some sort of
Caliban-like lower form of existence, we must contend with the way Mozart and
Schikaneder present him. Not only can we enjoy him more than the other
characters by being able to laugh with (and at) him, but musically he also
appeals to the audience much more engagingly than the dutiful Tamino or the
stiffly authoritarian Sarastro.

THEATRE AND CARNIVAL

Opposition to stifling cultural or political policies obviously did not have to be invented in the final quarter of the eighteenth century; some of the most effective means were already well established in the theatre, and Mozart's exposure to certain playwrights gave him ample ammunition to develop his own strategies. Sonnenfels may have disliked written comedies as much as improvised ones, but he and the censors had much greater difficulty slamming the door on some of the great comedies of the past century, works that often arose in an atmosphere not unlike the one Mozart now faced. These comedies did not come from northern Germany, where sophisticated comedy was not part of the mentality. English Restoration comedy failed to capture the German imagination, in part because few people knew the language. The two languages very much a part of the sophisticated or upper-class life of Vienna were Italian and French, and these two languages shared great comic writers, including Goldoni, Molière and Beaumarchais. Anyone involved in the theatre in Austria would have known a smattering of their plays, especially the Italian poets and librettists who wielded so much power in Vienna. Since comic opera flourished in Vienna under Joseph's rule during the 1780s, and numerous librettos were adaptations of the works of the great playwrights, familiarity with these plays came with relative ease. Mozart's friend Joseph Haydn set three of Goldoni's texts to music himself and knew numerous others through the vast operatic and theatrical repertoire at Eszterháza. Mozart's own discovery of the works of Molière from the gift of Fridolin Weber, an enormously important event for him, will receive full treatment in chapter 4.

It is, of course, one thing to discover some of the great comic works but quite another to know what to do with them – to have a sense of how one might adapt them strategically to one's own works. For that matter, it required an uncanny skill to recognize the subversive or protestant facets of these works and to see how subtly in some cases these were integrated into works written to be performed under the noses of the most repressive authorities, as was especially true in France. Two of Mozart's greatest operatic masterpieces, *Le nozze di Figaro* and *Don Giovanni*, owe their existence directly to Beaumarchais and Molière, and Mozart clearly learned much of subversion and subtlety from these two writers. Many of their works, along with those of Goldoni, brim with the spirit of Carnival, placing their subversiveness within a well-established tradition with which all levels of society could identify. This type of theatre could, of course, counterbalance some of the more odious aspects of the regime in a country such as France, and one suspects that at least to some extent those at the highest level understood and tolerated this. Mozart, in presenting his own challenge to Habsburg society, could do no better than adapt works that already served a subversive purpose, finding his own characteristic levels of subtlety and designing these to meet the issues and circumstances of the repressive benevolence of Joseph II and his ministers. Of special fascination is Mozart's recreation of Carnival in his works as well as the birth given to new descendants of Harlequin or even Hanswurst.

A tradition arose during the sixteenth century of using Carnival rites or carnivalesque theatre as a vehicle for protest, and this continued to be a factor in the eighteenth century.[28] It can be argued that the low forms of comedy, *commedia dell'arte* or the Hanswurst improvisations in German-speaking countries, shared that spirit of protest. The vulgarity of Hanswurst, his obscene speech or his fascination with gluttony, defecating and urinating, go too far beyond the bounds of decency; this is no longer good clean fun, and while he may have been somewhat sanitized during the eighteenth century, his offensiveness threatened many, prompting warnings to children of the immorality of gluttony.[29] The moral repudiation of the likes of Hanswurst and what he stands for – an attitude at the very heart of the ascent of modern bourgeois culture – may arise from a dread of (and simultaneous fascination with) the low and vulgar. Tom Cheesman places the issue sharply into perspective: 'The forms of "high culture" elaborated since the early modern period enact an unceasing dialectic between conscious repudiation of, and unconscious desire for all that is transgressive and "low".'[30] Because of this unconscious element, aspects of the low continue to surface in the fabric of high culture, raising fascinating issues in the attempts at marginalization. Carnival challenges authority, deliberately offending 'the Enlightened principles of reason and taste, virtue and decorum. So the vogue would be a kind of protest against repressive rationalism, a celebration of the flesh articulating a momentary popular collective resistance to official norms of propriety and property.'[31]

The nature of the conflict between these primary forces does not lend itself to a simple decoding of opposites, as Richard Sheppard argues:

> the relationship between 'high' and 'low' culture was extremely complex: 'high' culture took over and/or attempted to repress 'low' forms; representatives of 'high' culture (like students and lesser clergy) who had not been completely assimilated into that culture, together with 'low', popular culture in general, parodied and travestied 'high' forms (especially during the Carnival season). Consequently, 'high' and 'low' cultures interpenetrated with one another and 'the result has to be read as a palimpsest'.[32]

This sense of double reading, one erased to make way for the other, comes through brilliantly in the works of Molière, Beaumarchais and Goldoni. While Mozart discovered this through his own reading, he also gained access through his various librettists – especially Lorenzo da Ponte, who, like any Italian librettist, would have known the works of Goldoni intimately. Prior to Goldoni, Italy enjoyed a rich *commedia dell'arte* tradition but very little sophisticated theatre since opera dominated the theatre. Goldoni attempted to build a foundation for theatre in Italy, but in the light of existing practice, one should not be surprised that he borrowed heavily from *commedia dell'arte* and that he continued to write librettos for opera. With his dramatic instincts, various of his texts for opera, such as *Il mondo della luna*, *La buona figliuola* and *L'amore artigiano*, quickly rose to the top as sought-after texts by composers because of their enormous audience appeal. That did not prevent his other plays from being adapted to opera, and in the case of Mozart, *Don Giovanni*, while derived from a number of sources, owes much to Goldoni's *Don Giovanni tenorio o sia Il dissoluto*.

Along with the pervasiveness of *commedia dell'arte* in Goldoni's plays, Carnival also plays a pronounced role, in characters, situations and social out-look. Since he wrote many of the plays for *commedia dell'arte* actors, he strug-gled constantly to keep the actors to the script instead of doing what came naturally: improvising. Some plays, such as the early *Il servitore di due padroni* (The servant of two masters), which Mozart contemplated setting to music in 1783, started as an improvised drama, later to be given a fully written-out text to commit it permanently to the repertoire and to keep the *lazzi* or tricks and jests of the actors under control. The written texts took their cue from the improvised stage, using coarse or abusive language, lies, deception, acts of offensiveness, and reversals of expectation. The stock characters continued to wear masks appropriate to their social classes, as well as costumes to indicate class or attitudes to seriousness or gluttony. Servants usually outwit their masters, and the aristocracy often takes humiliating abuse in his plays. Women in some cases fare better than men, as they possess truth in degrees that men do not. In a way closely related to the sense of protest in Carnival, Goldoni gave his works a revolutionary character making those in authority appear inept, in placing virtue outside of the masculine domain, and in elevating characters at the bottom of the social heap, such as the despised *gondolieri* or starving serv-ants, to flesh and blood characters more human than their masters.[33]

Molière's plays contain nothing less of the spirit of Carnival than Goldoni's, and were most often intended for performance during Carnival and occasionally included specific Carnival scenes. One such Carnival scene, the finale to *Le Malade imaginaire* – a burlesque ceremony of the conferment of a doctor's degree on the invalid – shows an absurd medical examination with copious amounts of bastardized Latin, presentation of regalia, display of gigantic medical instruments, and assurance in song and dance that he will live eternally, with at least a millennium of defecating, eating, drinking and bleeding. Amid these wishes from the chorus, a surgeon prays 'may all his anni Be to him boni And favourable ever Et n'habere never Quam plaguas, poxas, Fievras, pluresias Bloody effusions and dissenterias'.[34] This imaginary victory over death, with its accompanying focus on disease and the lower part of the body, the mocking of a respected profession, and the frivolous use of prayer along with the defiance of death, struck many as blasphemy and sacrilege, preventing its first performance before the king at Versailles, where its intended première should have happened during Carnival season.[35] Along with Goldoni's *Don Giovanni Tenorio*, another major source for Mozart's *Don Giovanni* was Molière's *Dom Juan*, a work similarly imbued with a Carnival atmosphere with its focus on the underclasses, gluttony, seduction, deception, violence, coarse and vernacular language, as well as disdain for patriarchal authority.

The subversive element in the works of Goldoni or Molière lies not with outright challenges to authority of a physical or argumentative nature, but with subtle revelations of the true essence of authority figures or with non-overt relegation of them to a background against a foreground populated with peasants, servants and chambermaids. In Molière, for example, those in positions of power in some of his later plays can be seen to attempt to replace the independence of thought of their subjects with their own words of superimposition, creating a virtual ventriloquism – something he understood well from his own battles to resist attempts to silence him.[36] In the comic onslaught of Goldoni and Molière, laughter confronted authority, a laughter that even some of those it targeted could enjoy, never a vicious laughter but rather one that can transform unpleasantness in the spirit of Carnival, turning the world as we know it on its head and revealing that the upside-down world makes every bit as much sense as the other one, even though one may arrive at the conclusion through a parade of absurdities.

For Mozart, these writers, with their uncanny ability to balance on the line between Carnival and Lent, to satisfy the censors and ridicule them at the same time, stood foremost among his mentors. Aspects of Molière's treatment of this in *Dom Juan* will be discussed in chapter 4, and that spirit surely permeates *Don Giovanni*. Our sensibilities seem offended in the extreme by the opening scene, as Don Giovanni appears nothing short of a rapist, yet Mozart defuses both the tension and the offensiveness with the musical presence of Leporello. As Giovanni and Donna Anna remain locked in conflict, Leporello provides the audience with his own running commentary, contrasting their high, serious style with his own low style of vocal blather and buffa patter. Even after the Commendatore has been run through and gasps his last breaths, the patter from Leporello continues. How can we take these events seriously? Very simply, we must ignore Mozart's music if we do.

At the outset Mozart alerts us to a world turned on its head, where the most serious events seem not serious at all – where we feel inclined to laugh at a state of affairs that the least shred of decency should oblige us to find repugnant. This upside-down world, which starts with the opening scene and runs through to the final singing of the moral, this bombardment by the lowest *zanni* or *commedia dell'arte* or the ironic treatment of what should otherwise be taken as seriousness, is most assuredly the world of Carnival.[37] This opera brims with the most basic features of Carnival, especially seduction, masquerading, lies, coarseness, ascent of the lower classes, gender equality, abuse, disorder, grotesqueness, drinking, emphasis on the physical, foolishness and fascination with sexuality. In fact, there may be good reason to regard the opening scene as a small Carnival play in its own right, a possibility which would allow it to be taken lightly. Don Giovanni enters Donna Anna's chambers masked, and her horror does not immediately arise as she initially interprets the intrusion as a harmless Carnival prank, perhaps perpetrated by Don Ottavio or even an incognito friend, chiding him with no more than a 'gentle reproach'. As the beneficiary of a solid moral upbringing, unlike Zerlina, she has no doubt been warned about the perils of Carnival time, and on realizing her mistake about the intruder, she marshals her deepest moral fibre to find the strength to get rid of him. Don Giovanni, disappointed to have entered the sanctuary of a young woman not favourably disposed to the conventions of masquerade, attempts a graceful exit. She will have nothing of this, and even less so her moralist father, who insists on settling the matter with swords. Giovanni refuses but the old man leaves him no choice; with an insult of 'Misero! Attendi, Se vuoi morir' (Miserable wretch, prepare yourself, if you want to die), he finishes him off, fulfilling the familiar Carnival threat noted by Goethe in Rome that young men hurl at their authoritarian elders: 'Sia ammazzato il Signore Abbate [or Padre or Commendatore]' (Death to you . . .).

Social conventions take a battering throughout the opera as Don Giovanni thumbs his nose at religion, marriage, the law and honest or decent dealings with one's fellow beings. Unlike Molière's loquacious and free-thinking Don Juan, Don Giovanni's indulgences in sex, food and drink make him more of a Carnival character, having more in common with the *commedia dell'arte* Juans before Molière with their lustier, more animal-like features.[38] Mozart's revolt here struck broadly and cut deeply, challenging the entire fabric of enlightened society. It achieves this by wearing the mask of a morality play which the audience (and the censors) believed in the end could set everything right as heaven would triumph. The mask brilliantly deceived Mozart's contemporaries, and we still continue more often than not to miss the musical irony of the concluding moral.

Before being dragged down to hell in flames by spirits, Giovanni hurls his final insults at God: 'God is a fairy tale. . . . I scorn Him, I defy Him!' Could the opera end here, as it did for the earliest production in Vienna? Very unlikely. If it did, we might have cause to believe that Lent won the battle. Now, just as Bruegel marginalizes Lent and leaves Carnival centre stage in his painting, Mozart paints his followers of Lent into a corner of irrelevance. In a vaudeville they come forward singly or in pairs to tell what will happen to them next, and all become somewhat diminished in the act. They have been unable to tame Don Giovanni and even after his physical removal they find him laughing at them from beyond the grave. They can do nothing but cheerfully leave him in the realm of Pluto and Proserpina, but, as ignorant of myth as incompetent in retribution, they forget that Proserpina has only one foot in Pluto's hell while the other remains firmly on earth.

With the concluding proclamation of Lent in *Don Giovanni*, the statement that evildoers will come to their deserved end, Mozart perpetrated one of his most skilful deceptions on the censors and the audience. Lawrence Lipkin gets it right when he notes that the '*deus ex machina* that winds up the action relies on make-up and trap-doors and fire that could not singe a sleeve. In real life the aristocrat would bribe the officials and go scot-free.'[39] While he may not get off quite scot-free in the opera, Mozart at least gives him the last laugh as his derisive spirit infiltrates the singing of the moral. The style may be liturgical, but Mozart treats it ironically. The chorus has difficulty with the word 'wicked' as accents are misplaced or the wrong syllables are prolonged in the text 'E de' perfidi'. The word 'morte' (death) should be serious in the extreme, but it can hardly be that when four tied whole notes on the first syllable are followed by a quarter-note hiccough on the second. Most conductors refuse to treat this quarter note as Mozart wrote it, fearing that in the presto tempo it would sound ridiculous. Mozart knew exactly what he wanted and wrote it accordingly. If after the remaining examples of how not to write seriously in the liturgical style we have still missed the irony, Mozart does not let the matter go by, as the orchestral conclusion with its sparkling humour offers the final nose-thumbing gesture. In the end, Carnival wins.

Chapter 2
Leopold Mozart and the Republic of Letters

In the extraordinary correspondence between Mozart and his father, Leopold set the epistolary wheels in motion; he understood the nature of epistolary commerce and the power of the pen in relation to his contemporaries in Germany as well as abroad. As the instigator of what stands as one of the finest German-language correspondences during the eighteenth century, to say nothing of his role as teacher of the most brilliant of all composers, Leopold Mozart deserves our special attention as an intellectual, tutor and writer; questions naturally arise about his intellectual background, his literary models, and his other literary accomplishments. Since Wolfgang did not share his father's enlightened vision or enthusiasm for certain writers, and succeeded in demolishing Leopold's greatest literary project as an epistolary respondent, one needs to know who and what the targets of Mozart's darts were. Our knowledge of the various people and forces in Leopold's intellectual realm is murky at best, emerging in bits and pieces from letters and other documents, and because of this a kind of reconstruction becomes necessary – taking the major figures we know attracted his attention and identifying their ideas which may have especially appealed to him.

Biographers have recognized a number of anomalies in the few surviving records of Leopold's early life, such as his apparently dismal performance as a student at the University of Salzburg, but these become less troublesome as one accounts for his genuine intellectual models in relation to the education he received. For a Catholic thinker living in a town which escaped the Thirty Years War because it had had the foresight to expel its non-Catholics, and having attended a university so mired in archaic Catholic doctrine that the introduction of the thought of a conservative such as Christian Wolff seemed revolutionary, Leopold Mozart in many respects stood out as conspicuously on the leading edge, not in harmony with his surroundings. But the leading edge for Salzburg resembled thought in other parts of Germany and Europe from the beginning of the century, ideas that seemed painfully obsolete and irrelevant to the younger Mozart, ideas easily punctured by a young Turk cleverly wielding a

3   Leopold Mozart: portrait by Pietro Antonio Lorenzoni, 1765.

perspicacious rapier. Leopold had gone far to position himself beyond the salification of his adopted home, but unfortunately for him not far enough to remove the target of his son's wily – but at times acid – defiance.

LEOPOLD'S EDUCATION

From the beginning it appears that Leopold's family in Augsburg had in mind that he should become a priest. Leopold, who maintained a lifelong contempt for members of the clergy, regarding priests and monks as poor keepers of the religion he prized, resisted this with as much subtlety as he could muster, keeping his hand close to his chest so as to continue his education in the humanities as long as possible. His intelligence was never in question, and he made an excellent start in his home town of Augsburg at the Jesuit Gymnasium of St Salvator, which he entered at the age of eight in 1727. Two further years at the Lyceum (1735–7) added to his firm grounding in Latin, French and Italian, as well as a more sophisticated understanding of his native language, although he did not complete the programme – skipping the university preparatory class in theology. While the Jesuit education placed less emphasis on the sciences, he nevertheless received some instruction in astronomy, geometry, mineralogy and biology, enough ultimately to pass an enthusiasm for these on to his son.

For a promising student like Leopold, it should come as no surprise that he would enroll at the University of Salzburg. This major university ranked only behind Vienna and Leipzig in size among German universities, and attracted eighty per cent of its students from outside Austria, including many from Augsburg or other parts of Swabia. The student population numbered in the range of 2,000, and over 5,000 doctorates had already been granted. Leopold entered in 1737, completing his first year in the study of logic and jurisprudence, passing with commendation and gaining the baccalaureate. During his second year, however, things appeared to go badly off the rails, as the university record notes the demise of his university career apparently resulting from his own negligence:

> Don Johann Georg [Leopold] Mozart, a Swabian of Augsburg, has from the beginning of the civil year hardly attended Natural Science more than once or twice, and has thereby rendered himself unworthy of the name of student. A few days before the examination he was called before the Dean and informed that henceforth he would no longer be numbered among the students. Having heard this sentence, he offered no appeals, accepted the sentence, and departed as if indifferently; therefore he was not called for further examination.[1]

Considering Leopold's later obsession with productivity and dependability in letters of advice to his son, this appears badly out of character.

Various explanations for Leopold's behaviour seem possible. His father had recently died, and his mother, with whom he remained in conflict for the rest of her life, may have withdrawn the funding for his education, especially when it became evident that his studies were not leading to the priesthood. Leopold himself may have felt that the direction of his education could be concealed no longer, and withdrew (or lapsed into inertia) rather than continuing the deception. But that still fails to explain why someone of Leopold's intelligence and industriousness would allow his formal education at a major university to come to such a shabby end. Some allowance can perhaps be made for his age, and he would not be the first or the last bright student to see his higher education dissipate. Perhaps his educational decline resembled that of many others in his situation, students whose mental agility and capacity for broadening leave them thoroughly bored and repulsed by the stultifying nature of the instruction inflicted on them.

The University of Salzburg may have been large and appealing to many Catholics, but it stood at least a full generation out of synchronization with the rest of Europe. As a Benedictine institution serving an exclusively Catholic constituency, it did not attract professors who would come up with new ideas or for that matter even entertain new ideas when they arose. The likes of Professors Gregorius Horner, Godefridus Kröll, Andreas Gschwandtner, Eberhard Ruedorfer, Werigand Kogler, Aemilian Drahtzieher, Beda von Schallhammer, Friedrich Falzeder, Oddo Gutrath and Ambrosius Rieger, all of whom held positions there while Leopold was a student, have thankfully long since been forgotten, except in the annals of university historians.[2] The primacy of the medieval Catholic university held sway here, with philosophy and theology under the thumb of scholasticism and the Thomists, where the writings of Thomas Aquinas were adapted to suit the times, which, by the eighteenth century, allowed for an Aristotelian influence. Challenge to ecclesiastical authority was foreign to the culture, and Thomism itself had become part of the establishment.

By the early 1740s, after Leopold Mozart had already left, some slightly more recent thought began to creep in, such as Rektor Vogl's introduction of the systematic philosophy of Christian Wolff,[3] thought which itself was derived from Leibniz, but coming from a Protestant professor from Halle seemed revolutionary in the Salzburg scheme of things. Wolff, like Leibniz, saw the structure of the world and the objects in it as there to fulfill God's wise ends, and held that the best of all possible worlds arose from the free and wise choice of God. His argument that moral and judicial laws lie in natural reason, independent of God's will, along with his emphasis on logic and mathematics, was somewhat more difficult for Catholic theologians to swallow. By the time Wolff's ideas penetrated Salzburg, their grip on northern Germany had been tested for some forty years; the Pietists who succeeded in discharging Wolff from Halle had been forced to eat humble pie when the authorities ultimately brought him back and made him chancellor.

Leopold Mozart's inclinations towards logic and law revealed more of an affinity with Wolff's views than those of his own professors, and one suspects that had these been in the curriculum while he attended the university, he might have prolonged his stay. Certainly the absorption of Protestant thought into the Catholic realm accorded well with Leopold's own views, as his own religion did not succeed in drumming out of him the interdenominationalism he brought from his native Augsburg. Yet one suspects that even the introduction of Wolff or the historicism of the Italian Lodovico Muratori into the curriculum would not have been enough to challenge Leopold's questioning mind; the writers who interested him most, who ultimately became his literary models, were Protestants who would not gain the acceptance that Wolff had, and, having moved in that direction, he would always find himself as something of a renegade Catholic. That presented no conflict in his own mind, but his sense of tolerance far outstripped the religion to which he remained loyal.

THE MAN OF LETTERS

Aside from his formal Catholic education, we can safely assume that Leopold Mozart discovered another education – one which ultimately touched him much more deeply, this being a self-education through his own reading. That started in Augsburg, a city where Catholics and Protestants coexisted much better than elsewhere in Germany, and where Leopold came under the spell of the leading German Protestant writers of the early part of the century. Unlike the Catholic theologians who seemed to go out of their way to foster obscurantism, to write in a way that would not be understood by anyone but another Catholic theologian, Protestant writers addressed themselves to the world at large, to the emerging literate population from all classes and religions, and wrote so as to be understood by all. Both the medium and the message engaged the reader, as well as the linkage between the two. The enlightened message promoted morality and refinement leading to the ultimate goal of happiness. This should be available to all, and that could only be achieved through a use of language that anyone could understand, a language stripped of ostentation and formality, and spoken by ordinary people although not in a rough way or with local colour. Part of the exercise involved raising the taste of ordinary people, and in the process of refinement finding enlightened happiness.

Protestant German writers did not lead the way in this endeavour. During the first half of the eighteenth century they had numerous models from England and France to build on, and the Germans read these avidly – especially the English models. Shaftesbury's *Characteristics of Men, Manners, Opinions, Times* appealed to writers such as Hagedorn, Lessing and Weisse, and may have actually been better received in Germany than in England.[4] Similarly, the *Spectator* and *Tatler* of Addison and Steele engaged a large German readership through translations in Johann Mattheson's *Der Vernünfftler*, a moral weekly appearing in Hamburg as early as 1713. Developments in France paralleled those of England, although Germans much more grudgingly acknowledged this because of traditional rivalries with the French. Still, they were perfectly well aware of the literary activities in France, and in fact some notable Germans, such as Baron Grimm who became a primary source of information for Leopold Mozart on international literary developments, participated in these. Not only did France produce many of the literary giants of the century, but writing took on a social orientation through the literary outreach of the salons, placing women at the heart of the civilizing process. The various literary activities in France, including the *Encyclopédie*, the *Correspondance littéraire* and the letters to absent members of salons, all had the effect of fostering a vibrant climate of thought and refinement, drawing ever larger circles of those with a passion for letters. This appealed not only to the educated population but served to offer education, giving new meaning to what the seventeenth century had termed 'The Republic of Letters'.[5] The web of this 'Republic' extended well beyond

French borders, becoming a truly international phenomenon, carried into Germany by people like Grimm, by the outreach of the *Correspondance littéraire*, and by other active exchanges of letters.

By the mid-1750s Leopold actively engaged in correspondences with various individuals, although at this point he gave little thought to the preservation of letters for the purposes of posterity. The exception to that was Leopold's letters to his old friend Johann Jakob Lotter in Augsburg. Lotter, a publisher, had agreed to print Leopold's manual on violin playing, and a lively correspondence, of which twenty-nine of Leopold's letters have survived, ensued in 1755–6, covering various details of publication and some personal matters as well (MBA i 3–48). Leopold bore the cost of publication himself, although having been disinherited by his mother he involved Lotter in a plan to recover the 300 Gulden he believed he was owed:

> I wish to take this excellent opportunity . . . of telling you how you can assist me to carry out a scheme. All my brothers and sisters are now married and have all received in advance 300 Gulden of their heritage from my mother. Now it might well happen that in time to come, as I have as yet received nothing, matters might look very black for me. For this reason it has occurred to me that I now have the finest opportunity of likewise acquiring 300 Gulden for myself. I have therefore made a statement to my mother, but especially to my chief guardian, and represented to them that I absolutely must have the 300 Gulden for the publication of my book, hoping, as a result of this, to squeeze out the 300 Gulden, for otherwise, one day or other, the devil may fly away with them. Supposing now that you were asked questions! You must always say that you did not know how costly it would be, but that it might possibly cost as much as 300 Gulden. This is what I wanted to tell you.[6]

Only in a well-established friendship would Leopold be likely to confide such a scheme, one which put his credibility in Augsburg on the line. Leopold did not save Lotter's letters to himself, but the fact Lotter saved Leopold's marks the first indication of a prospect that Leopold himself only recognized some six years later. The fame of Leopold Mozart, as the author of a book, would spread throughout Europe, and his letters might some day be worthy of publication. Lotter's instinct about Leopold proved to be right in the extreme.

Most of these letters deal with pre-publication issues, revealing Leopold to be exceptionally well informed on aspects of the book trade, including typography, layout, paper quality and illustration,[7] but personal matters come up as well, most notably the birth of a male child in 1756: 'I must inform you that on the evening of the 27th January my wife was delivered of a boy and, moreover, successfully. She was surprisingly weak and the after-birth had to be removed. But now, thank God, the child and mother are doing well. She presents her compliments to both of you. The boy is called Joannes Chrysostomus Wolfgang Gottlieb.'[8]

We also learn in these letters of Leopold's other business arrangements with Lotter, that Leopold distributed Lotter's books in Salzburg, selling them on commission. On 28 August 1755 he referred to a group of books intended for this purpose, including Gottsched's *Redekunst, Critische Dichtkunst* and *Deutsche Sprachkunst*, and Gellert's *Fabeln* and *Lehrgedichte* (MBA i 14). Selling the books of these two Protestant authors in Salzburg was not simply business as usual for Leopold but a labour of love. In these writers more than any others at this time he found his own literary mentors – the literary principles he aspired to, the quality of writing and the approach to enlightened morality he endorsed. Here lay the missing link from his own Catholic education, and now, going much further than Professor Vogl's safe appropriation of Wolff into Catholic thought, Leopold took the much larger and more seditious step of emulating Protestant writers whose works did not lend themselves to Catholic isolationism or doctrine. At this point, Gottsched, Gellert's own teacher, had the greater impact on Leopold, and one notes a number of places in the correspondence with Lotter where Leopold invokes Gottsched's name in relation to the violin manual, pointing to matters of vocabulary, turns of phrase, or overall effect where Gottsched's own writing should be taken as the model (MBA i 4, 5, 8, 10, 20). Lotter surely needed little prompting to accept Gottsched as the authority in matters of German language usage, and these discussions as much as anything underline a shared enthusiasm.

Gottsched placed much emphasis on a clear, instructive and pleasant style; in his journal *Der Patriot*, addressed to women readers and professed to be written by a group of women, he noted ironically – knowing the state of academic writing – that not all scholars would be capable of cultivating such a style.[9] Above all, he stressed that writers should use naturalness in language, and in this way would find the greatest virtue. By the third decade of the eighteenth century he stood out as the undisputed arbiter of German language usage and mentor to the next generation of German writers. Leipzig, where he taught at the university, became the city best exemplifying the proper use of German, and not unlike the *philosophes* in Paris, he soon found himself surrounded by a society which shared his views and disseminated his linguistic ideas in writings that included prose and verse. Those who cultivated this branch of the republic of letters in Germany took strong notice of the leading French writers, from whom they found support for their development of a literary language.[10] As influential as Gottsched may have been, concerning poetry he had little more than a pedantic idea of the possibilities, although these ideas provided a critical start for German literature. Because of his conservatism and pedantry, though, he came under strong criticism from certain quarters, and from this he never entirely recovered. Towards the end of his life, 'old, fat and remarried', as Eric Blackall points out, he 'had become a laughing-stock'.[11] By the time Goethe came to Leipzig to study, Gottsched had nothing to offer his generation, but Gottsched's pupil Gellert did, and Goethe turned to him for tutoring.

THE VIOLIN MANUAL

Leopold Mozart gained citizenship in the republic of letters with the publication of his *Versuch einer gründlichen Violinschule* (*A Treatise on the Fundamental Principles of Violin Playing*), published in 1756 but formulated over a period of years prior to that date. Though he apparently hesitated to proceed with the project, this changed, he informs us in the Preface, when

> I received by chance Herr Marpurg's *Historic Critical Contributions to the Advancement of Music*. I read his Preface. He says at the beginning that one need not complain of the number of musical publications. He points out and regrets, moreover, that a guide to the violin is still lacking. This stirred my former resolution once more into life and was the strongest stimulus to send these pages to the publisher in my native city.[12]

Friedrich Marpurg commanded respect as one of the leading writers on music of the day, as author of numerous treatises, translator of French treatises such as d'Alembert's *Éléments de musique* into German, and writer of a journal, *Kritische Briefe*, with the format of letters exchanged among the members of an imaginary society, in a manner very much like both French and English moral weeklies.[13] Leopold's claim to have stumbled across Marpurg's *Historisch-Kritische Beyträge zur Aufnahme der Musik* seems unduly modest; Leopold knew the full range of writing on music perfectly well as he identified Glarianus, Zarlino, Bontemps, Kepler, Vogt, Neidhart, Euler, Scheibe, Prinz, Werkmeister, Fux, Mattheson, Mizler, Spiess, Marpurg and Quantz in a letter to Lotter dated 6 November 1755 (MBA i 19). Two decades later, Leopold referred to these and other writers in a letter to his son, suggesting he had a project in mind to incorporate their positions into a comprehensive study:

> There must be some good material in it [Vogler's *Kurpfälzische Tonschule*], since he could copy out the *Clavier Methode* from [C. P. E.] Bach's book, follow the instructions of the *Singmethode* of Tosi and Agricola, and the instructions for composition and harmony from Fux, Riepel, Marpurg, Mattheson, Spiess, Scheibe, d'Alembert, Rameau and a lot of others, and offer them as a shorter system, which I have long had in mind (MBA ii 374).

While exceptionally knowledgeable about the writings of music theorists, Leopold appears to have been more strongly influenced by the likes of Gottsched, whose mission was much greater than the transmission of information or rules. That, of course, does not exclude the possibility of some writers on music, including Marpurg, holding similar goals. Johann Mattheson, himself the editor of one of the first moral weeklies in German, carried the spirit of something larger into his treatise *Der vollkommene Capellmeister*, in which he claims 'it is the true purpose of music to be, above all else, a moral lesson [*Zucht-*

Lehre]'.[14] Leopold's dedication and Preface may not go that far, but his references to the need to grasp truth, purity and good taste, in the context of enlightened moral discourse, amount to the same thing.

As well as his references in the correspondence with Lotter identifying Gottsched as his model for language usage, other factors link this work with Gottsched. Not the least of these emerges from the title itself: *Versuch einer gründlichen Violinschule*. One of the Gottsched works noted above in a letter from Leopold to Lotter, *Deutsche Sprachkunst* (MBA i 14), has the more complete title *Grundlegung einer deutschen Sprachkunst*. In fact, various derivatives of the word 'Grund' (fundamental) appear in Gottsched's titles; aside from Leopold Mozart's treatise, this word seldom occurred in the titles of other writings on music.[15] The fundamental principles of natural language elucidated by Gottsched in his *Deutsch Sprachkunst* accorded well with Leopold's own goals:

> I often wondered greatly that nothing had been published as a guide to so popular and, for the greater part of music, so indispensable an instrument as the violin, in view of the fact that sound foundation, and in particular some rules for special bowings, coupled with good taste, have long been needed. I was often sad when I found that pupils had been so badly taught; that not only had I to set them back to the beginning, but that great pains had to be taken to eradicate the faults which had been taught, or at best had been overlooked. . . . I have here laid the foundation of good style; no one will deny this. This alone was my intention.[16]

In this manual, more for teachers than students, Leopold devised his own musical grammar of violin playing, linking technical correctness with the acquisition of good taste, just as Gottsched instructed in the area of language, making him an arbiter and enlightened purveyor of taste, refinement and happiness.

The *Violinschule* was soon translated into French, Dutch and even Russian, and Leopold anticipated a considerable market for it in Italy as well. In his letter to Hagenauer already cited in the Introduction (p. 5) about the possibility of Rochus Alterdinger, an administrator in the Archbishop's household, translating it into Italian, Leopold expressed his own Gottschedian view about what the nature of the language of a manual of instruction should be, avoiding a high-flown style and emulating the clear and intelligible style of the original German (MBA i 266–7). Leopold's 'clear and intelligible' come very near to Gottsched's ideals of '*Natur* and *Vernunft*' (nature and reason), the blending of plain middle style and civilized low style.[17] Some of those who wrote notices of Leopold's manual, much to his delight, corroborated that his treatment of language had been successful. Christian Daniel Schobart, for one, a fellow Swabian, confirmed in his *Ideen zu einer Aesthetik der Tonkunst* that 'by his *Violinschule*, written in very good German and with deep insight, he has earned great merit'. Similarly, Carl Friedrich Zelter, in a letter to Goethe, described it as 'a work which will be worth using as long as the violin remains a violin; moreover it is well written'.[18] But, just as Gottsched had his detractors on his approach to language, so did Leopold. Johann Adam Hiller, writing in the *Wöchentliche Nachrichten*, while praising the thoroughness and clearness, carped that 'the exceptional usefulness of the book may encourage its reading, even if the author's use of language might not always do so' (MDB 80).

Having entered the republic of letters by writing the work, Leopold found himself very much elevated as an honoured citizen through its reception. The success of the book allowed him to reach out to new correspondents, and also resulted in overtures made to him from other distinguished writers. One of these, Marpurg, who had provided the inspiration for proceeding with the project, praised the *Violinschule* lavishly in the 1757 issue of his *Historisch-Kritische Beyträge zur Aufnahme der Musik*:

> A work of this kind has long been wished for, but one had hardly dared to expect it. . . . The thorough and accomplished virtuoso, the reasonable and methodical teacher, the learned musician – these characteristics, each of which alone makes a man of merit, are all here revealed in one. . . . These are the matters of which Herr Mozart treats in the best and most natural order and in a pure German diction (MDB 10).

More importantly, Marpurg made Leopold a corresponding member of the *Berliner Gesellschaft der Musik Wissenschaft*, writing to Leopold in an open letter published in the *Kritische Briefe über die Tonkunst*:

> a certain musical society here, whose secret correspondent I have the pleasure of being, wishes to produce a musical weekly. . . . The society is minded to publish its periodical articles in the form of letters, and it proposes to take the liberty of addressing its letters to persons of merit, insight and taste. Could the aforesaid, in this endeavour, Sir, make a more auspicious beginning than with you? (MDB 11).

With that honour, bestowed in 1759, Leopold found himself free to explore the furthest reaches of the republic of letters, to behave like a master, and to lead others into the network.

LITERARY FRIENDS AND CORRESPONDENTS

Leopold appears to have taken immediate advantage of his new status, striking up correspondences with other famous writers, visiting them when the opportunities arose as happened during the early tours with the children, or broadening the horizons of his own reading. While in Zurich in 1766, for example, the whole family met Salomon Gessner, a famous poet whose idylls presented an ordered view of nature, taming the ruder aspects of country life much to the delight of his urban readership. Gessner and his brother Johannes the physicist, Leopold lamented, had made 'our stay very agreeable and our departure very glum. We took away mementos of their friendship' (MBA i 231). Aside from a set of his own works, Gessner also gave the Mozarts a copy of Christoph Martin Wieland's *Poetische Schriften* (MDB 61). Wieland, of course, held an elevated reputation among German writers; Leopold knew his works well and referred to them occasionally in his letters to Wolfgang and others, including *Die Abderiten* and *Sympathien* (MBA ii 72; iii 228). Leopold had never met him but enjoyed Wolfgang's realistic and at times unflattering description of him when Wolfgang made his acquaintance in 1777:

> I found him to be not what I had expected; his speech struck me as somewhat artificial. With quite a childish voice, a continual glazed look; a knowing look of pedantic rudeness, and even now and then with a stupid condescension. It does not surprise me, in spite of how he may carry on in Weimar or elsewhere, that he has come to be so condescending here [in Mannheim], since people see him as though he descended from heaven. People usually seem embarrassed on account of him, people keep quiet and do not even move; all listen intently to every word he speaks; and it's too bad they often must wait so long in expectation, for he has a defect of speech that forces him to speak very deliberately, and he can't say six words without grinding to a stop. Besides that, he is the way we all know him to be, a first-rate mind. He has an incredibly ugly face, covered with pockmarks, and he has a fairly long nose (MBA ii 207).

Leopold replied he could have given the same description, even though he had never seen Wieland. Another of Leopold's literary friendships from the early 1760s was with Baron Grimm, from which a sizeable correspondence grew, and aspects of this will be described in chapter 3.

Leopold's reading took him through a wide range of German writers, but his strongest allegiance remained with Gottsched and his school. Gottsched's successor at the University of Leipzig was Gellert, and while still a pedant in Gottsched's cast, Gellert had literary skills far exceeding those of his mentor; even the young Goethe as a student at Leipzig believed he could learn something from Gellert. During the early 1750s Leopold became an avid reader of Gellert, acquiring his works such as the *Fabeln* and *Lehrgedichte* from Lotter and also selling copies among his circle of friends. His enthusiasm brimming, he felt compelled to make contact with Gellert, which he did well before the publication of the *Violinschule*, approaching Gellert in early 1754 with a letter not as an established author but as an unknown person in Salzburg expressing his admiration. That letter has not survived, but its tone, quality of writing and contents were enough to evoke a response from Gellert, who wrote to Leopold in April 1754 expressing his sincere thanks, providing a model in epistolary style for its grateful recipient. Needless to say, Leopold preserved this letter, which has been published with Gellert's collected correspondence.[19] In it

4   Bölzlscheibe: Mozart and the Bäsle.

own branch of the republic of letters – meeting in salon-like fashion in the Mozart home to discuss matters of linguistics and morality as people did in Leipzig or perhaps even as in the great salons of Paris. Leopold may not have been the only thinking person in the group, but this most assuredly did not approach an extension of the republic of letters. To be sure, a circle of people existed, dozens of whom the Mozarts identify in correspondence beginning in 1762 for at least the next two decades. While touring with his children throughout Europe, Leopold, the prime force behind this circle, tried to keep it intact as a correspondent, addressing his letters to Lorenz Hagenhauer but intending that they should be read by all. These letters frequently end with words such as 'give my greetings to everyone in Salzburg', sometimes with individuals identified and always with the understanding that the letters would be circulated. Leopold may very well have seen himself as the Gellert of this circle, as an enlightened beacon capable of refining the local taste through discussion, stimulation to read the best writers, and through his own letters which vividly describe his travels abroad and cultivate a spirit of German good sense.

How much of that was possible in Salzburg? Perhaps some, at least with individuals like Hagenauer who could be trusted as the conduit for the epistolary commerce, or Abbé Joseph Bullinger, whose Jesuit education and university degree at Ingolstadt together with a previous position at a Jesuit Gymnasium placed him as Leopold's genuine intellectual peer. In fact this appeared to be the closest of all the friendships, and even Wolfgang on the night of his mother's death felt more comfortable confiding the truth to Bullinger than to his father, as will be discussed in chapter 5. But the intellectual activities of the circle appear to have been much less frequent than more basic entertainments such as card playing or the off-colour sport of Bölzlschiessen. Those involved formed a group not unlike a darts club, and the members, who met once or twice a week at the Mozarts' apartment, shot air-guns at targets designed and painted by the members themselves (including the Barisani, Robinig, Schidenhofen and Gilowsky families). The ingenious targets with their local significance and satire of the members or other acquaintances gave the game its special flavour. One depicts Katherl Gilowsky scarching for a husband, and another shows Wolfgang sadly separating himself from his 'little cousin' in Augsburg.[24] Another shows Emanuel Schikaneder (well known for his womanizing), who lived in Salzburg in 1780, trifling with one young woman while another waits patiently for him to come to her. Lest the point of any of these should be missed, captions appear in cartoon-like fashion above the heads of the characters.

In the days following the departure of Wolfgang and his mother on the journey that would take them to Munich, Augsburg, Mannheim and Paris, Leopold managed to find some consolation in Bölzlschiessen: 'On Wednesday Nannerl went to church early. In the afternoon we did our shooting. Herr Bullinger won most for Sallerl [Rosalie Joly], shooting for both Mamma and Sallerl. Mamma won eleven kreuzers as well, but Wolfgang lost four. Herr Bullinger and Katherl [the daughter in the Gilowsky family] played with us until six o'clock' (MBA ii 8–9). Two months later, when Mozart was writing from Mannheim, the possible scatological pleasures of Bölzlschiessen remained very much on his mind:

> Concerning the *targets*, if it is not too late, please do this for me. A small man with light hair, stooped over, revealing his bare arse. From his mouth come the words: *good appetite for the feast*. The other man should be shown with boots and spurs, a red cloak and a splendid, fashionable wig. He must be of medium height, and precisely in the position that he can lick the other man's arse. From his mouth come the words: *oh, there's nothing to top that*. So, please, if it can't be this time, another time (MBA ii 103).

Could one of these men have been Archbishop Colloredo or an official of the court? If so, it was a delightful way for disgruntled employees to let off steam. Leopold enjoyed these games as much as his son, and no doubt simply settled for what could be offered by Salzburg society, which even among its 'intellectuals' had difficulty escaping rude entertainments.

Carnival played no insignificant role in Leopold's life, and the harmless revelry of the season appealed to his own earthier instincts. Throughout the correspondence he makes frequent references to Carnival, usually with relish, and he occasionally disguised himself for dances and other Carnival events in a harlequin costume. During the Carnival of 1775 he and the children were in Munich, and, this being the performing season for opera, his energy was sagging. Twice before Ash Wednesday he expressed his longing for Carnival, which he felt lasted far too long, to be over, although at the same time he encouraged his wife to attend one of the masked Redoutes in Salzburg. On Ash Wednesday he thanked God that Carnival had finally ended (MBA i 523). To be sure, this comment to his wife concerns the lot of the professional musician/ composer at this hectic time, but something else may have crept in here, namely, his preference for Lent over Carnival. In the battle between Carnival and Lent Leopold may have been somewhere between the two, but leaning towards the more sober time of austere thought and behaviour. His subsequent letters of advice strongly reflect this preference.

Leopold succeeded in becoming a man of letters, but instead of the 'republic' of letters as those in Paris or Leipzig knew it in the 1750s and 60s, the territory he inhabited was decidedly more colonial, where citizens lacked equality and depended on benevolent literary despots to show them the way to happiness. Leopold, like Gottsched and Gellert, saw himself as one of the leaders, fulfilling a God-given duty of leading a receptive population by the nose to their enlight-ened happiness through his instructions to his son. By the mid 1760s, as Goethe and numerous others made clear, this sort of attitude had become obsolete. Gottsched and Gellert had ended up as pathetic creatures, the laughing stock of many of their literary contemporaries or pitied by those of more generous dispositions. In Habsburg territories Leopold thought with good reason that the approach of Gottsched and Gellert was still viable; it far surpassed anything of the Catholic theologians and steered clear of the sedition and blasphemy of a Voltaire or Holbach. But Wolfgang saw through it before he reached the age of fourteen, as his comment (noted at the beginning of chapter 5) on the death of Gellert makes clear. During his adolescence and early twenties Mozart escaped the siege of the colonial mentality and discovered the real republic. Derision could not be his tactic in responding to authority any more than it could be for the *philosophes* writing the *Encyclopédie*, who found themselves in 1757 vulner-able to heavy penalties, including death, if convicted of writing, publishing or selling any 'writing tending to attack religion, to rouse opinion, to impair Our [Louis XV's] authority, and to trouble the order and tranquillity of Our States'.[25] Having to coexist with the authority figure, his father, led to a strategy of irony, dissimulation and evasiveness.

Chapter 3
Leopold Mozart's Biography of His 'Miraculous' Son

Extraordinary people attract biographers. If the number of biographies of a given person is any measure of greatness, Mozart would surely be judged the most exceptional person who has ever lived. That method of measurement, of course, is faulty, since biographers need raw material; they need to have reliable sources of information about their subjects, or the biography turns into pure fabrication. A Shakespeare would surely have attracted as much biographical interest as a Mozart, but we know precious little about him, so little in fact that some have disputed that there ever was a Shakespeare, pointing to Marlowe or someone else using a pseudonym. All of this tried the patience of an exasperated Mark Twain, who finally set the record straight with the quip that the works of Shakespeare were either written by Shakespeare or by someone else with the same name. Perhaps one day documents will surface that will allow for a Shakespeare biography – letters, diaries, memoirs or sketches – although at this point not too much hope should be held out. Biographies of living people often attract us even more than those of the dead since the achievements of these notables remain fresher in our minds, but that type of biography presents different challenges. Living subjects can at times be fairly uncooperative, or may wish us to know them in ways that do not correspond with reality.

We of course have an insatiable appetite for biographies of extraordinary figures; naturally we are curious about the person behind the great achievements, to know what makes these sorts of people tick or whether they are remotely like us with faults, foibles, hobbies, favourite books, lovers or eccentricities. The problem for the biographer lies in the raw material itself, assuming, unlike the case of Shakespeare, that it actually exists. Letters are generally regarded as extremely valuable and authentic, giving us an inside view of the person, but unless we learn the critical modes for reading the letters themselves, we may naively end up with some very bizarre results.

No set of letters has been as overworked as the Mozart correspondence in this respect, supplying the lifeline to the dozens of Mozart biographers for over two centuries, and no set of letters has been as consistently misread as the letters

between Leopold and Wolfgang Mozart. Sorting that out will take more than
one chapter; the relationship between these two has come down to us – thanks
to Leopold's insistence through his epistolary commerce with his son that all
the letters should be saved – as an epistolary narrative, with all the ingenuity,
strategy and intrigue which that implied to the eighteenth century. Leopold's
insistence, which he dropped when Wolfgang killed the epistolary commerce in
1779, appears to have been directed towards a goal, one in which the letters
would be used as something other than a purely private communication. One
can presume that this went far beyond a simple desire for posterity; for him it
virtually amounted to the embracing of a new career, one with a distinctive
eighteenth-century nature. This chapter places Leopold's goals in that perspective, taking the source of the tension in the relationship out of the domain of
nineteenth- or twentieth-century psychology and placing it in the realm of
eighteenth-century letter writing.

A SURVIVING MOZART MYTH

Various of the Mozart myths surviving since the earliest biographies have been
debunked in recent years, but the one about Leopold abandoning his personal
aims to concentrate all his energies on his genius son remains very much alive.
Leopold himself provided the source of this impression, writing his thoughts to
Lorenz Hagenauer in 1766: 'God, who has been much too good to a wretched
sinner like me, has given such talents to my children that, aside from thinking
of my duty as a father, I am impelled to sacrifice everything for the success of
their education. Every moment that I lose is lost for ever' (MBA i 232). These
words should not be taken at face value. The letters to Hagenauer served a
purpose far beyond that of friendly correspondence, as will be described below,
and remarks such as this take on a very different meaning in that context. While
Leopold may have curtailed his own compositional activities after about 1762,
the notion that he abandoned his own ambitions and career at that time simply
does not hold water.

Two important events in Leopold's life in 1756 were the birth of a male child
– Johannes Chrysostomus Wolfgangus Theophilus (who would be one of two of
his seven children to survive to adulthood) – and the publication of his *Versuch
einer gründlichen Violinschule* (*A Treatise on the Fundamental Principles of Violin
Playing*). In both cases it took a few years to see how matters would be, and for
both the results were extraordinary. The child turned out to have had all the
qualities of a musical genius (one should note that the female child who
survived, Maria Anna or Nannerl, could have had the same potential), and
fostering this talent became a clear duty. The *Violinschule* similarly achieved
an outstanding success, making him something of a European celebrity. The
chance that the two might be linked in terms of career possibilities appears not
to have occurred to him until the early 1760s. As a court musician Leopold had

been unable to rise above the rank of assistant Kapellmeister in a minor and aggravating provincial court. On the other hand, publication had placed him in the public eye, elevating him among his peers, and it did not take an enormous leap to see which way his aspirations should be directed. For financial security he still needed the position in the Salzburg court, but as for his creative energies, these would preferably be spent on other bigger and better publication projects. That his son could be the focus of one of these projects, the subject of a large-scale biography, satisfied not only his musical inclinations but also his strong affinity for the issues of enlightened morality. Given that his formal as well as self-directed education had been in moral philosophy, it should come as no surprise that he would move in that direction, emulating his famous correspondent Christian Fürchtegott Gellert.

The shift Leopold hoped to make from assistant court Kapellmeister to writer did not go unnoticed by Wolfgang, who described it in 1776 in a letter (written in Leopold's hand) to their old friend Padre Martini in Bologna:

> My father is a music master at the metropolitan church, which allows me to write as much church music as I like. He has already been in the service of this court for thirty-six years, and since he knows that this Archbishop cannot and will not be considerate of people who are getting older, his heart is no longer in his work, and he has turned to literature, which always was a favourite study of his (MBA i 532).

Leopold had always read avidly, and the interest in literature described here surely suggests more than an extension of this. He undoubtedly intended to make the mark as writer he had not made as a composer or performer.

Leopold shared his admiration of Gellert with Joseph Haydn, who had called Gellert his hero,[1] and saw in the achievements of this great moralist a model for his own endeavours. While Leopold had no intention of casting his literary net as widely as Gellert had, he recognized that at the heart of Gellert's writing was the perfection of the epistolary style, most apparent in the treatises *Gedanken von einem guten deutschen Briefe* (*Thoughts on good German letter writing*, 1742) and *Briefe, nebst einer Praktischen Abhandlung von dem guten Geschmacke in Briefen* (*Letters, together with a practical treatise on good taste in letters*, 1751), as well as the large body of model letters accompanying the latter. Letters were central to other types of writing as well, including the epistolary novel *Leben der schwedischen Gräfin* (*Life of the Swedish Countess*), about which Gellert wrote to Leopold in 1754,[2] and various moral discourses which could be written as letters of advice. One of these, 'Lehren eines Vaters für seinen Sohn, den er auf die Akademie schicket' ('Lessons from a Father to his Son, whom he sends to university'), may have been of special importance to Leopold, whose biographical project focused on his own son.

Leopold's embrace of biography as a moral instrument emulated a widespread eighteenth-century practice. Sketches of moral characters of a biographical nature presented in the moral weeklies such as the *Tatler* and the *Spectator*, first popularized in German by Johann Mattheson in his *Der Vernünfftler*, were the foundation for this type of writing. Like the moral weeklies, the practice of moral biography flourished in England before coming to Germany, and Oliver Goldsmith explained it in the following enlightened way:

> Biography has, ever since the days of Plutarch, been considered as the most useful manner of writing, not only from the pleasure it affords the imagination, but from the instruction it artfully and unexpectedly conveys to the understanding. It furnishes us with an opportunity of giving advice freely, and without offence. It not only removes the dryness and dogmatical air of precept, but sets persons, actions, and their consequences before us in the most striking manner; and by that means turns even precept into example: whence arises the propriety of placing these volumes in the hands of youth.[3]

In presenting the lives of English worthies, a writer could, as one pointed out, excite 'an ardour of virtue'.[4] The influence of English writers on German literati, most notably of the Third Earl of Shaftesbury on a whole generation of German writers, appears to have been true for biography as well.[5]

LEOPOLD MOZART'S BIOGRAPHY OF HIS SON

Leopold informed the world of his intended biography of his son in the preface to the second edition of the *Violinschule* (1769), in which he speculated on the project with great enthusiasm:

> I might here take the opportunity of entertaining the public with a story such as probably appears but once in a century, and which in the domain of music has perhaps never yet appeared *in such a degree of the miraculous*; I might describe the wonderful genius of my son; circumstantially relate his unbelievably rapid progress in the whole extent of musical science from the fifth to the thirteenth year of his age; and I might, in so incredible a matter, call to witness the unanswerable testimony of many of the greatest masters, indeed even the testimony of envy itself. . . . I hope that after my return from Italy, where I now intend to go with God's blessing, I may . . . entertain the public with this story.[6]

Based on this description, the biography would necessarily be as much about the father as the son. While God may have been the origin of the 'miracle', it would not have been realized without the miracle of Leopold's instruction and his unleashing of this genius on the world. Leopold could surely take more credit than his maker for the 'unbelievably rapid progress', and could direct some of the envy of those who had it to its correct source.

That an exchange of letters could be the basis for a biography did not escape Leopold. For the early journeys with his children to courts throughout Europe,

Leopold sent vivid accounts to his friend Lorenz Hagenauer, and expected him to save these letters for the early part of the biography. Leopold referred to the project in a number of letters to Hagenauer in 1766 and 1767. In one, expressing his thanks to the Dean of the Cathedral in Olmütz for his concern and hospitality when the children fell ill, he wrote,

> I will only ask how many people there are of this kind who would receive into their house an entire family with a child who is in such a condition, and this from a purely humanitarian instinct. This deed will do Count Podstatzky no modest honour in the biography of our little one which I will have printed at another time. For here begins in a certain sense a new phase of his life (MBA i 247).

In the letter declaring his total sacrifice for the successful development of the children, he places his efforts and their industriousness in context: 'Should they with the excuse that one thing prevents another become accustomed to squandering their hours away, my entire plan [*Gebäude*] would collapse into pieces' (MBA i 232). The plan, 'my plan', or Leopold's plan, involved much more than Wolfgang's musical career. Leopold had much at stake here, extending far beyond the need to foster the reception of his son (or children) by persons in high places. The plan included the biographical project, the credit he could take for his son's progress, and the role he could play in the biography as a moral teacher.

Instead of attempting to extract the biography from these letters at some later point, with the enormous editorial effort that would require, Leopold appears to have had in mind that the letters themselves should be published, virtually untouched, and that the biography would be epistolary in the truest sense. Hints of this come in his separation in some letters of that which could go into the biography from routine practical or business matters as well as some personal opinions of a private nature. Matters not intended for the biography, or for people in Salzburg Leopold fully expected Hagenauer to share the letters with – whose enthusiasm for these letters could very well be the litmus test for publication – came under the subheading 'For you alone'. Generally the thoughts under this heading are neither contentious nor confidential; in those cases he would avoid the specific subject altogether, well aware of the dangers of letters falling into the wrong hands. On one such matter, he pointed out that it would have to be discussed when he could see Hagenauer in person in Salzburg: 'I will explain this to you the best I can. Though I must leave out some things which cannot be entrusted to my pen' (MBA i 254). In another case a few months later, he wrote, 'I could relate to you a weighty amount of all sorts of the most hostile plots and malicious persecutions. But I am too tired to recall these to mind and would prefer to keep them *for our forthcoming oral discussion in the near future*' (MBA i 269). Most of these cabals appear to have been much less malicious than they were in Leopold's mind.

In spite of his contact with the major cities and courts of Europe, Leopold, like many people from the provinces – during the eighteenth century as well as the present – felt nothing but contempt for the great centres of culture. Benjamin Britten associated London with dental work, and Canadians on the west coast revel in telling Toronto jokes. Leopold's view of the carnivalesque Viennese, who 'generally speaking, are not eager to see serious and sensible things, have little or no idea of them, and only want to see foolish stuff, dances, devils, ghosts, magic, Hanswurst, Lipperl, Bernardon, witches and apparitions' (MBA i 254), were carefully filed under 'For you alone'. Since Vienna would be a primary market for the biography, insulting the taste of potential purchasers was clearly a poor strategy. With exceptions such as this, he primarily used this subheading for matters of business too mundane to interest the local readers or broader public.

Writing at times required great effort, but the project depended on it: 'I can barely write; both pen and ink are wretched and I must steal time to write' (MBA i 54), he noted in Vienna at the beginning of the first trip. As the Mozarts travelled further from home the epistolary enterprise became more expensive, but still essential, as Leopold complained from London: 'You know that the farther away a thing is, the smaller it seems to the eye. Thus it is with my letters. My handwriting becomes smaller in relation to the distance I am from Salzburg. If we were to sail over to America, it would probably become totally unreadable. A plain letter without a cover from here to Germany costs a shilling and for the cover another shilling; consequently, it will cost two shillings for a letter with a cover' (MBA i 146).

In the letters intended for the larger audience, Leopold took great pleasure in registering the amazement of various observers, and with this he indulged his satisfaction in his role preparing the child as much as the achievements themselves. This gratification appears in the earliest letters, dating from October 1762, and continues throughout the entire correspondence with Hagenauer. At Ybbs, en route to Vienna, the six-year-old 'Woferl romped about at the organ and played so well that the Franciscans, who happened to be sitting with some guests at their noon meal, left the table and with their guests, ran to the choir, and were all but struck dead with astonishment' (MBA i 50). In Vienna at the opera, Leopold overheard 'the Archduke Leopold [the future Emperor Leopold II] say a number of things from his box to another box, that there was a boy in Vienna who so splendidly played the clavier, etc. . . . Mainly, everyone is amazed at the boy, and everyone says that his genius is inconceivable' (MBA i 52).

Comments of this sort abound in these letters, although from fellow musicians they seldom occur. Only from Georg Christoph Wagenseil could Leopold report a supportive declaration: '*As an honest person I can say no more than this boy is the greatest man now living in the world. It was impossible to believe*' (MBA i 257). Others, according to Leopold, avoided hearing Wolfgang altogether, so that if asked to appraise his achievements, they 'could always *say that they had not heard him, and that it could not possibly be true; that it was all smoke and mirrors*

and harlequinesque; that it was all for show; that he was given music to play which
he already knew; that it was absurd to imagine that he could compose, etc.' (MBA i
256). This aroused Leopold's pugilistic if somewhat paranoid instincts, and he
extended their stay in Vienna so that Wolfgang could prove himself by writing
an opera, *La finta semplice*. Leopold relished the embarrassment that this could
cause to other composers:

> Can you not imagine what sort of noise secretly erupted among these composers?
> What? Today one should see a Gluck and tomorrow a boy of twelve seated at the
> keyboard and conducting his own opera? . . . The consequences of this under-
> taking, if God helps us to make it happen, are so huge, but so easy to envisage,
> that they need no clarification. Now I must spare no money, for it will come back
> to me today or tomorrow. Nothing ventured, nothing gained; I must bring this
> thing to the light of day. We must succeed or fail. And where is Wolfgang more
> skilful than in the theatre? (MBA i 257–8).

In using 'I', Leopold does not mean to imply a collaboration. His role lay in
the musical preparation offered to his son, and whatever his involvement may
have been at this point, he takes offence at the accusation of his authorship:
'Then it was stated that not the boy, but his father had created it. But here too
the credit of the slanderers failed' (MBA i 271). Wolfgang passed their tests
with flying colours, and Leopold could proclaim,

> I owe this act to almighty God; otherwise I should be the most thankless creature.
> *And if I am ever to be charged with the responsibility of revealing this miracle to the*
> *world, this is now the time, when people are ridiculing whatever is called a miracle and*
> *denying all miracles.* Therefore they must be convinced; and was it not a great joy
> and an enormous victory for me to hear a Voltairian say to me in astonishment:
> '*Now for once in my life I have seen a miracle; this is the first!*' (MBA i 271–2).

Leopold took special pleasure in these comments from a so-called Voltairian,
probably Grimm, being convinced of Voltaire's atheism and hence his lack
of genuine moral foundation. Calling Grimm a Voltairian, as Leopold knew
perfectly well, surely stretched the bounds of credibility, and he scrupulously
avoids Grimm's name here to create the desired impression.

Already in these early letters to Hagenauer, Leopold emphasizes religion and
morality, drawing a connection between his miraculous child and these matters.
With morality in place, it followed that all else would be well too, including
musical ability, as Leopold believed of the Mannheim orchestra: 'The orchestra
is without contradiction the best in Germany, filled with upright young people
and people of good character, no drunkards, gamblers or slovenly riff raff, so
that both their behaviour as well as their performance are highly admirable'
(MBA i 79). In spite of Leopold's views on religious toleration, accepting
Protestants' embrace of morality still came hard, although there could be

exceptions, such as two fellow travellers encountered en route to England: 'Here you will see two men who have everything which honest men of this world should have; and, although they are both Lutherans, yet they are completely different Lutherans and people from whom I have often learned much. On parting, one of the fellow travellers, Baron von Bose, gave Wolfgang as a remembrance a beautiful book filled with spiritual contemplations in verse', and inscribed the book with a challenge to the seven-year-old Mozart to read it often and be inspired by its divine songs to create musical settings, 'so that the callous despiser of religion may read them – and take notice – may hear them – and fall down and worship God' (MBA i 140). The book in question, according to Georg Nissen, was *Geistliche Oden und Lieder* (1757) by none other than Gellert.[7]

Honesty and good taste were also seen as distinctly German traits, lacking especially in the French. Leopold, like his epistolary mentors and writing colleagues, realized that many of his potential readers would be women, and attempted to account for this in a letter to Hagenauer's wife Maria Theresa:

One must not always write to men but must also remember the fair and devout sex. If the women in Paris are fair, I have no basis to say; for they are painted so contrary to nature, like the dolls of Berchtesgaden, that even a naturally beautiful person with this horrible make-up is unbearable to the eyes of an honest German. As for devotion, I can confirm that it requires little effort to fathom the miracles of the French women saints; the greatest miracles are performed by those who are neither virgins nor wives nor widows, and these miracles all happen during their lifetime. We will speak more clearly on this subject another time (MBA i 121).

In this manner of addressing a larger audience, this letter continues at length with descriptions of French styles and behaviour, with even more contempt than he had shown for the Viennese. While his *Violinschule* had been translated into French and sold in Paris, Leopold apparently realized that his current project, in the style of Gellert, would not appeal to a French audience, making it safe to insult the French – to the delight of the German reader.

On returning to Salzburg in January 1769, the year of the published announcement of the biography in the second edition of the *Violinschule*, Leopold appears to have given the project more thought, as he made no attempt to publish his letters to Hagenauer or any other type of biography at this time. Perhaps on the home front in Salzburg not sufficient enthusiasm had been shown by the circle of friends. These letters by themselves would provide engaging reading, but would not fulfill the larger potential he saw for the project. In order for that to happen, his son would have to traverse adolescence, with his learned and wise father directing his moral development and ensuring his ability to handle all facets of his life and career. With such a work he could rival even Gellert's popularity, since not only could he provide the same degree of moral instruction, but it would have as its subject the brilliant young composer who had aroused the fascination of all Europe. To bring the project off in its full glory could take as much as another decade, during which time there would be ample opportunity for more correspondence because of the need for Wolfgang to travel and be displayed.

The next opportunity for travel and correspondence arose at the end of 1769 when father and son set off for Italy. As his wife did not make this journey, she became the recipient of the descriptive letters which should continue the epistolary biography. Leopold emphasized to his wife in more than one letter near the beginning of this journey the importance of preserving the letters. On 17 December 1769, mixed in with other instructions and comments, he noted, 'I will write to Herr von Schiedenhofen myself as soon as I have time. I hope that you are all well; I will write again from Bozen. You must keep all the letters' (MBA i 294–5). On reaching Milan in January 1770, he undescored the point: 'I have never in my life seen anything more beautiful of this kind; and as I hope *that you are diligently preserving all letters*, I will describe it to you later. It is no theatre, but a hall built with boxes like an opera house' (MBA i 306). Perhaps he intended to embellish this letter with details of the beauty of the theatre in question when he returned home and had more leisure time.

EPISTOLARY APPROACHES

During the next seven years father and son made a number of journeys together, to Italy, Vienna and Munich, allowing Leopold to build his epistolary portfolio. Once again Leopold addressed his letters to his wife, and occasionally sprinkled them with bits of advice for Nannerl. With a female readership in mind, these letters allowed him a fuller entry into the moral objective of the project. The French debate about the role of women in the Enlightenment – the idea that women might aspire to equality, the control that women had over salons during the middle of the century, the activity of women as writers, or the notion that women might provide a civilizing influence on men – had not reached Habsburg soil. German writers may have gleaned from England and France that women could be avid readers, an eager market for new styles of writing, but in no way did this suggest that women should be anything but subservient creatures to be shaped by the guidance of dominating men.

Male writers in Germany proceeded with the assurance that while some education for women would not hurt, this should not lead women to think of careers or of challenging men in any way whatever. While male intellectuals in France may have felt threatened by the likes of Louise d'Épinay, and those threats could be played on with misogynist responses by someone like Rousseau, German writers used the authority of their office to keep women in their place – to accept their role as wives, as providers of comfort to men, as social ornaments, as bearers of children, and as emotional caretakers of families.

A young woman could develop her talents – of which playing the piano was a notable and in many cases expected one – until she reached the age of marriage (about eighteen), and at that point, whether married or not, her cultural talents were not to interfere with her acquiescent social and interpersonal behaviour. The moral imperative here loomed strong: unlike some French women who had the option of a public or intellectual life, German women did not, and this received reinforcement from the precepts of the moral writers, whose circle now included Leopold Mozart.

Leopold very much underscores these attitudes in his writing. Recognizing the inherent dangers of the independence aspired to by some women in France, Leopold painted all French women with the same gaudy strokes, decorated unnaturally with detestable make-up offensive to honest German eyes and consequently lacking in piety: 'One has trouble enough to distinguish here who is the lady of the house. All live as they like, and, if God is not particularly gracious, the French state will go the same way as the former Persian Empire' (MBA i 122). This curious comparison with 'liberated' Persian women badly misses the mark, but that would escape his female German readers who should be duly appalled by women who do not cultivate the look of the 'woman of the house'. The painted look undoubtedly implies more than lack of domestication, evoking images of prostitutes roaming the streets of Paris, women so depraved that their description should cause any properly raised German woman to shudder.

Still missing from the project was a correspondence between father and son in which the father could demonstrate his highest level of enlightened morality. That possibility finally arose in 1777 when Wolfgang and his mother set out on an extended journey which lasted from September of that year until January 1779. The correspondence during this period between father and son proceeded intensely. Leopold typically wrote a lengthy letter twice per week at the early stages, noting after one month that 'Until now I have actually written to you by every post' (MBA ii 89). He expected Wolfgang to reply in kind: 'a letter takes six days, and if you do not write every post-day, we have no idea for too long a stretch of time where you are or what you are doing' (MBA ii 117). Mozart's mother confirmed the frequency of their letters: 'We write to you twice every week, so you should get as many letters as we do' (MBA ii 163). In late December she assured Leopold that all his letters had been arriving: 'We have in fact received all your letters and up to now have not missed a single one' (MBA ii 194). As the travellers got further from home the letters became somewhat less frequent, in part because of the expense; Leopold, though, always managed at least one letter a week, noting, 'I did not write to you last post-day; I too will write only every eight days, when nothing special happens' (MBA ii 223). The mere fact that so much of this correspondence has survived would seem to suggest that it arose from an epistolary commerce resulting in an agreement that it would be saved, in spite of the annoyances for Mozart of saving the letters on extended travels. In fact, Leopold appears to have kept a type of inventory of his own letters, and insisted that Wolfgang confirm in his replies that Leopold's letters had arrived.

After an initial flurry of letters in late September, Leopold demanded that 'you should at least write *whether you have received this or that letter*' (MBA ii 35). Periodic reminders of this come throughout the entire correspondence, although in letters of the next few weeks Leopold went out of his way to clarify the importance of the letters themselves and keeping track of them. On 15 October Leopold pointed out that 'with the letter which I enclosed to my brother, this is the third letter which you will get from me in Augsburg' (MBA ii 56). To prevent his letters from getting lost if they moved, Leopold insisted that they should 'always leave a note at each post office so the letter can be forwarded; otherwise it will be lost'. He reiterated this a few days later: 'I repeat that *on your departure from each place you should leave a note at the post office as to where your letters should be forwarded*' (MBA ii 89, 117). Furthermore, this had to be done in person to avoid the dangers of mischief by corrupt servants:

> we have known of hundreds of examples of hired servants and house boys who misappropriate and open many incoming letters in the hope of finding a credit note or draft; and of numerous letters, which should have been taken to the post, but were held back by the servant who stuck in his pocket and stole the six kreuzers which he should have paid for the postage. This last case happens very commonly (MBA ii 89).

As to how Wolfgang should respond and develop his own approach to letters, a lecture with detailed instructions followed in the same lengthy epistle:

> Many of my questions remain unanswered; and, you will observe that I reply to all of yours. Why? Because when I have written important matters to you, I then place your letter in front of me – read it through, and, whenever anything arises, I then answer it. Furthermore, I always keep a piece of paper on my table; whenever anything occurs to me, which I want to write to you about, I note it down in a few words. Then when I start writing, I cannot forget anything (MBA ii 61).

EPISTOLARY STYLE AND WIT

Various of Gellert's precepts outlined in the previous chapter applied to Leopold's letters to his son. Appropriate language and subject matter were of the utmost concern, especially for letters intended to be published. Occasionally he lets slip a scatological greeting to his wife, although he generally avoided such language in writing to his son. As for Wolfgang's letters, Leopold chastised him if his descriptions or opinions of persons went beyond good taste. When Wolfgang wrote that 'the Mufti H. C. is a prick [*Schwanz*]', Leopold, who held the same opinion of Archbishop Colloredo, replied with an entreaty not to 'write such nasty quips about the Mufti' (MBA ii 7, 15). To be sure, such letters could fall into the wrong hands, but on a larger dimension comments like this could render a letter unusable for public consumption.

Conscious of the need to make his letters interesting and engaging, Leopold followed Gellert's and Knigge's maxim of mixing advice with wit or humour. In many of his letters he describes something domestically touching, such as the family dog's anticipation of Wolfgang's return, or provides an anecdote about the ineptitude of Salzburg musicians before opening the floodgate to a torrent of advice. These touches of humour occur most often in the early letters of this journey, when all continued to go well and the project appeared to be on track. Even the description of their disconsolate lethargy following the departure of mother and son he laced with humour, including the dog's melancholy and the shooting party of the following day in which others had to shoot for Mozart and his mother.[8]

In the next few letters greetings come not only from Nannerl but Bimperl (the dog) as well. In describing a concert that had taken place in Salzburg in Eizenberger's hall, Leopold included a whimsical anecdote about the behaviour of the musicians after the concert: 'at the end, they all got drunk; they carried each other around on their shoulders in processions, bumping the lustres or the large chandelier, smashing the middle bowl and other pieces, which now must be sent to Venice for replacement' (MBA ii 18). A letter of 1 November 1777 contains a lengthy description of a performance conducted by Michael Haydn, Joseph's brother, including this example of the musicians' ingenuity: 'I should mention that Brunetti stood behind Ferlendis, Wenzl Sadlo behind the bassoonists and Hafeneder behind the other oboists; they watched Haydn throughout, and beat time on their shoulders; otherwise it would have often gone completely to the dogs, especially in the fugues and the running bass-obbligato parts' (MBA ii 96). Michael Haydn (unlike his brother Joseph) was often the butt of jokes in the Mozart household, although on this occasion Leopold reviewed him favourably.

GELLERT'S 'LESSONS FROM A FATHER TO HIS SON'

The range and volume of advice thrust by Leopold on his son in letters from September 1777 to the beginning of 1779 is nothing short of staggering. While Leopold needed no model, one nevertheless notes a remarkable similarity between his advice and the tone and content of Gellert's advice in 'Lessons from a Father to his Son'. Virtually all of Leopold's precepts appear in Gellert's epistolary essay (with the exception of the specifics on musical composition), with special emphasis on the cultivation of virtue. This letter genre was familiar not only in letter-writing treatises and model letters but in the novel as well. In Samuel Richardson's *Pamela* (letter no. 138), for example, sons or daughters were, aside from receiving instruction in the 'requisite style and forms to be observed in familiar letters', advised 'how to think and act justly and prudently in the common concerns of life'.[9] Parent moralists, believing their experience should help to shape the next generation, wrote these letters with the fervent intention of keeping their children on the straight and narrow, perhaps avoiding the pitfalls of the past, and certainly providing their offspring with stern warnings to shun the temptations lurking about at every turn. Gellert's text begins with a comment on the transformation of spoken advice to a written code of conduct, establishing the appropriate tone of authority:

> My Dear Son,
>
> I shall, in this letter, repeat to you those instructions in writing, which I have given you from your earliest years, or when I was already preparing you for your course of academic studies. Let it be a constant testimony of my affection for you, and a continual encouragement to you to fulfill the new career which will bring you nearer to the end you ought to have ever in view. You enter the world as a stranger, and will lead in it a life quite new to you. The attention with which I have thus far conducted you, seconded by the cares of your worthy preceptors, has had for its object to enable you henceforward to need no other guide than yourself, and to make your first step out of your paternal mansion as beneficial to you as possible. I know the goodness of your heart, your attachment to me, your decided taste for the sciences, the desire you feel to deserve the esteem of the well-informed and virtuously disposed. But I also know the faults of your age and temperament. The errors into which want of experience may lead you, the seductions to which you will be exposed, in a world where vice puts on its brightest allurements, and whose attractions are so powerful that the most virtuous heart finds great difficulty in resisting them, unless daily armed with courage and circumspection. Listen, therefore, my son, to the voice of a father, who proposes to himself nothing less than to point out to you the path you must follow in this life to lead you to a happy eternity.[10]

The son does not have a choice when it comes to following the advice, as he risks eternal damnation for any acts of subversion: 'The God who has entrusted you to my care, will one day call me to account for my instructions to you, and you will be also required to answer as to what use you have made of these instructions' (6).

What follows is a series of extracts from Gellert's patriarchal letter, culled from the lengthy original to give a sense of the breadth and tone of the father's authoritarian advice:

> You are of that age which is, properly speaking, most likely to decide on the future good or evil of your life (6). Apply yourself to them [your studies], therefore, from motives superior to the desire of surpassing others in learning, of getting a worldly reputation, of obtaining an eminent station, and of finding your application rewarded by the acquisition of a brilliant fortune. . . . Study then

with a view of the glory of God, that is to say, consecrate your talents to the acquisition and constant practice of wisdom and virtue (7). He who not only studies from taste, but also from a principle of piety, will be more disposed to economise his time, more capable of resisting whatever obstacles might arise to his progress (9). Be always the sincere friend of virtue; it will make you still more the worthy friend of letters and of men. You may be learned without being pious, but know that he who has the most knowledge unaccompanied by virtue, is of all beings the most despicable and the most unfortunate (12). Repeat frequently to yourself, 'it is my duty and my happiness to be industrious, as much as laziness would be my shame and misery' (14). But fly carefully from those dreadful scenes in which the passion of gaming rages, and in which many a well-disposed young man has lost his taste for study, his fortune, and contaminated his morals. I say nothing of those houses in which, under pretence of a country excursion, young men give themselves up without shame to libertinism and drunkenness (15–16).

Associate easily with everybody, but restrict your friendships to few (16). Be as much on your guard, my dear son, against every kind of intimacy with the declared infidel, as with the canting hypocrite, and always consider that man as unworthy your friendship, who has not sufficient virtue to be the friend of God (17). It is a bad omen when a young man can find no pleasure except in the society of persons of his own age, and never seeks the company of men of a mature age, and even of those still farther advanced in life. He ought to make use of the gravity of their well formed characters, to repress his fickleness and impetuosity (18). If the respectable man . . . deigns to admit you to the free use of his library, to make you share in his amusements, and invites you to his table, form yourself on his example (19).

With regard to your female acquaintances, I can only give you general instructions. Watch over yourself narrowly, my dear son, and resist every inclination which you would blush to own to the friend from whom you would expect the severest censure. O my son! love is a seducing passion, but religion and vigilance furnish us with such arms of defence as are proof against all its seductions. . . . You are as dear to me as myself, and I would prefer death to the overwhelming knowledge of your being abandoned to vice (20). Abstain from reading those books in which vice is disguised, clothed with the charms of poetry or eloquence, and presented in the most dangerous manner, seducing the understanding in order to corrupt the heart (21). Be therefore always on your guard, my beloved son, and feel always some mistrust of your heart in your most allowable intimacies with women, whose society is however the best calculated to form and polish your manners (23).

The ancient authors which you have already gone through must still occupy you . . . and you should make it a rule to read some portion of them every day, particularly those that have most merit. Dedicate one particular hour to this employment. . . . In the ancients we find the sources and models of history, eloquence, and poetry (24). From this time you ought, with the assistance of a good guide, to form your epistolary style, and try your abilities in other compositions (30). You must not suppose, my dear son, that I wish to impede your amusement; . . . But wit displayed in licentious writings, however exquisite, were it even the wit of a Crebillon, appears to me fit only to be compared to a beautiful woman in a house of prostitution, and who is the more seducing in proportion as she disguises vice under the exterior of virtue and innocence (33). The affectation of wit and fine talk, is often a dangerous malady to many young men (34).

My son, be a good economist. Economy is not only commendable in itself, but also from the influence it has on more essential virtues. . . . Economy is consequently a distinguished virtue, and I recommend it particularly to you, as it is not often the virtue of young people. Learn, then, to be economical even in trifles, which, taken singly, cost little, and by this means more easily seduce; but, in the long run, and taken altogether, come to be a considerable sum squandered away (35–6). Order is as necessary in a family, as a good articulation is in a well-framed discourse; and order is not less the fruit, than the source of economy (39).

Advice flows on numerous other subjects, including cultivating the arts, exercise, meals, recreation, sleep and the enjoyment of nature. In the end, these moral lessons will afford the advisee his highest degree of happiness, bringing true enlightened sentiment and refinement. Gellert concludes his letter with the ultimate in guilt-laden entreaties:

So conduct yourself, my dear son, at the university, as you would wish to have done when you arrive at old age. Live so as to recollect without shame, or rather with heartfelt satisfaction. . . . I implore the Almighty to restore you to my arms, enriched with all the treasures of learning and virtue, which may make you a useful member of society. . . . if, added to great improvement in useful knowledge, you have also improved in religion and virtue, I shall receive you with transport. Were you the greatest genius of the age, without being a pious and a virtuous man, I should grievously lament having given you birth. Adieu, my beloved, my worthy son (41).

LEOPOLD'S ADVICE

Unlike Gellert's litany of advice, contained in one extended and overbearing letter, Leopold spread his over some seventy letters during a period of a year and four months. In the end he covers every subject Gellert had, and some others besides, such as the prerequisites for success as a composer. In providing advice over such a long span of time, he addressed real situations as they arose, giving the set a much more engaging and immediate flavour. The personal issues did not disqualify them from the public domain, but heightened their appeal as emotions could come into sharper focus. When this correspondence began, Mozart was already twenty-one years of age, a few years older than the typical recipient of such a barrage of advice would normally be. In the case of Gellert's letter, for example, the son has just set out for university, making him about eighteen years old, and both more in need of and receptive to this type of advice. For someone twenty-one (about to turn twenty-three on his return home), in contrast to Gellert's son, it was insulting to have this forced on him at this age. That, along with certain other factors, puts a different stripe on Leopold's advice, suggesting in many cases he played up to the larger audience instead of speaking directly to his son. One of those other factors was his awareness by 1778 that most of his advice fell on deaf ears, but this knowledge did not prevent it from flowing. Posterity should know Leopold as a man of great acumen, capable of solving any problem, dealing with any person, assessing any situation, upholding the highest moral tradition, and defending God and the Catholic church.

Curiously, Gellert's paternal letter stands as a fairly humourless outpouring, lacking in the wit that Gellert himself advocated as necessary to hold the reader's interest. In this respect Leopold's letters actually surpass in quality those of his learned correspondent, although some of Leopold's also lack anything but advice. Along with wit, one of Gellert's other persuasive means, as he explained in his treatise on letter writing, was emotion, and here too Leopold surpasses his mentor, often incited by Wolfgang's evasive or dissimulating responses. In launching into this project, Leopold may very well have realized that the end result could be superior to that of the best German moral writer of his age, both for its subject matter and quality of writing. His would be instructional not only in morals and practical matters of life, but as a new, exemplary standard in epistolary language and style. Add to that the fact that the recipient of the advice had been the childhood darling of all Europe, known and admired, thanks to his father's efforts, in every corner of the continent; Leopold knew that he had a potential blockbuster on his hands.

In his first letters to his son and wife in September 1777, Leopold primarily describes events and conditions in Salzburg after their departure, not without touches of wit and humour, and certainly with genuine emotion arising from the separation. Advice in these letters comes in very small doses, a mere trickle which in a few weeks would open to a torrent. In his first letter he confines himself to advice on the least expensive lodging in Augsburg, Wolfgang's need to display his cross of the Golden Spur at court, and to remember to ask for letters of recommendation in Munich (MBA ii 8–10). On 28 September the matter of health arises:

> I only beseech you, dear Wolfgang, not to indulge in excesses; you have been accustomed to an orderly life from your youth, and you must avoid heating drinks, as you know that you are likely to get hot and that you prefer cold drinks to warm ones. This gives clear evidence *that your blood tends when heated to surge through your veins*. Strong wines and too much wine drinking are therefore bad

for you. Imagine yourself in what unhappiness and distress you would place your beloved mother in a far distant country. I would never hope to receive such an announcement (MBA ii 19).

If Wolfgang knew these things himself, especially the dangers of strong drink, they did not need to be said, except of course for the larger audience. This letter, mostly jovial to this point, turns exclusively to advice as he continues writing the next morning:

> You must make a major issue with Count Seeau of what arias, etc., you are prepared to write for his theatre, and ballets, without requesting remuneration. With the courtiers you must be extremely respectful, since each one has his face in the affairs. . . . If you are expected to write something for viol da gamba, [Woschitka] could tell you how it should be and suggest what types of works the Count prefers, revealing to you his sense of taste (MBA ii 19).

Composing to meet the taste of certain cities or nobles recurs as a theme for the next half year. While these passages may seem to us distinctive to the concerns of a budding composer, of no great interest to anyone else, nothing could be further from the truth. Virtually any decent employment, along with that in music or the theatre, including clerical, teaching, law, medicine or just about any other profession one might imagine, depended on securing the protection of a suitable patron, and the means of achieving this were not fundamentally different for a composer or a court secretary or a lawyer. Leopold knew perfectly well the steps involved, having been through that himself and having observed the various levels of court administration and professional activity as well as the steps necessary to secure these positions. Young men from the full range of the middle classes – and these were surely the target audience Leopold hoped ultimately to reach – had to concern themselves with the etiquette and propriety of dealing with classes above themselves from the lower nobility all the way up to the most elevated aristocrats. Insolence to any of these (such as 'the Mufti H. C. is a *Schwanz*'), regardless of how one felt about them, must be avoided at all cost, most of all in writing intended to instruct those who would be seeking court employment.

As the advice began to flow more freely, it also took on a more insulting tone. In assuming that Wolfgang would wish to avoid the composer Joseph Mysliveček in Munich, Leopold recommended as an excuse not to visit him that 'your Mamma forbids it of you' (MBA ii 26). One wonders what Mysliveček would have thought of a man twenty-one years old who took orders from his mamma on anything. A ruse of this type would be much more useful to a youth a few years younger. Concerning a scheme for employment coaching singers in Munich, Leopold saw nothing of value in it: '*If the arrangement can be readily implemented, good! then you should take it*. But if an agreement cannot be finalized quickly, then you cannot just sit about, squandering your money and wasting your time; for in Munich, despite all the compliments and professions of friendship, you cannot hope to make a single kreuzer there' (MBA ii 34). The diatribe against the Munich scheme continues on 6 October: 'You are right that if alone you could live in Munich. But it would do you little honour, and how the Archbishop would joke about us! *You can live that way anywhere, not just in Munich. You must not reduce yourself to that and throw things away in that way. Surely we have not yet fallen so low*' (MBA ii 35). The letter ends, '*Addio, keep well! But take care of your health*, for the other would be the worst thing that could happen to you; and save the best you can, for travelling costs money' (MBA ii 37). Advice breeds advice; the main focus here concerns securing employment at court, but why not toss in words on health and economy at the end for good measure?

On reaching Augsburg, Leopold's home town, Wolfgang began to receive letters addressed to himself alone, the floodgate of advice now completely raised. The first of these, a long letter dated 15 October, covers an extraordinary range of topics. It begins with a reminder that concerts need to be announced a week in advance and that favourable reviews should be collected. Following this, Leopold tells him to refrain from using the term 'Lutheran' but instead to call the people in question Evangelicals. If no more money can be made in Augsburg, he should move on, preferably to Mannheim. And, if they wished to be in Mannheim by 4 November,

the thought should not be entertained of going from Wallerstein to Würzburg. Rather, you should hurry straight to Mannheim, which is a considerable distance; it's a distance of about twenty miles, and therefore a journey of two days. *Mamma will find it on the postal maps*; much depends on whether the route is good, or whether many detours must be made. From Wallerstein it will be only fifteen miles to Würzburg, and from Würzburg also fifteen miles to Mannheim. Now the days are already getting shorter. So you should always try to depart *early in the morning* to avoid having to travel late at night. . . . Towards strangers who also reside at your inn, you should not be too forthcoming about your journey, for there are many adventurers and rogues. . . . I should have thought to tell you that immediately after your arrival in Munich, you should search for a copyist, and the same at any place where you will remain for any length of time. For you must really try to make headway with your composition, and that can happen if you have symphonies and divertimentos already copied to present to a prince or some other notable music lover. The copying should therefore be organized so that *the copyist writes out the first violin or another leading part at your lodgings under your supervision* (MBA ii 57–8).

In one paragraph Leopold plays the roles of travel agent, protector, and musical and career supervisor. Did he imagine his son could not read a map? Probably not. A young man seeking to elevate his place in life should concentrate on the main task ahead of him, leaving such mundane matters as travel arrangements

to someone else. For anyone from a higher class that would be readily understood, but middle-class readers might not have the sense to realize they should
not waste time on such matters. Ideally one should have a trustworthy servant
to take care of this, but if one's only travel companion happened to be one's
mother, she should become servant, secretary and chief map reader.

The importance of patronage receives emphasis throughout the correspondence, not only for long-term employment but in the short run as well. With
some form of patronage while travelling, he would have the

> advantage, *which is not slight*, that you would not have to pay for food, drink, etc.,
> and landlords' bills surely make a hole in one's purse. Now you understand me.
> *These principles are of the greatest necessity for your well-being*. . . . You have with
> you the big Latin prayer book, which you will find very useful, not only because
> all the Psalms and other church texts are in it, . . . but also because it will serve
> you *in practising the Latin language*; sometimes for a change you should say your
> morning and evening prayers from it, as these are easy to understand. There are
> also some confession and communion prayers here. . . . Now it is time to think
> ahead and try to move on. . . . You really should not concern yourself on account
> of the opera in Mannheim, which you can see during Carnival time. *But you must
> not neglect to see Prince Taxis at his estates*; and when there, you must allow
> circumstances to guide you. How you should set things in motion in Mannheim
> I will write to you another time (MBA ii 59–61).

He follows this with instructions on remembering important points concerning
letter writing already cited. Mozart probably said few prayers of any description
at this time; Leopold's advice to use his prayer book, not only for devotional
purposes but to improve his Latin, corresponds in Catholic fashion to Gellert's
Protestant directive to routinize the reading of the classics.

In Leopold's next letter, dated 18 October, the barrage continues, now with
a barrister's tone:

> First of all, *concerning October 11th, I must complete my defence*. I am clearly in the
> right and you got it wrong. . . . You yourself do not know how well you play the
> violin. . . . You must never play carelessly, or people will believe that from some
> foolishness you imagine yourself to be a great player. . . . Anyone who lowers
> himself even a little to their [the sons of Augsburg patricians] common level
> simply prompts them to fall into their mockery, which they usually practise only
> with people of their class. You made yourself too common with that lad. You
> went together to the theatre! You played the fool! You were not reserved enough,
> and were too familiar! In short, you were too easygoing with such a *puppy*, and he
> believed that he could poke fun at you. That should serve as a lesson to you, *to
> associate freely and naturally with grown-up people*, instead of with such ill-
> mannered, underdeveloped boys who can claim nothing greater than that their
> fathers are the town councillors. *With such fellows one must always exercise*

restraint, their acquaintance should be strictly avoided, and, consequently, familiarity with them. . . . When you arrive in Mannheim, the principal person, one whom you can completely trust, is *Signor Raaff*, an honorable *God-fearing* man, who appreciates things German and can offer you very valuable advice and help. . . . You must not reveal your intentions to anyone but Herr Raaff, who will tell you whether you should seek an audience with the Elector, and who perhaps can facilitate such a thing for you himself. *Initially you should only attempt to gain a hearing; afterwards you should first have an audience and then set things in motion.* . . . In Mannheim, too, an opportunity exists of writing for the German theatre. But remember the importance of not confiding in anybody. . . . I entreat you, hold firmly to God, who must be your guide since all men are villains! The older you get and the more you have associated with people, the more you will experience this sad truth (MBA ii 71–5).

Mozart learned his lesson well concerning horseplay with the likes of the sons of the Augsburg patricians, but not the lesson that Leopold expected. This one backfired, and he had been a fool to tell his father about it; in future he would continue the behaviour but with much less generous descriptions in the correspondence.

Various other letters to Augsburg include certain topics not previously covered. A name-day greeting and wish never to lose the grace of God become much more than that:

and it will never leave you, if you are diligent in fulfilling the responsibilities of a true Catholic Christian. You know me. I am no pedant and no praying zealot and even less a hypocrite; surely you will not refuse the request of your father, which is that you should be concerned about your soul, so that in the hour of his death you will cause him no anxiety, and that in that dreadful moment he may have no reason to reproach himself for having neglected the salvation of your soul. Farewell! Be happy! Be sensible! (MBA ii 79).

Here he virtually could have been copying Gellert's words, laying on the guilt in a way that invokes eternal damnation.

Economy stands next to godliness, and this returns more than any of the recurring topics:

Because of your prolonged stay in Munich and Augsburg you have consumed over 100 florins. If you had been in Munich for a shorter time, you would now have a surplus and profit. . . . Now you must be well on your guard, for Mannheim is a dangerous spot concerning money, where everything is expensive. . . . The court is filled with people who look on strangers with covetous glances and who put cudgels under the feet of the most skilful. Here economy is most essential; and if Herr Danner or some other friend could take you from your inn to a private lodging, you would save half your money (MBA ii 91–2).

Leopold, like Gellert, put enormous emphasis on economizing; this reflected his attitude about money, but it probably had less to do with his actual finances. While Leopold had to borrow to finance the initial stages of the trip, he had sufficient capital in investments to back it.[11] His own finances were fairly secure thanks to the displaying of his children in courts throughout Europe in the 1760s, clearly more secure than he would let on to anyone – including his son. Obviously he did not want to see this money squandered, but things were likely not as tight as he often suggested. Once again he directed his advice as much to his larger middle-class audience as to his son, readers whose need to economize might very well be more urgent.

Mozart's stay in Mannheim lasted much longer than either father or son anticipated, and during his four months there a new range of topics for advice arose, particularly involving writing music designed to meet the local taste. Here too Mozart tasted love and fell in with some fairly unsavoury companions, and Leopold felt compelled to address both issues. At this time Leopold became more conscious of Wolfgang's deceptive treatment of his letters, resulting in a more impassioned tone in some of Leopold's responses. The advice sent to Augsburg could be treated in a straightforward and rational manner since there were not yet any serious indications of it being ignored. In Mannheim the challenge became much more apparent and called for a somewhat different strategy, involving greater emotion. The responses now put the moral teacher to the test, and if he could succeed in keeping his son on track, his glory would be the greater and his credibility in the world would be all the stronger. Receiving the appropriate responses from his son therefore became crucial, requiring not only instruction in letter writing but the requisite acceptance of authority and proof of making the correct choices based on the father's advice.

On composition, Leopold firmly believed that little other than gaining approbation mattered. If Wolfgang should get a contract to compose an opera in Mannheim, he should 'follow the natural and popular style, which everyone finds easily comprehensible; leave the grand and elevated sound for grand matters. Everything in its place' (MBA ii 99). In Paris, Wolfgang should follow the same course: 'Should you be engaged to write a contrapuntal work or something of that sort for the concert spirituel, work it out with the greatest care, and listen in advance to what is being composed and what people like best' (MBA ii 325). Leopold now takes the matter of pleasing the public to the extreme: 'When composing your *opera you must be guided by the French taste*. If you can only *find approval and get well paid*, the devil can take the rest' (MBA ii 341).

This may be a little more crass than even Leopold intended, but on the matter of approbation he remained firm, insisting two weeks later that Mozart should

follow my advice and remember that *your whole reputation depends on your first work*. Before you write it, listen and think about the taste of the nation [France]; hear and observe their operas. I know you well; you can imitate anything. *Do not*

5   Letter from Leopold to Wolfgang in Mannheim, from
Salzburg, 12 February 1778, page 1.

compose in a hurry, for no person of sensibility does that. Discuss the text in
advance with *Baron Grimm* and with *Noverre* and make sketches and let them
hear them. Everybody does that. Voltaire reads aloud his poems to his friends,
listens to their judgement and makes revisions. Your object is to make your
reputation and to take in money (MBA ii 354).

Whether Leopold recognized his son's genius or not appeared to be irrelevant;
approbation and success superseded all else, and to achieve his end Mozart
should happily ape the dregs of French culture (Leopold himself had sneered

mercilessly at the mediocrity of French opera). Here he clearly spoke in the voice of the old school, the earlier attitude of the Enlightenment which insisted on gaining the audience's favour before presenting something challenging. Starving geniuses in garrets had no place in Leopold's scheme of things. Mozart appears to have invented the work in question, a nonexistent opera, for the purpose of convincing his father of his own industriousness. Leopold continued to harp on the issue of the French taste, continuing two weeks later: 'Once again I say to you *consider the subject matter well, read through the text with Baron de Grimm, and come to an understanding with Noverre* as to how the affects should be expressed, and *follow the national taste in singing*, which your modulations and vocal settings will raise and distinguish from the others' (MBA ii 365). If one wished to succeed in that country, he must, Leopold believed, outdo the French at being French.

The pretence of an opera could not be maintained indefinitely, and after Mozart buried the nonexistent opera, Leopold turned his advice to smaller types of works:

> Even if there is less return, if it is God's will, it will surely make you better known. But make it something short, easy, popular. Discuss with some engraver what he would most like to have – perhaps some easy quartets for two violins, viola and basso. Do you imagine that you would be doing something beneath yourself? Absolutely not! Did [Johann Christian] Bach, while in London, ever publish anything but similar trifles? *What is small can be great*, if it is written naturally, flowingly and easily, and follows the fundamentals. . . . Did Bach lower himself in that way? Absolutely not. Good craft and discipline, il filo – these separate the master from the duffer, even in trifles. If I were in your place I would first work on something like that and then apply all means to get an opera commissioned (MBA ii 444).

Leopold was not Wolfgang, and he wasted this advice on deaf ears, as Mozart, now in Paris, moved neither mind nor pen in response to it.

Aside from his friendship with Fridolin Weber, Mozart's encounter with the Weber family resulted in an infatuation with Fridolin's daughter Aloysia, an attractive and talented singer of seventeen, and his attempts to endear these people to Leopold met with immediate and persuasive resistance. Two matters arose here for Leopold to set straight: Wolfgang throwing his life away at too early an age for an unsuitable marriage partner, and his preference for the company of her undesirable family. Mozart's mother, usually tolerant of her son's activity, could not restrain herself on this matter, complaining to Leopold (while Mozart was at dinner and would not see her note) that

> you will have seen from this letter that when Wolfgang makes a new acquaint-ance, he promptly wants to give everything he has to such people. It is true her singing is unrivalled; although we should never lose sight of our own

good. . . . But as soon as he got to know the Webers, he quickly changed his
mind. In a word, he endears himself to other people more than to me. . . . You
will have to decide what should be done (MBA ii 255).

Leopold responded swiftly and forcefully, mustering the strongest of his
epistolary emotions, persuasive rhetoric and moral imperative. The thought of
providing any financial support to the Webers, of course, was ludicrous, and
Leopold described at great length his own precarious situation. As for Aloysia,
arousing guilt seemed at first the best strategy:

> One slides without notice into this type of situation and then doesn't know how
> to get out. I will say nothing about women, for one needs to use the greatest
> reserve and good sense where they are concerned, since Nature herself is our
> enemy; and whoever does not summon all his reason to maintain the necessary
> reserve, will exert it in vain later on when he tries to disentangle himself from the
> labyrinth, *a misfortune, which most often ends in death*. How blindly we may often
> be led on by apparently meaningless jests, flatteries and fun, etc.; meanwhile
> reason, when awakened later, is ashamed; you yourself perhaps have learned a
> little from the experience. I do not want to reproach you. I know that you love
> me, not only as your father, but also as your most certain and surest friend; that
> you understand and realize that our happiness and unhappiness, indeed, my long
> life or conversely my hastening death are, aside from God, so to say, in your
> hands. . . . Live like a good Catholic. Love and fear God. Pray with devotion and
> trust to him with full inner passion, and lead so Christian a life that, if I should
> never see you again, my hour of death may not be full of anguish. From my heart
> I give you my fatherly blessing and remain until death your faithful father and
> your surest friend (MBA ii 258).

Gellert could not have said it better; Leopold could now address the issue of
women with a real one on the horizon. The style and rhetoric of this letter
suggest less an addressing of the specifics of Wolfgang and Aloysia than a more
generalized moral stance he would wish to impress on his larger audience.
    Whether or not Leopold fully understood the situation, his first letter on the
subject leaves the impression that he had not yet grasped that his son had
more than sexual interest in this appealing young woman. When that sank in,
generalized epistolary rhetoric gave way to genuine emotion and focus on the
problem. Once again he could use the guilt strategy, but now in an intense
and personal way:

> My dear son, I beg you to read this letter with care – and take the time to think
> about it. Great merciful God, those pleasant moments are gone when, as a child
> and boy, you never went to sleep without standing on a chair and singing *oragnia
> figatafa* to me, and at the end kissing me repeatedly on the tip of my nose and
> telling me that when I became old you would put me in a glass container and

protect me from every waft of air, so that you would always have me with you and would hold me in honour. . . . it now depends entirely on you to raise yourself to a position of high reputation, which no musician has ever reached. You owe that debt to the extraordinary talents which you have received from the merciful God; and now it depends entirely on your common sense and behaviour whether you remain an ordinary musician, completely forgotten by the world, or become a renowned Capellmeister, of whom posterity will also read about in books – whether, ensnared by some woman, you carry on in a garret full of starving children in a straw bed, or whether, as a Christian, living in serenity, honour and fame, you die with your family well provided for and a position of eminence secured (MBA ii 273–4).

Leopold had now reached his epistolary zenith; he could invoke nostalgia, hope for the future, loyalty, God's beneficence, and the horrors of the garret with high emotion and rhetorical sting, persuading, he was certain, the most prodigal child to find the right path. Aloysia, Mozart discovered later in 1778 on his return from Paris to Salzburg by way of Munich where she now lived, did not share his affection, and the danger signalled by Leopold temporarily receded.

Before Mozart's late and grudging return to Salzburg, various other issues surfaced which required Leopold's firm treatment, and for some of those already noted, he repeated advice at various times. On travel this includes which roads to take, dealing with innkeepers, and the dangers of familiarity with guests. On composition he makes numerous comments on individual matters, but he emphasizes the essential point of writing in such a way that approbation will be secured. As for career advancement, he lays out strategies on how most effectively to achieve a position or find a patron. He discusses dealings with people of all ranks: avoid familiarity with lower classes and defer to the whims of the nobility. Reflecting von Knigge with great accuracy, Leopold wrote, 'with people of high rank *you can always be completely natural*; but with everyone else I beg of you to *behave like an Englishman*. Do not be so trusting and naive! Never let a friseur or any other domestic see your money, rings or watch, or even less leave them lying about' (MBA ii 272). Leopold warns him to be careful with women who may have designs of marriage, and avoid women of ill repute; he should manage his finances carefully, always frugal in choices of lodging, meals, clothing and conveyance; resist spending money frivolously and fend off the temptations of gambling.

As the journey proceeded from Munich to Paris, Leopold's advice on money turned to outrage because of the excessive amounts Wolfgang seemed to be spending. Advice flowed freely on how time should be spent, on the importance of being industrious, on how to make the best impression on those in positions of authority, on showing respect to persons with more experience than himself – most notably his father. On religion Leopold admonished him to keep his trust in God and uphold his tradition, and in matters of morals he must always maintain sound judgement and decorum. If Gellert, who had died in 1769, had seen this correspondence, one suspects that his admiration might have been tinged by shades of jealousy, since Leopold had surpassed his mentor in style, passion, rhetoric, wit and breadth – in short, in all facets of epistolarity, setting Leopold's letters apart as probably the best to come from the pen of any German writer in the eighteenth century.

THE FATE OF LEOPOLD'S BIOGRAPHY

If Leopold had such a grand epistolary moral and biographical project in mind, one that could have placed him among the leading German writers of the eighteenth century, one must, of course, ask what happened to it. Leopold, as he had noted he intended to do on various occasions, should have sought its publication himself, but the evidence (or lack of it) suggests that he did not pursue it in any way. This was certainly not for lack of opportunity. As a previously published author, one with a sizeable reputation, Leopold could have gone from respectability to best-seller status with this project; he already had a publisher eager to keep him in print, Johann Jakob Lotter of Augsburg, the publisher of the *Violinschule*, who brought that work out in second and third editions in 1769 and 1787 during its writer's lifetime (two more German editions appeared in 1791 and 1804). Leopold could surely have published the letters as an epistolary biography – with a strong element of travel literature – especially if he had approached it in the way he had the *Violinschule*, by taking the financial risk himself.

Speculation on what some may have deemed a missed opportunity will come in the following chapters, in a discussion of Wolfgang's complex responses to his father. As an epistolary biography the writings of both correspondents would need to be included, and for it to serve its intended purpose the son's letters would need to show an obedient and inquiring son, who seeks sound advice and then can be seen to be implementing it, confirming his father's moral authority.

The correspondence between Leopold and Wolfgang, of course, did not cease in January 1779, but continued until 1787, the year of Leopold's death, although progressively in decline. The set of letters following the Mannheim-Paris period, from November 1780 to January 1981, when Mozart worked on *Idomeneo* in Munich, is telling. The advice which had flowed so freely during the previous two years now vanished almost completely. The occasional points of advice that do creep into this set appear to get there by force of a habit hard to break; for the most part Leopold goes out of his way to resist the temptation. The reason for the absence of advice in these letters is surely not that a twenty-four-year-old son needed it less than one aged twenty-two. On the contrary, Mozart had succeeded in turning his father's long-term project into an epistolary game, a contest in which he played his side with such virtuosity that no father-moralist, regardless of how intelligent and enlightened, could possibly win. Leopold knew what was happening; his own letters progressed from control to bewilderment by late 1778. Wolfgang so completely subverted the project that the letters were rendered unpublishable; what could have been a grand and noble project was dissolved by its subject, who did not share his father's embrace of the Enlightenment.

Chapter 4
The Road to Dissolution: September 1777 to January 1779

Before we move on to Mozart's dissimulating and evasive written replies to his father, a glance at the circumstances of his life during this period of response would be useful, recognizing of course that the life as we know it can only be constructed from Mozart's letters to his father, chronicles that at times foster intentional unreliability. The epistolary narrative that emerges seems to suggest that Mozart, in his pastimes and associations with other people, now travelled on the road to dissolution – probably even further than the letters indicate since the correspondence belonged to an epistolary commerce driven by Leopold's moral objectives. Complete candour would have been foolhardy; what Leopold did not know would not give him cause for grief, and even more to the point, would not unleash torrents of chastising advice or worse.

Setting out with his mother on 23 September 1777 on an extended journey that lasted over sixteen months, a quest intended to secure an appointment that would free him and perhaps the whole family from the drudgery of Salzburg and elevate him to a position worthy of his talent, Mozart found himself for the first time in his life without his father looking over his shoulder, directing his productivity, career, beliefs and morals. Leopold, for his part, attempted to continue this with a powerful pen in the correspondence just described in the previous chapter, but since the postal system took six days to deliver a letter and since his wife, as Mozart's travel companion, avoided prodding or enforcement, the role of director fell into decline, in spite of the fact that the letters now recorded it for posterity. Mozart sensed very quickly the new freedom that had fallen his way, and he did not hesitate to take advantage of the independence that became possible. His changing strategy for communicating this to his father will be the subject of chapter 5, and in part this strategy unfolded in relation to the events, friendships, actions, indolence and influences that ensued. As time elapsed Leopold became progressively aware of the dissolution that gradually swallowed his son, and he fought bravely with all his moral resources and worldly experience to prevent it. But Mozart very much liked his own new course, and he was not about to allow his sensible father's wisdom and righteousness to derail it. What we have here is not a case of a prodigal son sowing some wild oats before returning to his birthright of enlightened morality; for Mozart the shift proved decisive and longlasting, shaping the person and artist at the deepest possible level.

FRIENDS AND LOVERS

Mozart's friends in Salzburg were family friends, people known to and approved of by Leopold, and any questionable activities, such as Bölzlschiessen with its sometimes scatological overtones, were family activities, indulged in by Leopold with as much relish as the others. Now unable to control his son's choices of companions, Leopold could do nothing but sound the alarm when Mozart appeared to be falling in with the wrong crowd, as happened during the visit to Augsburg in October 1777 with the sons of local patricians. With these 'ill-mannered, underdeveloped boys', Leopold scolded, 'you were not reserved enough and, you were too familiar. . . . That should serve as a lesson. . . . *With such fellows one must always exercise restraint, their acquaintance should be strictly avoided and, consequently, familiarity with them*' (MBA ii 73–4). No amount of advice could keep Mozart from choosing the wrong friends; for the next year he persisted in doing precisely that, enjoying the company of an assortment of characters who could not possibly win Leopold's favour. To be sure, Mozart learned a lesson at this early stage of independence, only a few weeks into the correspondence, realizing he must be much more circumspect in the information he provided his father. He also learned to avoid displaying the cross of the Order of the Golden Spur – which Leopold had advised him to wear – in situations where it would likely cause the kind of embarrassment it had in Augsburg.

The incident with the son of one of Augsburg's leading citizens may have soured Mozart on the city of Leopold's birth, but not entirely:

> I will be decidedly happy to arrive in a place again where there is a court. I can surely say that if it were not for my good uncle and aunt and my truly adorable cousin, I would regret as much having come to Augsburg as I have hairs on my head. Now I must write a little about my lovely young cousin. But I will save that until tomorrow, for one must be in a very cheerful mood if one wants properly to praise her as she deserves (MBA ii 66).

That praise came the next day: 'Our petite cousin is beautiful, intelligent, adorable, clever and merry. . . . The two of us hit it off perfectly, since she too is a bit naughty. We both make fun of people and have a merry time doing it' (MBA ii 66). In fact, Maria Anna Thekla had qualities that he hoped Leopold would not discover, and he avoided describing the nature of the 'fun' they had. Leopold appears to have known more about this than Mozart suspected:

6   Maria Anna Thekla Mozart ('the Bäsle'): pencil drawing,
1777–8.

'She repeatedly protests against the accusation of being *intimate with rakish clerics*. . . . between yourself and your young cousin there was a very sad and disconsolate departure' (MBA ii 90). But members of the clergy interested in more than her soul were not her only enticement, as Leopold wrote chastisingly a few months later: 'In Augsburg too you had your little scene, indulging in a good time with my brother's daughter, who must now send you her portrait' (LMF 476). Leopold could hardly tell his son to avoid his cousin, but his accusation appears to have hit the mark, evoking the appropriate indignation from Wolfgang: 'What you wrote so bitingly about my merry indulgence with your brother's daughter wounded me deeply; but since the situation is not like that, I do not have to answer your accusation' (MBA ii 286). On the contrary, matters stood exactly as Leopold thought, and the nature of this, again known to us exclusively through letters – some of the most impishly scatological, nonsensical and lascivious letters in the epistolary canon – will be described in chapter 6.

Mozart, much to Leopold's annoyance at the overstay, wasted the two weeks he spent in Augsburg in career pursuit, but not in gaining a taste for the pleasures of life. The career prospects were not much brighter in Mannheim, but Mozart managed to prolong this stay with all sorts of excuses for four and a half months, finding diversions here perhaps not as instantly gratifying as Augsburg, but undoubtedly more appealing in the long run. The first of these diversions took place shortly after his arrival in the household of Christian Cannabich, concertmaster and conductor of the famous Mannheim orchestra and Mozart's principal contact in that city, as he described in the form of a facetious confession to his father:

I, Johannes Chrisostomus Amadeus Wolfgangus Sigismundus Mozart, plead guilty that yesterday and the day before (and already many other times) I did not arrive home before midnight; and that from ten o'clock until the designated hour at Cannabich's house, and in the presence and en Compagnie of Cannabich, his wife and daughter, Herr Treasurer [Gres], Ramm and Lang, I frequently, without difficulty, but with ease, spouted rhymes, and, in fact, complete garbage, namely, about dirt, shitting and arse-licking – and actually in thoughts, words and – but not in deeds. I would not have behaved so godlessly, though, if our ringleader, namely the one named Lisel [Elisabetha Cannabich], had not incited and agitated me into it; and I must confess that I heartily enjoyed it. I confess all these sins and transgressions of mine from the bottom of my heart, and in the hope of having to confess them often, I strongly resolve to improve on the sinful life I have embarked on. Hence I beg for the holy dispensation, if it can be easily secured; if not, it's all the same to me, for the game will carry on anyway (MBA ii 123–4).

Under other circumstances Leopold – no prude when it came to such language and games or even the satirizing of priests (most of whom he deemed corrupt) and confession – might have been amused, but not when it appeared that Wolfgang was squandering precious time and money:

the most beautiful autumn that anyone can remember has gone by, and so far you on the other hand have just turned it into a holiday, spending your time living it up and having fun. . . . But to live in Paris, you must assume an entirely different way of living, and a different way of thinking. . . . Such a journey is no joke; you have not as yet experienced anything like it. You should have other important things on your mind instead of just fooling around; you should be trying to set up a hundred things in advance, or in an instant you will find yourself sitting in the muck, without money – and where there is no money, friends will also disappear . . . instead of taking care of important things, you mess around in the filth from ten o'clock until midnight (MBA ii 143–4).

Diversions and games with the Cannabichs were no doubt fairly innocent, but that proved less true of other friendships. The outstanding flutist Johann Wendling, whose performance skills Leopold had admired as early as 1763, opened his home to Mozart late in November – lunch there became a matter of routine, and Friedrich Ramm, oboist in the orchestra, frequently joined them. Early in December Wendling proposed that they should travel together to Paris where he would help Mozart to launch his career, and Mozart wrote to his father with enthusiasm for the plan. Mozart aborted these arrangements early in February as he had now met new and stronger friends, the Webers, but the reason given to Leopold concerns the life that Wendling led: 'Wendling is a fundamentally honest and good man, but unfortunately lacking any religion; and the same with the whole family. . . . Ramm is a decent person, but a libertine' (MBA ii 252). Leopold's wife corroborates their lack of religion, disappointed that Wendling's wife and daughter prefer the theatre over church (which they found unhealthy), but in response to Leopold's chastisement for not letting him know sooner about Wendling's way of life, she pleads ignorance: 'The reason we didn't write you about it sooner is that for a long time we knew nothing about it' (MBA ii 291). To be sure, she may not have known, but the chances that Mozart did not after two months of almost living at his home seem unlikely in the extreme. Undoubtedly he not only knew but approved, and now needed a convenient excuse not to go to Paris with Wendling and Ramm, one that he could be certain Leopold would endorse.

FRIDOLIN WEBER

In January 1778 Mozart met Fridolin Weber and his family, and the association could not have had a more profound effect. For conspicuous reasons much has been made of Weber's daughters Aloysia and Constanze, as the former was Mozart's first true love and the latter his wife, but very little has been said of Weber himself and the nature of Mozart's friendship with him. The reasons for this are obvious since we know little of Weber himself, and only one letter survives of his correspondence with Mozart; the glowing descriptions of Weber supplied by Mozart to his father, of course, cannot be trusted. Yet, one could argue that Fridolin Weber provided the initial and chief cause for Mozart's attraction to this family, and this particular friendship played a pivotal role in Mozart's development. Curiously, Mozart, in his own state of unemployment and lacking solid prospects, attempted to play the part of protector to the Weber family; this may have been a misdirected form of repayment for the new way of looking at the world that Weber inadvertently offered him.

Mozart was drawn to people like Weber, particularly at this time as he attempted to shed the baggage of a disagreeable appointment and the influence of an enlightened father. Weber did not lack an education, having studied law at Freiburg University, and he had held a respectable position in the government bureaucracy at Zell im Wiesental; in spite of that he now found himself eking out a meagre and precarious living as a singer, music copyist and prompter in the court theatre at Mannheim. When his former employer, Baron Schönau, fell into financial difficulties, he dismissed Weber from his position, ostensibly because of Weber's dealings in a shady business transaction – which the baron himself had initiated. To avoid worse than a dismissal, Weber fled from Zell im Wiesental with his wife and children in the middle of winter, taking nothing more than could be carried in the escape. Like his father before him, he sued the baron, and his case ended in a settlement.[1] As a man forced from respectability, he lived on wit and ingenuity in the theatre, on the fringe of society, not only in a profession associated with Carnival but as the living example of someone transformed from a place of standing to marginal protest. In short, he curiously represented what the roguish Mozart may have wished to identify with at this time.

Unlike our century, where actors – particularly those from cinema – have become the new aristocracy, the theatre held little glory and certainly no honour during the eighteenth century. In fact, a career in the theatre represented the strongest possible alternative to a life of respectability. Theatrical troupes frequently found themselves at odds with authority, possibly because of the satire and ridicule of prominent figures they dished out in *commedia dell'arte* performances. The line between serious actors of the high theatre and comedians could not always be clearly drawn; Emanuel Schikaneder, a leading comic actor, had won great success playing Hamlet in Munich, while Friedrich Schröder, another of Mozart's future friends and perhaps the leading serious German actor of the late eighteenth century, had frequently played roles in *commedia dell'arte* productions.

No profession stood in lower regard than the theatre, as actors, singers, managers, and others in these troupes were held up to the world by moralists as the prime example of what one should strive to avoid. A curious contradiction existed here, in that enlightened morality could be inculcated in the theatre, yet the practitioners of the trade were considered to be so far off the scale of moral acceptability that some moralists represented them as nothing short of monsters. In the division between Enlightenment and Carnival – or moral refinement and coarse licentiousness – people of the theatre clustered at the extreme low end of the polarity. While numerous eighteenth-century writers espoused this view, one of the most articulate and popular in Germany was Adolf von Knigge; his *Über den Umgang mit Menschen*, topping the best-seller list in Germany, appeared in English translation as *Practical Philosophy of Social Life* in 1799. As for people of the theatre, von Knigge warns his readers 'that the more eminent their talents are the more they are given to libertinism. I would therefore advise my readers, particularly those that are of a lively disposition, to form no intimate connection with people of that class. . . . Singers, poets, dancers and players are fond of good living; and we need not be astonished at it.' The rigour of the profession 'frequently impels them to inebriate themselves by excess in sensual pleasures. To this we must add, that most people who have once devoted themselves entirely to the polite arts, very seldom retain a relish for serious occupations.' Their lives become warped by what they do on the stage, forcing them to abandon rational and prudent principles; they feel 'more attached to the man who procures them sensual pleasure, than to the sage who endeavours to lead them back to the road of wisdom and regularity. They intrude upon the former and flee the latter.'[2]

This contemptible profession attracts those who love idleness and dissolute-ness, although von Knigge readily accepts that 'music, poetry, the theatre, dancing, and painting undoubtedly produce a salutary effect upon the heart', and even 'mollify our morals and promote social virtues'. In spite of the numerous fine qualities the theatre can offer, one should not judge it 'by what it *might be*, but take it as it *really is*', and in this respect not only actors can be dangerous but the plays themselves, promoting exaggerated notions of love, thoughtlessness and profligacy. Decent people should be wary of actors because of 'the liberty and independence on the restraints of civil life which they enjoy', among other things. In a final diatribe against the profession, he asks

> what sort of people are these theatrical heroes and heroines in general? People without education, principles or knowledge: adventurers and wanton harlots. . . . They are, besides, not connected with the state, and consequently have to pay less consideration to the public opinion of their moral character. . . . The daily change of the parts which they have to act, deprives their character of all originality; custom leads them at last to assume the charac-ters which they are in the habit to represent: their profession obliges them frequently to pay no consideration whatever to their disposition of mind, but to act the buffoon when their heart aches, and to appear sad and melancholy when cheerfulness and hilarity expand their bosom: this accustoms them to dissimulation; . . . poverty, sickness and disappointment are generally the last scene of the theatrical life.[3]

To make his invective even more stinging, von Knigge adds a gender bias, heaping special scorn on women of the profession whom he regards as 'harlots', as well as likening the seductions of drama itself to inferior feminine qualities. In distorting reality by overromanticizing feeling and actions, the theatre has the potential of transforming sensible men into creatures who react like women, susceptible to every impression and emotion: 'A too tender and effeminate mind, which may easily be agitated by real or imaginary distress, by its own sufferings of the misery of others is, indeed, a most lamentable acquisition'. These would be 'extremely burdensome to us, when firmness, an unshaken manly courage and perseverance are required'.[4] Reinforcing gender inequality placed von Knigge squarely on one side of the question of women: using misogyny to make his case placed him in the camp of official high culture, the authority which the Enlightenment now underscored.

Von Knigge's book, which came fairly late in the century, summed up earlier enlightened German attitudes, and Mozart had heard all these thoughts many times before, from his father to be sure, and his reading of Gellert and others. His disenchantment with this type of thinking drew him towards these objects of scorn from the enlightened moralists, seeking out people like Weber and forming the most intimate ties with them. The friendship with Weber was genuine and deep, as Mozart's letter to him from Paris, advising Weber on career matters, makes clear. Weber's own precarious position with the Elector and the exploitation of Aloysia's talents called, Mozart recommended, for cunning and deception, a strategy that should convince the Elector of their indispensability. If that did not work, they would surely have other prospects. As much as Mozart would have liked them to join him in Paris, he advised against that, since it was too late in the year to make performance arrangements for the coming season. Mozart did not hesitate to confide information to Weber he would offer to no one else, including his own father, concluding the letter with, 'if I didn't have a father and a sister, for whom I must provide more than I do for myself, always worrying about supporting, I would completely neglect my own fate with the greatest pleasure – and concentrate entirely on your affairs – since your well-being – your pleasure – your happiness, would be all that I would think about' (MBA ii 419). While carrying some rhetorical emphasis, this probably came fairly close to the truth.

Presenting the Webers to his father required an inventive strategy, considering that Mozart wished to take them to Italy where he believed Aloysia could make a career, and he needed Leopold's permission for this decidedly half baked scheme. Having expounded Aloysia's virtues as a singer, he promoted all of them as 'fundamentally honest, good Catholic Christian people. I am very sorry that I did not get to know them long ago' (MBA ii 252). As for Weber, he 'is just like my father, and the whole family like the Mozarts' (MBA ii 253). His mother protested, complaining that

> when Wolfgang makes new acquaintances, he promptly wants to give everything he has to such people. . . . But as soon as he got to know the Webers, he quickly changed his mind [about travelling with Wendling and Ramm]. In a word, he endears himself to other people more than to me, for I raise objections with him about this and that which I do not approve of; and he does not like this (MBA ii 255).

Leopold, of course, was livid. Knowing Weber's profession, Leopold did not imagine for a moment that they had anything in common. Like his wife, he found the shifting friendships to be frivolous: 'Then you made the acquaintance of Herr Wendling. Then he was the most honourable friend – and then what happened next, I need not repeat. Suddenly along comes your new acquaint-anceship with Herr [Weber]; then all the others are left behind; now this family is the most honestly Christian family . . .' (MBA ii 275). The Italian travel plans all but forced him to lose his reason: 'My dearest son! How can you have let yourself be taken in even for an hour by such a repulsive idea! Your letter reads like nothing other than a romance – and could you really decide to go schlepping about the world with these strange people? To set aside your repu-tation – your aging parents, your beloved sister? Then cause me grief, if you can be so cruel!' (MBA ii 276, 279). Leopold, well aware of the conventions of literary romance, immediately recognized the stylistic thrust in Wolfgang's strategy; his fear aligned precisely with that expressed by von Knigge, as he perceived his son being seduced by ill-bred and conniving actors and singers who would corrupt his morals, warp his sense of reality, and leave him with a much lighter purse.

WEBER'S GIFT TO MOZART: MOLIÈRE

Just before Mozart left Mannheim for Paris, Weber gave him a copy of Molière's comedies (which Mozart had not yet read) as a parting gift, with the inscription 'Ricevi, Amico, le opere del Molière in segno di gratitudine, e qualche volta ricordate di me' (Receive, my friend, the works of Molière as a mark of gratitude and sometimes think of me) (MBA ii 328). This small gift, presumably the German edition noted by O. E. Deutsch in Mozart's estate (MDB 588), proved to have been fateful. The long and excessively boring journey from Mannheim to Paris no doubt allowed time for reading. If Mozart did not know these works before, he now, of course, discovered the play which would become the basis for *Don Giovanni*. But this gift undoubtedly struck him with much greater immediacy, as a quality in these plays surely would have reminded Mozart of Weber. No writer for the seventeenth-century established theatre had done as much as Molière to infuse a spirit of Carnival in his works, and here Mozart could recognize his friend who had progressed from a respect-able existence to the fringe of society, living a type of marginal protest through the theatre.

The spirit of the carnivalesque has not gone unnoticed in recent studies of Molière, most notably in Thérèse Malachy's *Molière: Les Métamorphoses du carnaval*, and particularly the chapter 'Le Carnaval solitaire de *Dom Juan*'. Molière himself was an actor, well versed in the skills of *commedia dell'arte* and familiar with the stock characters of the Italian improvisatory tradition. The sense of disorder associated with Carnival, turning things upside-down, and the emphasizing of absurdity, run rampant in his plays, and he goes so far as to include actual Carnival scenes, such as the burlesque ceremony which con-cludes *Le Malade imaginaire*. Similarly, the appearance of the spectre at the end of *Dom Juan*, entering in the form of a veiled woman and changing to Time with scythe in hand, invokes the spirit of Carnival plays. Throughout this play he turns normality on its head as Don Juan uses deception to gain his subversive ends: effusive politeness to Monsieur Dimanche, a creditor, succeeds in delaying payment of his bills; he plays the hypocrite to his father, convincing him of a new-found religion; and Elvira's pleading for his soul simply arouses new sexual desire for her, as he attempts to persuade her to stay the night.[5] Throughout Molière's works one finds an enjoyment of laughter, and no backing away from the grotesque – a fascination with aspects of life that include crudity, indecency, unreality and improbability. Respectable society vulnerably crouches in constant danger of attack, falling prey to satire and irony, and this goes far beyond gentle ridicule into areas of unacceptability. In *Dom Juan*, for example, where morality suffers blow after blow, Sganarelle, the sometimes gullible and on other occasions dissimulating low-bred servant, has the role of trying to persuade Don Juan to change his ways; to use W. G. Moore's words, 'Molière confides the cause of God to a dolt'.[6]

Another decade would pass before Mozart would add his own contribution to the Don Juan myth, yet at this point in his life, in seeking to become his own person but with stinging letters of reprimand and moral judgement and advice from his father in his pocket, he must have found the allure of Molière's Don Juan overwhelming. This character took every imaginable moral precept and vestige of decent society and made a mockery of them. It may have seemed especially attractive to Mozart that Don Juan too had a father intent on reforming him, a father who represented conventional moral society, and gladly turned to threats when persuasion failed. A long speech by Don Luis to his son on virtue, behaviour and changing his ways evokes no response from Juan other than an invitation to sit where he might speak more comfortably. On his father's departure, Juan expresses his true sentiments: 'The sooner you die the better. Every dog has his day, and I have no use for fathers who live as long as their sons.'[7] Juan does not wish to hurt and insult his father, or to challenge his authority openly: he wants only to get the old man off his back. What better way than convince him he has been converted to virtue, that heaven itself interceded, and henceforth he would make amends for his sins? Don Luis exits in a state of ecstasy, now convinced he will meet his son in heaven, never suspecting the ruse.

In playing the hypocrite, Juan outdoes the real hypocrites, the subscribers to religion and conventional society who perpetrate their own forms of evil, for a very definite purpose as he explains to Sganarelle: 'When I talked of mending my ways and living an exemplary life it was a calculated hypocrisy, a necessary pretence, which I had to assume for my father's benefit because I need his help, and as a protection against society and the hundred-and-one tiresome things that may happen to me.' The method proved effective and painless, one Mozart recognized as useful for himself, one he in fact applied with great skill in his letters over the next ten months. In the works of Molière he undoubtedly discovered a whole new world, reminding him of the presenter of the gift, prodding him in the subversive direction in which he was already heading.

PARIS

After a tedious journey from Mannheim lasting nine and a half days, Mozart and his mother arrived in Paris on 23 March 1778. As early as November Leopold had urged his son to put his affairs in the hands of Baron Melchior Grimm in Paris, to listen to Grimm's advice on all matters including behaviour, dealing with the French aristocracy, and Parisian musical taste. On arrival in Paris he should waste no time in establishing this contact; he should drive to Grimm's house forthwith to announce his presence, which Grimm would expect, having been informed by Leopold through a series of letters. Grimm was travelling early in 1778, making it impossible for Leopold to establish his whereabouts, although at one point Grimm crossed paths with the Mozarts without their recognizing him. On his return to Paris, Grimm replied to Leopold's letters, noting that he had seen his wife and son at a concert in Augsburg:

> I put myself so into the line of sight that he and Mme Mozart could see me, but neither he nor *Mme sa mère* recognized me: and as I was in a great hurry to depart, and everyone told me that they were on the point of going to Paris, I decided to remain unknown, since we should meet in Paris. I shall be very glad to see him again; but I am very sorry that he is coming without his father. . . . nobody can take the true place of a father (MDB 173).

Leopold had the utmost confidence in Grimm, referring to him regularly as 'our bosom friend', a fellow honest German living in Paris as the Russian ambassador of Catherine the Great and respected (so Leopold assumed) in the highest cultural and literary circles. Grimm, who should have been an obvious aid to Mozart's professional endeavours, assured Leopold that Wolfgang would be safe in Paris: 'I believe your son's conduct to be sufficiently good to have no fears for him from the dangers of Paris. If he were inclined to libertinage, he might no doubt run some risks; but if he is reasonable, he will take precautions against all trouble, without thereby leading the life of a hermit' (MDB 173).

Mozart's relationship with the reasonable Grimm did not fare well; by late July, Grimm complained to Leopold that his son was 'too inactive, too easy to catch, too little intent on the means that may lead to fortune' (MDB 177). Mozart, for his part, complained of Grimm's stinginess and that he had done nothing to help him make contacts. Their disagreement came to a head in September over a small loan made by Grimm to Mozart. Insults and accusations were thrown by both, and Grimm summarily dispatched Mozart by the least expensive (and most inconvenient) conveyance out of Paris before Mozart had

had a chance to conclude his financial affairs. Grimm's haste annoyed even Leopold. Before matters had reached that point, Mozart wrote to his father that 'Grimm may be in a position to help *children*, but not grown-up people. . . . Do not form an impression that he – is the same as he was. . . . And he need not be so proud of this deed [his hospitality] – for there are four houses where I could have had lodging and board; the good man doesn't know that, if I *were to remain here*, I would have cleared out next month, and settled in a less simple-minded and stupid house than his – where people can do you a simple favour without always making a huge issue of it' (MBA ii 474). Mozart's impressions of Grimm bore similarity to those of others in Paris, who, observing his social climbing, dandified attitudes, excessive grooming, embroidered coats, white silk stockings, powder, scent and wearing of a sword, seriously doubted his ability to understand the minds of the great French intellectuals.[8]

MADAME LOUISE D'ÉPINAY

Acquainting his son in February with the names of the most important people to contact in Paris, Leopold noted that if Grimm should be travelling, 'Madame d'Épinay will assist you with everything, or send you over to one of her friends'. She, in his terse description, is 'a very intimate friend of M. Grimm, from whom Mamma got that beautiful fan' (MBA ii 270), 'very intimate' in this case his euphemism for mistress. Mme Louise d'Épinay has been an unfortunately marginalized figure in eighteenth-century French history, but that impression has recently been corrected in a book by Ruth Plaut Weinreb outlining her extraordinary intellect and literary achievements.[9] Unlike the stiff, morally stolid and autocratic Grimm (called *Tyran le Blanc* by Gauffecourt because of his habit of dabbing his cheeks in white), she was a free spirit. After the early demise of her marriage, she took to society under the tutelage of women who discouraged prudence. Meeting Grimm changed the course of the society she kept, and she soon numbered Rousseau, Diderot, the Baron d'Holbach, the Abbé Galiani and Voltaire among her most intimate friends (and in some cases lovers).

This was no light-headed woman, as she has sometimes been characterized (a lingering impression for which Rousseau can claim some responsibility), cultivated by Encyclopaedists as their diversion from more lofty pursuits of criticism, philosophy and descriptive writing. A woman of great intellectual prowess, we have now finally recognized her as one of the first to redefine the position of women in France. Aside from her monumental *Histoire de Madame de Montbrillant*, a 2,000-page fictional account of her life which surveys the place of the upper-class woman, or her three-volume *Mémoires et Correspondance*, she participated actively in the *Correspondance littéraire*. She contributed essays on politics, philosophy, economics and the theatre, as well as book reviews, verse and letters. Grimm frequently travelled for extended periods to fulfill his duties as ambassador, during which time she, with Diderot's assistance, assumed responsibility for the entire operation. She co-authored articles with Diderot and Jacques-Henri Meister (Grimm's secretary), initiated new areas of discussion, and brought in new contributors such as Voltaire.[10]

Recognition of her place in history has suffered from her vilification at the hands of Rousseau, whose famous falling out with her over his period of residence at her Hermitage is known to the world from his side only, as described in the *Confessions*, marking, according to its author, a turning point in his life. As a leading *salonnière* she played a strong role in the intellectual life of Paris, although Rousseau disparaged this too, disputing the contribution of women to the Republic of Letters and accusing men who frequented the salons of ingratiation and social climbing. His problem with Mme d'Épinay arose in 1757, when poor health forced her to leave Paris to take a lengthy convalescence in Geneva, and various people pressured Rousseau to accompany her as a gesture of gratitude for her hospitality. His response was vitriolic; he claimed he owed her nothing and that in fact she had been the main beneficiary of his residency at the Hermitage. In the end it turned out for the best that he did not accompany her, since this sojourn opened a new vista in her life. Under the care of the physician Tronchin in Geneva, doctor and patient were frequent guests of Voltaire at nearby Les Délices. The friendship of Mme d'Épinay and Voltaire quickly blossomed, as Voltaire recognized the intellect and personal qualities of this extraordinary woman. On her departure in 1758, he wrote to her expressing his regrets: 'Tronchin performs miracles; everything is upside down; I will canonize him for this one which he has worked upon you, and I join with all Geneva in praying that God will immediately afflict you with some trifling ailment which will bring you back to us. . . . Ah! Madame, you must only trust "solitaries" like myself or Grimm.'[11] They nevertheless remained in contact, through occasional visits and their active correspondence, sometimes concerning the *Correspondance littéraire*, or sometimes personal, in which he affectionately calls her his 'belle philosophe'.

In contrast to the inhospitable attitude of Grimm, Mozart received very different treatment from Mme d'Épinay. Shortly after their arrival in Paris, Mozart's mother wrote to his father that their son, if he likes, 'can take lunch every day with Noverre or also with Madame depine' (MBA ii 329). After his mother's death early in July he moved into the Grimm household, but, he carefully explained to Leopold, not the quarters of the mean-spirited Grimm:

Madame d'Épinay certainly has a better heart; the room where I stay belongs to her, not him. . . . I would have written to you about this long ago, but I was afraid that you would likely not believe me. But, I cannot keep silent any longer, whether you believe me or not – but – I feel confident that you do believe me – for I still have sufficient credit with you to convince you that I am telling the truth. I also take my meals with Madame d'Épinay; but you must not imagine that he pays her anything, since I cost her practically nothing.

In the same letter, he also clarifies that 'if it were not for Madame d'Épinay, I would not be in this house' (MBA ii 474–5).

In what appears to be the relatively large amount of pleasurable time Mozart and Mme d'Épinay spent together, taking meals and in other social interaction, one can only assume that he learned much from her about her own background and struggles, her epistolary and other literary endeavours, as well as something of the lives and thinking of a few of the notable people in her intimate circle, such as Diderot, Holbach and Voltaire, the last having died shortly before Mozart moved into her rooms. Like Mozart, she had had cause when younger to rebel against an oppressive parent, in her case her mother, and this received literary realization in her novel. In *Montbrillant*, Mme Gondrecourt, closely modelled on her real mother, obsesses over appearances, reputation and virtue, and exercises her maternal authority severely, expecting obsequiousness and ingratiation in return. In the process of growing up and ultimately assuming maternal authority herself, Émilie, the heroine of the novel, comes to embody the modern view of liberation in contrast to her own conventional and mis-guided mother.[12] Yet at no time does Émilie exhibit outright defiance, animosity or blame, revealing instead in her letters admiration and respect.[13] She secures her independence in more skilful and subtle ways, without her mother realizing that the transformation takes place.

It seems unlikely that Mme d'Épinay would have discussed her novel with Mozart, but she may very well have acquainted him with aspects of her own past. Throughout her life she had had difficult people to deal with aside from her mother, including her libertine husband, the irascible Rousseau, and now in the 1770s an increasingly cold and distant Baron Grimm, something Mozart appears to have recognized. On Grimm's phlegmatic behaviour towards her, involving his plan to move abroad, a plan about which he failed to inform her, she revealed her plight to her intimate correspondent Abbé Galiani:

> I was told that silence had been maintained exclusively out of discretion. . . . He concluded by emphasizing that he would be distressed if I raised the subject again. Meanwhile, he did not even tell me what proposals were being made to him. . . . But we have to take people with their virtues and their faults. . . . my feelings would not have made an ounce of difference to him.[14]

Mozart's relations with Grimm, moving from cordial to strained, seemed to parallel hers, and his passive manner of dealing with it was also similar: 'Recently he spoke to me quite severely, crudely and stupidly, and I lacked the courage to reply, since I was afraid of offending him, that he need not be concerned on account of his fifteen louis d'or. I could do nothing but endure it – and asked him whether he had finished speaking. And then I said: your obedient servant' (MBA ii 475). A strategy appropriate for dealing with Grimm could be applied to dealings with Leopold as well, although in the end he could not restrain himself from an outburst of his disparagement towards Grimm.

Through her many complex dealings with the above-mentioned people, Mme d'Épinay had developed a sense of wariness and even scepticism, aware that complete candour could be counterproductive. Her faith in virtue had been very much shaken by the licentious behaviour of her husband, but that did not prevent her from writing a highly moral epistolary discourse to her own son, in the hope that it would counteract the negative influence of the child's father.[15] Virtue and religion were important to her, but as with Voltaire, this did not always show. At one point in *Montbrillant*, she takes a decidedly irreverent tone, relating a parable which mocks not only church dogma but the Trinity as well.[16] Similarly, her own high morals do not entirely square with the fact that she spent much of her life in two adulterous relationships.[17] In these complexities of life she had developed modes of discourse in conversation and correspondence to cover all instances, to be the appropriate person or wear the right mask in dealing with different people. She also succeeded in building this into a literary style, writing a novel which could have been offensive to some. Through Mme d'Épinay Mozart discovered a mastery of language he had not previously encountered, and her lessons were surely not lost on him.

MME D'ÉPINAY'S FRIENDS

The *philosophes* who surrounded Mme d'Épinay, these intellectual giants of the age whose lives and works she surely discussed with Mozart, were in a number of cases on the fringe of an intolerant France, in danger of authoritarian wrath if their views offended and if they could be identified. Aside from Voltaire, Diderot, Holbach or Galiani, Rousseau too may have been discussed, although she undoubtedly still felt rankled following the complete breakdown with him in 1757 after a very close relationship. Mozart may have retained some interest in Rousseau since his childhood, as he wrote an opera at the age of twelve, *Bastien und Bastienne*, based on Rousseau's *Le Devin du village*, first performed at the residence of Anton Mesmer in Vienna. But Rousseau, especially following his break with d'Épinay and the *philosophes*, seemed the least likely of the people in question to strike a sympathetic chord with Mozart at this time. Contrary to the social pessimism and religious scepticism evident in the thinking of his foes, Rousseau clung tenaciously to a faith inspired by nothing more than feeling and a naive sense of optimism. For Rousseau, dissimulation was neither necessary nor significant.

Unlike Rousseau, Voltaire, according to Norman L. Torrey, 'was a constant double dealer, he lied and believed in lying that he might live to lie again another day'.[18] To be sure, he intended much of this for the benefit of humanity. Also, in an intolerant society, it could keep a nonconformist out of serious trouble. On more than one occasion Voltaire had tasted the hospitality of the Bastille, and he disguised his true sentiments as an obvious protection. As a specific precaution he avoided signing his own works; Voltaire regarded Rousseau's insistence on signing his own works as foolhardy, something Rousseau persisted in doing even after various condemnations of his works and silencing.[19] Dealing with the church could be an especially delicate matter in eighteenth-century France. To Père de la Tour, Voltaire promised that he would 'tear up any page of his works that was hostile to the church and would live and die in her bosom'. Anyone who knew him well would see through this deception, and Voltaire himself pointed out that 'it is a sad business making hypocrites'.[20] Voltaire wished to protect not only his public image, but also the impressions of his closest friends. In his vast correspondence one often sees letters to his most intimate acquaintances, including Mme d'Épinay, which hold a position utterly contrary to that expressed to someone else.

For Diderot the question 'What is the world?' evoked the following reply: 'A structure subject to revolutions which all indicate a constant tendency to destruction; a rapid succession of beings which succeed one another, displace one another and disappear; a fleeting symmetry; a momentary order.'[21] If world order defied detection, the notion of God as architect was not likely to fare well, to say nothing of a god intervening in the affairs of people. Voltaire the deist could accept the idea of a god who had placed the universe in motion and then stepped out of the way. Others, such as Holbach, went much further, frightening even Voltaire with their rejection of Christian tenets. Holbach had no use for the traditional conceptions of God, life after death, the soul, original sin or salvation, dismissing all of these as superstition and supernatural idolatry that interfere with morality.[22] An interventionist god who willed things for the best had ceased to be an operative notion.

In traditional enlightened thought the presence of evil had a place, but only as a countervailing force which should in the end allow the victory of good to be all the stronger. As these notions were passed from generation to generation, more acquiesence than thought was required of the younger generation. For the better minds of the eighteenth century, maintaining these principles became increasingly difficult. Scepticism had ample opportunity to ferment, either as a natural intellectual consequence of precepts grown stale, or as the result of events that could not be reconciled in such an orderly scheme of things. Without question, wars fell into this category, with people of Christian nations or denominations perpetrating the most heinous cruelty against each other. These actions of people, though, could perhaps be explained as moral lapses or as forces of evil that would eventually be conquered by good. Extraordinary so-called 'acts of God' proved much more difficult to explain, such as the great earthquake of Lisbon which took the lives of thousands of people, many of whom were at worship when the quake struck. How could a caring, benevolent deity allow this? Numerous theories came forward, ranging from God punishing the sins of the victims to God sending a warning to the rest of Europe. But sinners and the righteous perished side by side, with no distinction between the two, suggesting that a god responsible for this act must be unusually cruel and senseless. Voltaire responded sceptically to this event in his *Poème sur le désastre de Lisbonne*, and in *Candide* the notion of all intended for the best receives its final blow. Increasingly disorder and evil were recognized as powerful forces in their own right, not about to be dissipated by a system requiring their sublimation.

While Voltaire, contrary to the belief of many of his critics (including Leopold Mozart), never embraced atheism, his censure of Christians could be severe. As early as 1722, in the poem *Épître à Uranie*, a piece excluded from his works until 1772, he launched a reasoned attack:

> Enter respectfully with me the sanctuary of the god who is hidden from us. I want to love him, and I am shown a monster whom we must hate. He created men in his own image in order to abase them; he gave us evil hearts in order to punish us; he made us love pleasure in order the better to torment us. He created the world and then drowned it, not to create a purer race, but to people it with brigands and tyrants. And then, having drowned the fathers, he died for their children, but without effect, and punished a hundred nations for the ignorance in which he had kept them of his own death on the cross. In all this I do not recognize the god I must adore.[23]

The actions of church authorities in the name of Christianity came in for special disparagement; writing to the banker Tronchin with more reaction to the earthquake, he lamented,

> what a wretched gamble is the game of human life! What will the preachers say, especially if the palace of the Inquisition is still standing? I flatter myself that at least the reverend fathers inquisitors have been crushed like the others. That ought to teach men not to persecute each other, for while a few holy scoundrels burn a few fanatics, the earth swallows up one and all.

Taking a decidedly anti-Leibnizian stance, Voltaire asked one critic to show him 'why so many men slit each other's throats in the best of all possible worlds, and I shall be greatly obliged to you'. And further, 'Leibniz does not tell me by what invisible twists an eternal disorder, a chaos of misfortunes, mingles real sorrows with our vain pleasures in the best arranged of possible universes, nor why the innocent and the guilty suffer alike this inevitable evil.'[24] Ultimately argument succumbs to irony, as one sees in *Candide*, a work Mozart must surely have known (he knew Paisiello's *Il re Teodoro*, vaguely based on *Candide*).

Aside from Voltaire, the person Mme d'Épinay would have been most likely to discuss with Mozart was Diderot, her close friend and colleague on the *Correspondance littéraire*. Unlike Rousseau, who had hurt her deeply, or Galiani, with whom her correspondence had gone beyond friendship, she would have no reason to suppress her thoughts on Voltaire and Diderot or conceal her admiration for their achievements; passing this on to someone of Mozart's intelligence and receptivity would surely have been a labour of love. Diderot's name also appears in the Mozart correspondence, as Leopold had a letter of introduction for him concerning his son.

Irony proved essential to Voltaire's literary language, and the same could be said of deception for Diderot, although not necessarily in the way that English-speakers understand the meaning of the word 'deception'. Instead of an injurious or maligning act perpetrated by a deceitful person against a wronged victim, the semantic sense of the French *déception* implied a shift away from the deceiver to the object of deception, the person or persons who find themselves deceived. Unlike the more traditionally understood direct progression from deceiver to deceived, from the guilty to the innocent, this involves a much more complex relationship, described by Thomas M. Kavanagh as 'an always dialectical movement presupposing the active complicity of the other. Deception, like language, has become a dialogic exchange in which closure depends on the desire of the other.'[25] Few writers developed this exchange as well as Diderot, who showed himself partial to the ploys of tricksters. In a work such as *Les Bijoux indiscrets*, he can present situations, Kavanagh writes,

> in which the deceptive or destructive illusion is able to establish itself only because the other, the person deceived, was an active participant, thanks to his misplaced desire, in the consolidation of an illusion. Tricked and trickster alternately lead each other in a dance whose figures are impossible without the synchronized evolutions of both deceived and deceiver.[26]

The relationship of deceived and deceiver may go well beyond the characters of a literary work, extending to the interplay between author and reader as well. Through an epistolary strategy, as Diderot accomplishes in the *Préface-annexe* of *La Religieuse*, the nature of the relationship between author and reader may blur considerably, as the author's various masks obscure his stance, leaving uncertainty as to who is the target of the ruses and whether the author has fallen into the trap of his own deception. In this work Suzanne Saulier (alias Diderot, perhaps) writes to the Marquis de Croismare, attempting by a ruse to entice him to return to Paris. Grimm explained the events of the plot in the *Correspondance littéraire*, although in all probability Diderot wrote this as well, drawing Grimm into a larger deception in which no clear line between reality and fiction exists.[27]

Diderot adopts other masks in this work, introducing another character, Mme Madin, who becomes a conduit for information which most effectively reaches the Marquis indirectly, as she is sure to pass it on to him. Thus the epistolary range multiplies from dual to triangular, providing a strategy of communication between two people through a third person. When Diderot, so the reader perceives, can no longer laugh at his sentimentalizing but appears to be drawn into the emotion, and Grimm (alias Diderot) duly reports this, a virtual breakdown occurs among author(s) and reader, in which the sense of distance between them vanishes, the reader now at a loss whom to believe.

Referring to Michel Foucault's social use of the 'author-function', examining it as a type of outside imposed process capable of suppressing the subversive power of fiction, Rosalina de la Carrera notes that 'Diderot, for his part, already foreseeing this possibility, attempts to prevent his reader from imposing the author-function by explicitly subverting it from within.'[28] In this work he gives the reader an inside view of the author's function, appearing to protect the reader from the subversive power of fiction, but all the while drawing the reader further into the web. He uses gender roles as part of his strategy, as he assumes female roles in the correspondence allowing a seductiveness in corresponding with a man, and similarly makes shifts in addressing female and male readers.

We, of course, have no proof that Mozart spent hours with Mme d'Épinay listening to her descriptions of the intricate thoughts of the *philosophes*. Unfortunately, his only continuing correspondence during this time was with his father, and one cannot imagine Mozart sharing these ideas with him if he in fact received them. Instead of proof, the best we can hope for is adumbration, the indirect representation or putting into practice of ideas that he may have been receiving. Mozart's letters to his father open a possible avenue in this regard, and the chapter which follows will place these in the context of possible French literary and epistolary influences. One passage from his mid-1778 letters to his father, which bears mentioning here since it concerns one of the writers just noted, involves Mozart's comment on the death of Voltaire. This comment, short in the extreme, for a number of reasons touches a raw nerve; not only incongruous in its placement, it appears entirely inappropriate.

Leopold himself had commented on Voltaire's death in a letter of 29 June, gloating that 'Voltaire is dead too! and died without changing; he should have done something to improve his reputation with posterity' (MBA ii 386), but Mozart had not yet received this when he wrote his excoriating barb a few days later. Mozart's letter to his father of 3 July 1778 may very well be the most famous of the entire correspondence, and will be examined in greater detail in the following chapter. Mozart wrote this letter a few hours after his mother had died, as he admitted to Leopold on 9 July, and in it he urges Leopold not to give up hope for her recovery or trust in the will of God. One can only be stunned that in a letter written at that moment, surely the saddest in Mozart's life so far, he should not only discuss at length his composition of the Paris Symphony, K. 297 [300a], a nonexistent opera, and aspects of the Parisian audience, but should include this churlishness about Voltaire: 'Now I have a piece of news for you which you may already know, namely, that the godless arch-rogue Voltaire, so to speak, has kicked the bucket like a dog, like a beast! That is the fruit of his labour!' (MBA ii 389). The news of Voltaire's death may have just reached Leopold in Salzburg in time for him to comment on it in a letter dated 29 June, but Mozart, living in Paris and in regular contact with one of Voltaire's close friends, would have known about it within days of it happening on 30 May. Why should it take him over a month to pass on this piece of news, and to do it in such a rude manner?

Leopold's remark about Voltaire seems to have been a fairly accurate reflection of his opinion; as a devout but enlightened Catholic he was not about to split hairs on the fine distinctions between theism and deism, or for that matter to separate these from atheism. The free-thinking Voltaire had gone too far for Leopold beyond the boundary of religious acceptability, and while that could have been corrected by an embrace of Christianity before his death, Voltaire's admission rejecting atheism – without a broader confession – did little to dissuade those convinced of his lack of belief. While Leopold was entirely capable of recognizing Voltaire's greatness, he could not forgive him for abandoning God and the church: without these Voltaire's reasoned morality proved in the end not only of little use but dangerous as well. Notwithstanding the fact that Archbishop Colloredo admired Voltaire, which provided reason enough for Leopold to reject him, the world was now undoubtedly a better and safer place with his expiry.

The odds that Mozart actually shared his father's view of Voltaire seem small in the extreme. Voltaire, as the following chapter will discuss, achieved consummate mastery of epistolary deception – of writing opposite views to different correspondents depending on what the addressee would prefer to hear. Mozart appears to have learned the technique well, and in berating Voltaire even more than Leopold would be likely to, committed the ultimate Voltairianism. One month earlier, when Voltaire actually died, Mozart may not have yet formed his own opinion about him sufficiently to react one way or the other, and he probably still knew little of Voltaire's own epistolary virtuosity. On 3 July, with his mother's deceased body still warm on the bed beside his writing table, he could write with genuine duplicity, belying his own admiration for Voltaire, paying Voltaire a final tribute, if somewhat crudely, by emulating his deceptive approach.

Chapter 5
The Virtuosity of Deceit

When as a child Mozart received a gift of Gellert's *Geistliche Oden und Lieder* from Baron von Bose, Leopold proudly quoted the inscription to Lorenz Hagenhauer: 'Take this book, little seven-year-old Orpheus, from the hand of your admirer and friend! Read it often – and feel its god-like songs and lend them (in these spiritual hours of feeling) your irresistible harmonies: so that the callous despiser of religion may read them – and take notice – may hear them – and fall down and worship God' (MBA i 140). Leopold's sentiments exactly. When the not yet fourteen-year-old Wolfgang learned of Gellert's death in 1769, the influential Christian Fürchtegott Gellert, moralist, teacher of German youth, professor at the University of Leipzig, correspondent and model to Leopold, he drolly commented to Nannerl, with a pun on Gellert and gelehrt (learned), that, 'I have nothing new except that Herr gelehrt, the poet from Leipzig, died, and since his death has composed no more poetry' (MBA i 309). Nannerl, too, had been plagued with more than her share of learned moralizing à la Gellert, and undoubtedly shared her brother's immense relief that no more would be coming from that quarter. In one terse sentence to the appropriate addressee, Mozart dropped the obsequious mask he frequently wore, exploding the image of the child receptive in all respects to his father. Already at this tender age he could manage this with consummate skill, not shrieking defiance and disgust, but subtly and humorously turning the rapier in a way leaving the intended victim uncertain of the wound. From this one sentence we learn legions about the young Mozart, in particular that we should be wary of believing everything he writes, especially to his father.

The difficulties in establishing that Leopold had career plans as a writer involving his son become even more nagging in probing the extent of Wolfgang's knowledge of the project. As reporters in centres of political intrigue such as Washington, D.C., can attest, establishing who knew what and when they knew it can be all but impossible in recent cases like the Watergate or Iran-Contra scandals, where live but often dissimulating respondents still abound. In attempting to clarify these points in matters from over two centuries ago, we have nothing but correspondence to build the case on, and the veracity or biographical authority of that correspondence can crumble very quickly when put to the test. In all likelihood, Mozart was never entirely privy to his father's apparent plan, since full knowledge would spoil the spontaneity of his responses, resulting in a correspondence too contrived to convince the reader of its genuineness and moral authority. Yet Mozart must have been made aware of it on certain levels, knowing of his involvement in an epistolary commerce, or his suspicion would surely have been aroused. The matter of saving letters, for example, which Leopold had always insisted on not only in early correspond-ences with Hagenhauer or his wife but after September 1777 with his son as well, would have left little doubt that these letters had a purpose beyond the immediate addressee. While the latter correspondence progressed, complicated by Mozart's frequent moves from city to city, or from lodging to lodging within a given town, Leopold's constant admonitions about the security of the post and enumerations of letters sent (noted in chapter 3) similarly showed something of the father's hand.

EARLY STRATEGIES

Well aware of his father's literary aspirations, as noted to Padre Martini in 1776 (MBA i 532), Mozart undoubtedly felt admiration at this point for the direction in which Leopold's career appeared to be turning. Mozart could readily accept that their common enemy, the Archbishop of Salzburg, had been as detrimental to his father's career as his own, and to see his father circumventing his patron and establishing an international reputation through the wiles of his literary skill no doubt gave him much satisfaction. But this took a different turn late in 1777, when the paternal pattern of the correspondence became patently clear. Mozart had frequently traversed with his father's guidance down the moral avenues of Gellert's writing, and he did not have to be the genius he was to recognize in the bombardment of advice the genre of these letters with their advice intended for someone considerably younger than himself. Judgement on the truthfulness of Mozart's responses at the earliest stages of the correspondence must for the moment be reserved, but most assuredly his replies were compliant, so much so that one suspects collusion in the project. While he was in Augsburg during October the advice flowed freely, and Mozart responded near the end of the month that 'I too will certainly make a great effort to live most exactly by your orders and the advice which you have been so good as to give me' (MBA ii 85).

These were exactly the words a father would wish to hear and they were eminently printable in a published moral biography, not only these words, but the ones that follow as well: 'Papa can live without worry. I always have God before my eyes. I recognize his omnipotence, and I fear his anger; but I also recognize his love, his compassion and his mercy towards his creatures. He will

7   W. A. Mozart: portrait by Joseph Lange, 1789.

never forsake those who serve him. If it stands according to his will, it also stands according to mine.' The final point, seeming innocent enough at this time, proved more troublesome as the correspondence continued, as God's will and Mozart's will became increasingly indistinguishable and God's will offered a convenient hedge against points of more questionable judgement. As it became more difficult to explain his actions on certain matters a month later, Mozart invoked this defence again, writing, 'What after all is the point of useless speculation? What will happen we do not know – but yet we know it! – the will of God. So now a cheerful Allegro, non siate so Pegro' (MBA ii 146). Early in December he tried it one more time, with the equivocation 'incidentally, regardless of what comes, it can never be bad, if it follows the will of God; and it is my daily request to be thus' (MBA ii 170). He did not know that a letter in the post saw through the ruse of this line of defence. Three days earlier, on 4 December, Leopold had pricked the balloon:

> But that you, my son, write me *that all deliberation is useless and without any point, since we do not know what will happen,* that must have popped out of your head without any reflection – and was certainly written down rashly. *That all things will and must proceed according to the will of God,* no sensible man, to say nothing of a Christian, will deny. But does it follow from this that we should deal with things blindly, always live without caring, make no preparations and just wait until something flies down from above on its own? Does not God himself and all reasonable people demand that in all our dealings we should consider, according to our human reason, the consequences and their outcomes, and should strive to plan ahead as much as possible? If this is necessary in all our actions, then how much more crucial is it in your present circumstances on a journey? Have you not already met with some of the consequences of your conduct? (MBA ii 166).

Leopold was either generous or naive to call his son's approach 'rash'; Wolfgang by this point had developed his own strategy, and this time it did not work. When he used the 'will of God' stance in the future, as he would half a year later in relation to his mother's death – knowing his father had deciphered his own deceitful use of it – the implications appeared much more ominous.

While Mozart attempted for a few months to maintain an obsequious tone, he found this all but impossible to continue in the face of the often insulting advice Leopold heaped on him. If this correspondence was to be published, as Wolfgang had some inkling it would, it became all the more important to adjust or skew the impression posterity presumably would have of him based on these letters, as an incompetent fool. An early strategy involved being facetious, as he attempted from Mannheim on 14 November, in a 'confession' quoted in full in the previous chapter (p. 89):

> I . . . plead guilty that yesterday and the day before (and already many other times I . . . frequently . . . spouted – rhymes, in fact of garbage, namely, about dirt, shitting and arse-licking – and actually in thoughts, words and – but not in deeds. . . . Hence I beg for the holy dispensation, if it can be easily secured; if not, it's all the same to me, for the game will carry on anyway (MBA ii 123–4).

Not being a hypocrite, Leopold probably enjoyed the sport in this; the game, however, no doubt went further, beyond the good humour of the Cannabichs, to other facets of behaviour Wolfgang omitted in his description. He had by now encountered his cousin Maria Anna Thekla in Augsburg, and also appeared to be falling in with some less than savoury characters in Mannheim; the confession may have been only partly facetious.

Another early strategy involved trivializing advice with light comments, such as those written on 22 November:

8   Mozart's postscript to his mother's letter to Leopold from
Mannheim, 8 November 1777.

What you write about Mannheim I already fully know – but I never like to write about anything prematurely; everything will go fine. Perhaps in a future letter I can write you something *very good* for you, but only *good* for me, or something *very bad* in your eyes, but something *passable* in my eyes, or perhaps also something *passable* for you, but *very good, dear and valuable* for me! That's somewhat oracle-like, don't you agree? – it's cryptic, but still intelligible (MBA ii 138).

Hardly an oracle and certainly not intelligible; if anything, this approaches the style of a *commedia dell'arte* harlequin, bordering on the totally nonsensical. In garble such as this, the intelligibility certainly escaped his father: 'I've almost racked my brain out of my head – and written myself blind. I would like to take care of things in advance. And you see everything as a trifle, you are apathetic, you tie my hands when I try to advise and help you' (MBA ii 149).

As Leopold's advice and chiding became more upbraiding, Wolfgang became less inclined to let it pass without response. By the end of November he had had enough: 'You make many reproaches to both of us – and without our deserving it. . . . But if you ascribe the cause to my thoughtlessness, carelessness and laziness, I can do nothing but thank you for your good opinion of me, and regret with all my heart that you do not know me, your son' (MBA ii 152–3). Later in December came more of the same:

> I had written to you that your last letter gave me much joy; that is true! But one thing annoyed me a little – your question of whether I wasn't becoming some-what negligent about confession. I have no great objection to this. Just allow me one request: and this is not to think so miserably of me! I like to have a good time, but rest assured that I can be as serious as anyone else. . . . Once again I entreat you, most humbly, to have a better opinion of me (MBA ii 199).

By the end of December, responding to Leopold's travel plans for his mother, the tone of Wolfgang's opinion had now moved beyond facetiousness to a darker mode of irony: 'That is only what I believe; what I most certainly know is that whatever you find appropriate will be the best for us, for you are Herr Court Kapellmeister, and a pillar of good sense! [to quote Madame Robinig]. I kiss Papa, if you know him, on the hands a 1,000 times' (MBA ii 207). Leopold was not Court Kapellmeister, only an assistant, but could anything be more insulting than invoking his mediocre position in the Salzburg court as the basis for his authority? Indeed there could, and that lay in putting the words recognizing Leopold's superiority in the mouth of Mme Robinig, a woman Mozart groaned about on another occasion that it had been 'a long time since I spoke with such a fool' (MBA ii 536).

THE TRUTH?

Following these few outbursts of filial frustration late in 1777, one finds virtually nothing in Mozart's subsequent letters with an accusatory or insulting tone. As a tactic it simply did not work; instead of stemming the tide of censure from Leopold it had the effect of making his disapproval even more excoriating. In the first two and a half months of 1778, before arriving in Paris in mid-March, Mozart returned in his letters to a more obsequious tone, but now handled with greater style and sophistication. Instead of the irony and insolence noted above, he now made these types of comments seem like genuine compliments, such as, 'I am much obliged to you, my dear Papa, for the fatherly letter you wrote me; I will keep it with my treasures and always make use of it' (MBA ii 281). Later in February, the tone of filial devotion continued:

> My chief purpose was, is and forever will be to strive to bring us together soon and happily – but we must have patience. . . . We can trust in God, who will never forsake us. I will not be found lacking. How can you possibly doubt me? Is it just for myself that I work with all my strength, so that I may have such honour,

such joys of love and pleasure to embrace with all my heart my most worthy and dearest father? . . . I have placed my confidence in three friends, and these are powerful and invincible friends, namely in God, your head and in my head. Our heads are admittedly very different, but each in its own way is very good, workable and useful; and I hope that in time my head will little by little begin to approach yours in those areas in which yours is superior. Now all the best! Be merry and light-hearted. Be aware that you have a son who certainly has never, knowingly, neglected his filial duty to you, who will take the trouble to become always more worthy of so good a father, and who will remain unalterably your most obedient . . . (MBA ii 306).

Shortly before leaving for Paris, Mozart reiterated the semi-deification of Leopold: '*Near to God comes Papa*; as a child that was my motto or axiom, and with that I remain firm' (MBA ii 318).

The truthfulness of these expressions remains very much in doubt; instead of being placed on that type of scale, they must be looked at more in terms of epistolary strategy. On numerous other matters over the previous few months, Mozart's truthfulness came very much into question, and on more than one of these Leopold called his son's bluff. In one case, involving a young singer, Mlle Kaiser in Munich, Mozart admitted to lying, although his motives for both lying and admitting to it seem less than clear. Early in October, he had praised her singing highly (MBA ii 29), but in February Leopold doubted his sincerity about this in light of Wolfgang's apparent turnaround on German and comic opera. Mozart's curious admission of deception appeared on the surface a humbling experience:

About your reproach concerning the little singer in Munich, I must admit that I was an ass to write you such a bold lie. In fact, she does not yet know what *singing* means. . . . The reason I praised her so highly may well have been because from morning to night I heard nothing but: there is no better singer in all Europe. Whoever has not heard her, has not yet heard anything. I certainly did not dare to contradict them, partly because I wished to make some good friends, and partly because I had just come straight from Salzburg, where we have been cured of contradicting anyone. But as soon as I was alone, I laughed until my sides ached; why didn't I also laugh in my letter to you? That I really do not understand (MBA ii 286).

The explanation does not ring true; in fact, it seems designed to put Leopold off the track. He did not tell Leopold the truth on a number of subjects, and admitting here what was more contradiction than lie may well have been intended to divert Leopold from scrutinizing other matters, especially involving his interest in young women.

Compositional productivity and opportunities for making money were particularly sensitive subjects for Leopold, and Wolfgang's casual treatment of the commission from De Jean, the Dutch amateur flutist, drove Leopold, ever conscious of the state of their finances, to distraction. On these concertos and quartets, Leopold finally exploded in February 1778:

> When I believe that everything is now on a better footing, and taking a correct course, in a flash again along comes a foolish, unexpected notion, or matters are revealed ultimately as having being different from how you reported them to me. So once more I have guessed it? In fact you have received only 96 florins instead of 200? – and why? – because you finished only two concertos and only three quartets for him. How many were you to have written for him, that he would only pay you half? Why do you write such *a lie* to me, that you had to compose only three short easy concertos and a pair of quartets? And why did you not follow my directive when I *specifically* wrote you: *You should satisfy this gentleman completely as quickly as possible*. . . . Have I not in fact guessed everything? It appears that I see more and judge better from a distance than you do with these people right in front of your nose (MBA ii 293).

As to his honesty on various subjects, Mozart could merely protest, 'I beg you, believe anything you want of me, just nothing bad' (MBA ii 290). Leopold's refusal and the resultant nagging and carping called for other strategies, ones he would perfect in France under the apparent tutorship of one of the great French minds and *épistolières*.

FRENCH EPISTOLARY MODELS

In what appears to be the substantial amount of pleasurable time Mozart and Mme d'Épinay spent together, one can only assume, as the previous chapter suggested, that he learned much from her about her own background and struggles, her epistolary and other literary endeavours, as well as something of the lives and thinking of a few of the great people in her intimate circle, such as Diderot and Voltaire. Considering the importance of epistolary style to her, especially in her novel *Histoire de Madame de Montbrillant* – an epistolary novel like those of Richardson, Fielding or Laclos (in fact preceding the last's *Les Liaisons dangereuses*) – as well as her contributions to the *Correspondance littéraire* and her enormous correspondence with numerous people, in all probability she exposed Mozart to epistolary concepts and approaches he had no idea existed. While German epistolary masters such as Gellert developed their styles in part in response to French influences, fundamental differences existed. The evolution of German as a literary language depended on a new, simpler and less encumbered style,[1] one ideally suited to moral discourse. France already had great writers in the seventeenth and early eighteenth centuries, Racine, Corneille and Molière to name a few, and French was poised as a much more sophisticated language in the second half of the eighteenth century, one capable of sustaining higher levels of irony, intrigue, double entendre and various modes of indirect or dissimulating expression. The role of letters proved crucial to this sophistication, and few understood the potential and achievements as well as Mme d'Épinay.

In matters of epistolary breadth and sophistication, arguably Voltaire had no equal in any country or language; even Gellert – who probably detested him – learned much from him about style and form. The known correspondence of Voltaire includes some 1,200 correspondents and as many as 17,000 letters, spanning a sixty-year period. In such an enormous correspondence one should not be surprised to find the writer perfecting his own style and devising forms and strategies appropriate to the addressee(s), the subject matter, his persuasiveness, how he wished to be perceived, or what enduring impression he wished to leave. He moves strategically between seriousness and humour, or sincerity and subterfuge, using whichever best suits his calculation of distance or intimacy, and he places his shifts of emotion or mood at the most suitable point in a letter to carry the addressee through a progression or development designed to have the desired effect. Wearing the appropriate epistolary mask, or putting on the desired persona, became the trademark of his letters, a process Samuel S. B. Taylor describes in the following way:

> Voltaire's pursuit of an image or a disguise through his letters was normal and frequent. He uses a form of ventriloquism, a verbal play of *personae* that borrows clothing from the Biblical text, from medicine, philosophy, literary allusion. He 'dials' a disguise, almost as a game, and invites the recipient to a form of complex epistolary dance. It is here that his virtuosity of style is so evident, since he borrows styles as a temporary convenience, but, even more, as a kind of performance art, a verbal pantomime.[2]

Similarities with conversation remain, but a fundamental difference lies in the fact that while letters may at times cultivate an improvisatory style similar to conversation, the letter writer retains the ability to determine strategies and approaches, controlling reception in ways impossible in direct interaction.

Of course one cannot say that upon setting foot on French soil Mozart acquired an entirely new epistolary approach, either in writing to his father or to his various other correspondents. Yet, he may have become more conscious of the strategic possibilities for shifting his mask from one correspondent to another, transforming moods within a single letter, and particularly, in dealing more effectively with his father – to maintain the impression of filial duty and intimacy while at the same time putting up less perceptible means of distancing. Unlike Voltaire, Mozart engaged in relatively little correspondence with the exception of his letters to his father, although it included enough people to give one a sense of the diversity of masks he could wear. His letters to one of these others, his cousin Maria Anna Thekla, stand at the opposite end of the spectrum from those to his father. These letters continue to be troubling to some of today's readers, and a separate chapter therefore seems useful to put them in their eighteenth-century setting. His letters to other friends will be considered in chapter 8. Since the letters to his father take a somewhat different turn from Paris onward, showing greater skill in manipulating the reader – sometimes bordering on epistolary fiction – it is well worth devoting a separate section to them.

LIES MY SON TOLD ME

Mozart's most skilful use of correspondence – his finest epistolary virtuosity – came in the letters written to his father from late March 1778, on his arrival in Paris, to January 1779, when he finally and reluctantly returned home to Salzburg. Leopold had not yet given up on the project during the summer of 1778 since the advice still flowed freely, but by autumn his replies to Wolfgang were so distressed, angered and out of control that one can no longer imagine publication as a possibility. In the end, Leopold hoped for little more than to survive the sojourn of his son with a modicum of his own credibility in Salzburg intact. The process by which things came to this was not one of defiance on the part of Wolfgang; in fact, Wolfgang achieved the direct opposite of that, feigning obedience while widening the gap between words and deeds. Success could be measured by Leopold's happy responses, which occasionally were forthcoming, although this could not always be so since Leopold had ways of knowing that certain words and actions did not correlate. In spite of periodic angry responses, Wolfgang maintained his obsequious strategy to the end, ingratiating, thanking, praising, calming, stroking, cajoling – in short, lying his way through ten critical months of correspondence.

As a primary objective in these letters, Mozart attempted to give the impression of pleasing his father, and he occasionally uses words to this effect in a direct manner, as he does early in April: 'But I am prepared to do anything to give you pleasure' (MBA ii 332). As a formality it remained crucial to end letters in the appropriate manner, with words such as 'Farewell and best wishes. I kiss your hands a thousand times . . . and remain your most obedient son' (MBA ii 358). Success appeared to be in hand if he could write as follows: 'Your last letter drew tears of joy from me – in that it completely revealed to me more than ever your true fatherly love and concern. I will strive with all my strength to deserve more than ever your fatherly love' (MBA ii 422).

The evidence, however, places these words in a context suggesting anything but true filial devotion or obedience, and one finds this demonstrated in a number of matters, some in response to Leopold's questions and others strategically invented and placed by Wolfgang. One of these, a longstanding concern for Leopold (as it was for Gellert in his epistolary discourse to his son), involved Wolfgang's productivity, which should have been considerable during this sojourn if he hoped to secure a position. Old works by a young composer would not always be suitable; they might in fact give the wrong impression to a court searching for a mature and able composer, making necessary the composition of new works which should, of course, according to Leopold, follow the Parisian taste about which Grimm should be consulted. To satisfy Leopold's concern in this matter, Wolfgang periodically informed him of works in progress, sometimes breaking off short on a letter claiming the need to get back to work on a composition in question, works there is not the least shred of evidence existed or for that matter were ever started. The first of these phantom works was a large project, an opera: 'I will not write an act for an opera, but instead an opera entirely by me, en deux actes. The poet has already completed the first act. Noverre (at whose place I eat as often as I like) has taken it over, and in fact came up with the idea' (MBA ii 332). A week later he sends more news, although now slightly less definite: 'Soon now, I believe, I will receive the libretto for my opera en deux actes. Then I must first present it to the Director M. de Huime, for him to accept it. But that is not in doubt, for Noverre initiated it and De Huime can thank Noverre for his position' (MBA ii 357). Two months later it became clear the project would not get off the ground:

> With the opera, this is how things stand just now. Finding a good text is very difficult. The old ones, which are the best, are not convertible to the modern style, and none of the new ones are of any use. For poetic texts, which alone the French can take pride in, become worse every day – and yet the poetry is the single thing that remains good here – because they do not understand music. There are now two operas in aria which I may write, one en deux actes, and the other en trois. The one en deux is Alexandre et Roxane – but the poet who is writing the libretto is still in the country – the en trois is Demofont (translated from Metastasio). . . . Of this one I have also not yet been able to see anything (MBA ii 389).

Clearly no libretto existed to begin with, nor would there be one in the foreseeable future. In the meanwhile, Leopold had felt useful by giving all sorts of advice on operatic writing and the French taste.

Other phantom works continue to pop up with clockwork regularity. The ruse has been as successful for many subsequent music scholars as for Leopold himself; much energy has gone into identifying certain of these works such as a concertante noted on 5 April 1778,[3] and a second symphony he claimed the French performed on 8 September (MBA ii 473). Neal Zaslaw has expressed some doubts about the existence of a newly composed second symphony,[4] and Alan Tyson has been much more prepared to doubt Mozart's veracity, suggesting Mozart used the reference to mislead Leopold.[5] Tyson also picks up on Mozart's means of covering his tracks; Mozart offered this explanation of why he would not have two symphonies in hand on his return to Salzburg: 'Le Gros purchased from me the two overtures and the sinfonia concertante. He imagines that he alone has them, but that is not true; I have them still fresh in my mind, and, I will draft them again as soon as I get home' (MBA ii 492). It is much more likely that if Mozart were to write them out, it would be for the first time.

Other works referred to seem even more obscure or unlikely to have ever had pen set to paper. These include a scena for Giustino Ferdinando Tenducci, a male soprano (MBA ii 458), six trios (ii 476), and yet another opera: 'Why must I be brief? Because my hands are full with things to do. Just to please Herr von Gemmingen and myself I am now writing the first act of the declaimed opera (which I was engaged to write) *for nothing*; I will bring it with me and then complete it at home' (MBA ii 516). Once again no evidence exists to suggest that Mozart ever started to write it. In one other case of a claimed work, a concerto for violin and clavier, he actually did write an initial fragment of 120 measures. It should also be noted that certain works long believed to have been composed in 1778, including the piano sonatas K. 330, 331, 332 and 333, come from some time later.[6]

Leopold very much looked forward to seeing some of these works, making his request in July: 'If you could delight us with something of yours, then do so! When will such a convenient opportunity come again to send us something?' (MBA ii 413). On the same day Mozart had written to his sister, apologizing 'that I cannot offer you a piece of music, as in other years' (MBA ii 411). By October, no longer in Paris and possibly en route to Salzburg, Mozart realized that he had built a large phantom repertoire, and he had better begin to revise this list to something closer to the truth: 'I have not produced very much. I do not have the three quartets and the flute concerto for M. De Jean; when he went to Paris, he packed them into the wrong trunk, and they consequently remained in Mannheim. . . . Therefore I will be bringing nothing completed with me except my sonatas' (MBA ii 492). The works quickly evaporated through various vanishing tricks, in wrong trunks (he had written only two quartets for De Jean) or the purchases of Le Gros, existing now only in his memory. Along with not writing, he similarly took few pupils in Paris, and worded his explanation as follows: 'For giving lessons here is no joke – you can easily exhaust yourself at it; and if you do not take *many* pupils, you cannot make much money. You must not think that this is laziness – No! – rather because it goes entirely against my genius, against my manner of life' (MBA ii 427).

EVASIVENESS

Evasiveness also proved to be a fairly effective strategy in these letters – simply avoiding discussion of certain topics or issues or not replying on certain points raised by Leopold. A more drastic form of evasion involved not writing at all, as occasionally happened for an entire month. During August Leopold heard nothing from his son, and expressed his concern on 3 September: 'I wrote to you on the 3rd of August, the 13th and the 27th. . . . Yet since your short letter of July 31st I have seen nothing from you. This makes my oppressed heart even more troubled' (MBA ii 463). By 10 September he had still heard nothing: 'The anxiety that I feel, not having received a letter from you for an entire month, is indescribable' (MBA ii 468). Referring to a later hiatus in writing, Mozart made the following apology: 'Concerning two things I have to ask your forgiveness, first, that I have not written to you for so long, and second, that this time I must be brief' (MBA ii 516). The reason: he was too busy working on his (nonexistent) opera.

That, of course, was a crude form of evasiveness, not like the type he usually practised, such as a letter to his father from Paris dated 12 June 1778, a fairly long chatty letter which goes on endlessly about certain friends and singers but says very little of substance, and certainly not the substance concerning activities or plans Leopold hoped to hear. In his reply of 29 June, Leopold insisted on receiving some real news:

> But there are no more announcements about *your composition students* – nothing more about *the ballet with Noverre* – nothing more about *your opera*. Also no word whether *Wendling* is still in Paris? – whether Wolfgang has seen Baron Bach? – whether Piccinni is still in Paris? – whether he [Wolfgang] has met the two *Staymetzes* [Stamitzes]? – whether he has seen *Grétry*? – whether the performers at the concert spirituel and the production are any good? I would be very pleased to have some mention of all these things with just a few words (but without covering whole pages on them). . . . My dear son can easily imagine that it is a little like torture for me to know that in the meanwhile he has been composing many works – and that I, alas! cannot hear any of these, which at one time afforded me my greatest pleasure (MBA ii 384).

At this point Wolfgang's evasiveness had not yet become a matter of frustration, and Leopold accepted the stories about composition.

Another technique of evasion involved changing the subject, first used by Mozart in letters dealing with the disagreeable subject of his mother's illness and death. In his letter of 9 July 1778, after giving only a few details of the death, Mozart quickly moves to other happier subjects: 'Let us therefore say a devout Our Father for her soul – and now get on with other matters; everything has its appropriate time' (MBA ii 394). This, of course, could not possibly satisfy Leopold, who wanted details: 'Write to me soon – with everything – what day she was buried – where?' (MBA ii 404). But Wolfgang remained taciturn: 'I hope you have safely received my last two letters. Now we will no longer talk about their main contents – it is all over now – and were we to cover whole pages about it, the events could not be altered' (MBA ii 405). Wolfgang proceeds with a profusion of anecdotes of little interest to Leopold, although one comment suggested something of the current working of Wolfgang's mind: 'Only a very clumsy story-teller not of the first rank would avoid some fabrication – I'm saying, some fictionalizing' (MBA ii 406). In writing to Fridolin Weber at about this time, Mozart advised him on a professional matter concerning Aloysia's performance career, attempting to teach his older friend how to work a deception to his advantage: 'then you will see what effect this thing can have; – but this must be done with great subtlety and cunning' (MBA ii 415). This scheme would require Weber to act his role convincingly – curious advice to be given to the professional actor.

ON HIS MOTHER'S DEATH

Undoubtedly the most famous of all Mozart's deceptions is also his most benevolent, his letter written to his father immediately after the death of his mother. Even though she had died a few hours earlier, he described her as being ill and that hope should not yet be forfeited. On the same night, he also wrote to the close family friend, the Abbé Bullinger in Salzburg, telling him the truth and asking him to break it gently to Leopold. This Bullinger did, and Leopold was prepared to accept what Mozart described as 'this small and very necessary deception' (MBA ii 393). While the deception may be regarded as benevolent, a type that the influence of Mme d'Épinay or Diderot may have helped Mozart to write, it nevertheless has some disturbing aspects that one finds difficult to reconcile with his good intentions. One of these concerns his sudden changing of the subject in the two primary letters. In the first, dated 3 July 1778, he abruptly shifts from the discussion of her illness, with the words 'Now on to other things; let us dispel these melancholy thoughts', moving on to a lengthy description of the performance of the Paris symphony as well as details concerning his nonexistent opera. In the next letter, he launches into chitchat that seems entirely inappropriate in a letter describing his mother's death. Leopold had recently passed on some amusing anecdotes about Salzburg musicians, and Mozart now responds at length to these descriptions. Again this letter goes on and on, with little real news, seeming altogether too frivolous for the letters whose main subject concerned the most monumental loss possible to Leopold.

The other disturbing element in these letters, particularly the first in which he claimed she was still alive, involves his discussion of the will of God. Mozart had used reference to this before as a ruse and Leopold had chastised him for it. Now Mozart uses it again as a deception, his mother already having died, and he uses it in a repetitive way seemingly designed to underline its deceit. In the space of half a paragraph, he makes reference to God, and the will of God especially, eight times, giving these words a rhetorical sense detached from the writer's genuine sentiments. Even then, at the moment of his mother's death, which surely aroused the deepest emotion in Mozart, he wrote to his father with consummate epistolary skill and style.

The various deceptions of this letter, dated 3 July 1778, do not end with his suspension 'day and night between fear and hope', his having 'submitted myself completely to the will of God', or his equivocations about a nonexistent opera. In the middle of this letter he dropped his scurrilous view on the death of

9   The Mozart family: painting by Johann Nepomuk della Croce,
1780–1.

Voltaire, 'the godless arch-rogue' who 'like a dog, kicked the bucket like a
beast!' (MBA ii 389). He immediately preceded this with a comment about
honest Germans, Christians and husbands, and followed it with a note of
agreement on the wages owed to Theresa the maid, all in the same long paragraph. With this short, detached, punctuated remark, Mozart, on the night of
his mother's death, demonstrated perhaps his highest achievement as an
épistolier, as a true disciple of the French letter-writers, as a beneficiary, it would
appear, of the mentoring of Voltaire himself. In dismissing Voltaire so contemptuously to his father, Mozart appears to have paid him the ultimate
compliment. Voltaire's own first epistolary dictum was to write appropriately
for one's addressee, and this Mozart did – although perhaps with a touch of
overkill.

With this shot at Voltaire, Mozart wore his Christian-moralist mask, as he
already had in the sentence leading up to it: 'for I always am and always will be
happiest in the house – or with a good, true, honest German who, if he is single,
lives alone as a good Christian, or if married, loves his wife and raises his
children properly' (MBA ii 389). Speaking words such as these occasionally, as
he did, affirming his adherence to the standards of morality his father had so
often admonished him about, would surely help to deflect constant nagging and
probing into his behaviour. When subjected to this type of scrutiny or when

chided for fearing his father's reproaches, Mozart protested with righteous indignation, such as in his reply on 8 January 1779: 'I know of no transgressions that should cause me to fear your reproaches. I have made no mistake (by that I mean a mistake which does not befit a Christian and honourable man)' (MBA ii 536). Leopold's fears of unsavoury travel companions who might lure his son into licentious situations were similarly met with pacification: 'Concerning the businessman who travels with me, you can banish all your worries; he is the most honourable man in the world, more concerned about me than for himself, travelling, to please me, to Augsburg and Munich, and perhaps even to Salzburg' (MBA ii 502). To clear the air completely about this unidentified traveller, he continues, 'We always weep together when we think that we will eventually have to separate. He is not a learned man, but a man of experience; we live together like children. When he thinks of his wife and children, whom he has left behind in Paris, I try to comfort him; when I think of my family he attempts to console me.' The truest statement here is probably that they lived like children; as for the mode of consolation, one can only speculate.

BEHAVIOUR UNBECOMING

The details of some of Mozart's escapades did reach Leopold's ears, including whatever indulgence there had been with Maria Anna Thekla in Augsburg, news we can presume that Leopold's brother had passed on to him. In the letter of 12 February 1778, in which Leopold assumed that his son's intentions toward Aloysia Weber were less than honourable, he also raises the romp with the 'Bäsle', taking it as yet another example of Wolfgang's irresponsible behaviour with women, accusing him of amusing himself 'with my brother's daughter, who must now send you her portrait' (MBA ii 274). Mozart's indignant reply to his father's cutting remarks 'about my merry indulgence with your brother's daughter' in which 'the situation is not like that' (MBA ii 286) proved one of his weaker efforts in refracting the truth.

How matters actually were, perhaps in this case or in other escapades from this time, we get some idea when Mozart lived in Vienna early in 1781, and again reports reached Leopold about the unbecoming behaviour of his son. In order to deflect these admonitions, he compared his present aspirations with those of his more youthful and reckless adventures of 1777–9. On 4 April 1781 he assures Leopold that he need 'think no more of my stupid actions, of which I have repented long ago with all my heart. With misfortune comes wisdom, and I now have very different thoughts' (MBA ii 103). One such assurance proved not to be enough, as the next one came a month later: 'You surely must believe me that I have changed completely. . . . You certainly must have confidence in me, that I am no longer a fool. And even less should you believe that I am a godless, ungrateful son' (MBA ii 121). Even this did not suffice, as the protests continued in June:

Incidentally, you can rest assured that I genuinely hold my religion securely – and should I ever have the misfortune (which God forbid) to fall into misdirected ways, I shall speak of you, my upright father, as entirely blameless. For I alone would be the scoundrel – as I have you to thank for all good things and for both my temporal and spiritual well-being and salvation (MBA ii 130).

This is not what Leopold would want to hear, and reveals a much more independent-minded Mozart than the one in Paris. These protestations appear to show that Mozart had behaved dissolutely on the Paris sojourn, and lied about it at the time, simply wearing morality as one of his many epistolary masks.

WHERE IN THE WORLD IS WOLFGANG AMADEUS?

Throughout 1778 Mozart had seldom been more than vague in discussing his travel plans with his father, but after he left Paris in late September, at which time Leopold expected him to come home, his vagueness, silence or misinformation became much more contentious. Knowing that the plan to find a new appointment and relocate the family had all but run its course and the pressure to return was intensifying, Mozart decided to prolong his freedom as much as possible, and also to spend more time with his favourite people such as the Weber family, which he assumed was still in Mannheim, and perhaps his cousin in Augsburg. Since the Mannheim court had moved to Munich, and no prospects remained for making money in that city, Leopold advised him strongly not to return to Mannheim. After departing from Paris, Mozart prolonged his stopover in Nancy, and not informing his father of this drew an angry response:

> Now comes a stab in the heart! *A horrible stab in the heart!* I had written to the brothers Frank at Strassburg on October 1st, reporting your arrival and my money order to Herr Scherz. They replied on the 9th, *that you had not yet arrived, that the conductor of the coach reported that you had stayed behind in Nancy with some travelling companions, etc.* But you wrote to me from Nancy on about the 3rd, *that you and the businessman with whom you travelled had left the coach behind at Nancy, and that you were setting off on the following morning to Strassburg if the opportunity of a reduced cost should arise* (MBA ii 499).

Mozart's long and convoluted explanation for staying longer, his being persuaded to stay and play a concert to which virtually no one came, simply does not ring true. Similarly, his staying longer than expected in Strasbourg because of floods may simply have been an inventive excuse.

When he then popped up in Mannheim in November, against his father's wishes, Leopold's exasperation began to spin out of control: 'Frankly, I don't know what I should write – I will lose my mind, or die of emaciation. It is impossible to remember all your projects which since you departed from Salzburg you have kept in your head and also written about to me, without losing my wits. They have all amounted to proposals, empty words, in the end resulting in *absolutely nothing*' (MBA ii 508). The berating continues.

> During your stay in Nancy you literally threw money out the window, when instead of squandering it uselessly, you had a number of opportunities to travel to Strassburg, where you could more readily apply your money to good use. . . . I could not possibly imagine the crazy notion that you would remain in Mannheim, where there is no court, and consequently believed that you must have come to Augsburg on the 10th at the very latest.

He finally left Mannheim in mid-December, again saying very little to his father, and explaining his silence in the following way: 'The reason why I did not reply to you right away was because I wanted to report to you the most certain and precise information about my departure from here, and I did not know it myself at the time' (MBA ii 520). All of this vexed Leopold beyond the limit:

> I have already written you repeatedly that our interest and my prospects demand that you should return forthwith to Salzburg, and I believed that you would give more consideration to reason, and frankly that you would be more familiar with your father's insight, rather than relying on your own futile wishes. So I hadn't the slightest doubt that finally by the New Year you would then surely be back in Salzburg. However, when I least anticipated it, and was already expecting to see a letter from you from Augsburg, you give me the news that you will be travelling to Munich with the Prelate on the 26th or 27th at the earliest. Good! The opportunity justifies it. But do not imagine that you can loaf about in Munich doing nothing. . . . But what is the point of my saying more? You yourself, if without prejudice (setting aside all your merry dreams) you consider everything, will have to be so good as to accept that I am right; and so what if I give an explanation of my opinion, reproaching you about one thing or another, as I am heartily sick of writing so much that during the last fifteen months my eyes have almost popped out of my head from writing. . . . Therefore you must follow my order and depart immediately, for you have been loathsome, and I am shamed before the whole world for having given assurances that you would most certainly be home by Christmas or by the New Year at the very latest. Good heavens! How often have you made a liar of me! (MBA ii 528).

By this point, it should be clear, the biographical project had come to an end. These words do not belong to a staunch if stern moralist, writing to edify an audience; these are the screams of one totally defeated at an epistolary enterprise which could have made his fame and fortune, to say nothing of being deeply in debt, consigned to patriarchal oblivion and facing the grim prospect for the future of business as usual in Salzburg.

THE PRODIGAL'S RELUCTANT RETURN

Yet, for Leopold one more blow remained, connected with his son's circuitous and prolonged travel, perhaps harder than any of the above to accept since it involved him most personally. Not only was his son's return to Salzburg a matter of professional pride and necessity; at the heart of the matter stood his relationship with his son which appeared by the end of December to have vanished into the void. Wolfgang's happy return to his father's arms had been a frequent topic throughout the entire correspondence, and it took on a new urgency about the time he left Paris. Lest Mozart should not fully appreciate the depth of his father's sentiment about this, Leopold began to put it in stronger, more guilt-evoking terms: 'You may rest assured and believe it well, my dearest son, that without you near me, I will die much sooner, and that if I could have the pleasure of having you with me, I would live many years longer' (MBA ii 435). While still in Paris, in what seemed an eternity from Salzburg, Mozart could assure his father that 'when we finally have the joy and pleasure (which is my single endeavour) of living together in one place – when this happy time eventually comes – God grant it – soon! – then the time will have come – and then it will be only up to you' (MBA ii 425).

As the physical distance to Salzburg diminished, these assurances became much more difficult to make; at the same time Leopold's need for affirmation and insistence on the fulfillment of filial duty multiplied accordingly. While still in Paris, such as in his letter of 11 September 1778, Mozart could even write of how he looked forward to returning to his home town, the 'one place where I can say I am at home – can live in peace and quiet with my finest father and my dearest sister – can do as I like – where apart from the duties of service I am my own master – I have a permanent salary – can go away when I like – and can make a journey every two years. What more could I want?' (MBA ii 472). Only hints of discontent about working for the Archbishop surface in this letter, but as he gets closer to home this moves from the present *pianissimo* to a resounding *fortissimo* as the grim reality of it returns. He attempts to assure Leopold that his loathing applied only to the Archbishop and the low inhabitants of Salzburg – not his father – although in this he does not entirely succeed. In spite of outpourings of emotion, demands, threats or doses of guilt, nothing seemed to be bringing his son closer to home; Mozart always found one more reason for staying away longer, awakening in Leopold his deepest fears.

Not wishing to confront his father directly with a discussion of the possible barrier between them, Mozart resorted to the triangular epistolary approach he had used before to break the news of his mother's death, this time explaining his position to their common friend Johann Baptist Becke, who in turn wrote to

Leopold as the buffer for Mozart's feelings. Leopold, in his reply to Mozart, appeared to be surprised by Becke's letter:

> If your tears, your melancholy and heart-rending anxiety have no basis other than that you doubt my love and tenderness for you, then you can sleep peacefully eat and drink peacefully and travel home even more peacefully. I now realize all too well that you do not entirely know your father. It seems from our friend's letter that this is the main substance of your sadness; oh, I hope there is no other! Then you have no other reason to fear a reception lacking in tenderness or unpleasant days with me and your sister. . . . The main thing that places me in a state of angst and makes me anxious is your extended absence. As it is already four months since I received in hand your interim certificate [of appointment] – as people know that you left Paris on September 26th – as they know that I have been forever writing you that you should come – that people believed they would see you here on my name-day – then at Christmas – and finally with absolute certainly by the New Year, therefore I must tell you that people are saying to my face that you are treating the Prince – and, even worse, your father, as a fool . . . I will embrace you with joy. I am quickly becoming a fool as I write this . . . (MBA ii 532).

To this, Mozart replied,

> I assure you, my dearest father, that I am now looking forward with all joy to returning just to *you* (but not to Salzburg), since I am convinced by your last letter that you know me better than before! There never was any other reason for my long delay in travelling home – for the sadness which finally I could no longer hold back, and therefore completely opened my heart to my friend Becke – than this doubt. What other possible reason could I have? I am not aware of any guilt that should cause me to fear your reproaches (MBA ii 536).

Not only does he employ the strategy of the epistolary third party here, but he also resorts to the language of novels, of 'opening his heart' to someone who could be the conduit, taking off the sharp edge of emotion in a dispassionate transmission of the source of the sadness. These words, though, did not hasten his departure, as he found yet another reason for delay, this time waiting for his cousin in the hope of travelling together with her to Salzburg.

Leopold's last words on the subject cascaded with as much dismay as ever:

> But you cannot stay on [in Munich] to wait for an answer from my brother about this, *for I am absolutely determined that you will leave with Gschwendner.* I have told everyone that you will come with him, and you must not drive this thing any further, making me sound like a perpetual liar. If my niece wants to honour me with her presence, *she can follow on the 20th by the mail coach.* . . . Now you have no more excuses. You have seen the opera, and consequently you have done

everything you wanted to do. I am therefore expecting you to arrive with Herr Gschwendner without any more delays (MBA ii 539–40).

While this may have been his last word on the matter at hand, he more pointedly and ironically expressed his resignation to the way he had been treated in the letters a month and a half earlier: 'I want, if it is God's will, to live yet a couple of years more, pay my debts – and then, if you have the appetite, you can run your head up against the wall. But, no! you have too good a heart! You have no vices – you are just rash! Everything in its time!' (MBA ii 515).

Chapter 6
Scatology and the 'Bäsle' Letters

Stefan Zweig, who at one time owned the scatological letters written by Mozart to his cousin Maria Anna Thekla (the 'Bäsle' or little cousin), sent a copy of these previously suppressed letters to Sigmund Freud in 1931, believing they would be useful for a psychoanalytical study:

> I hope that you, as one who understands the heights and depths, will find the enclosed private printing, which I am making available only to a *narrow* circle, not entirely irrelevant: these nine letters of the 21-year-old Mozart, of which I publish *one* here in its entirety, throw a psychologically very remarkable light on his erotic nature, which, more so than that of any other important man, has elements of infantilism and coprophilia. It would actually be an interesting study for one of your pupils, for all the letters revolve consistently around the same theme.[1]

Freud, to his credit, could read these letters for what they were, as it appears he declined Zweig's invitation for his pupils to subject them to analysis. It was, alas, too much to hope that subsequent psycho-biographers or analysts would not fall victim to pathological interpretations of these letters, reading them as a 'fixation on a quasi-infantile stage of development', or worse, as reflecting a fear of incest,[2] or as evidence of Tourette's Syndrome.

SCATOLOGY IN EIGHTEENTH-CENTURY THEATRE AND WRITING

If Mozart's use of scatological language in his letters points to pathology, then one must assume the same of the hundreds of his contemporaries and predecessors who used similar language, or the notable writers including Rabelais, Martin Luther, Jonathan Swift and even Goethe who presented it in their works. Imputing pathology to literary genres may be more difficult than to persons, and scatology lay at the heart of certain genres. The dislike that

Sonnenfels and Gottsched shared for *commedia dell'arte* went far beyond matters of linguistic form; the crudity they found so repugnant extended not only to the scatology common in *commedia dell'arte* dialogue but to the preponderance of faeces in the *commedia*'s *lazzi* – the comical business, stage tricks, or theatrical foolishness in words and actions. These extremely popular *lazzi* were the stock in trade of *commedia dell'arte* in the sixteenth and seventeenth centuries, although the more prudish scholarly treatments of the subject in the nineteenth and first half of the twentieth century completely avoided discussing this. Performances saw no end of excrement-throwing, urinating, mixing food and faeces, placing one's buttocks in another's face, or the telling of dirty jokes. Arlecchino and Pantalone frequently find themselves the unwilling recipients of enemas from the Doctor, and the enema may result in some very strange items coming from the player's buttocks. Servant girls empty chamber pots out of windows, and the contents usually hit Pantalone (or the Captain) as he serenades Isabella. *Lazzi* of urinating, vomiting and spitting with all sorts of bizarre results occur. The Doctor bows to Arlecchino, and after Arlecchino insists that the Doctor bow lower, he shoves his buttocks into the Doctor's face.[3] Traditionally male characters wore an exaggerated leather phallus, pointing upward so as not to go unnoticed.

While these routines may have been common for the Italian versions of *commedia dell'arte*, they became mandatory for the German Hanswurst counterpart. Much more than Harlequin, Hanswurst liked to eat – to gorge himself on everything edible (or nonedible if necessary), and excessive eating resulted in equally inordinate defecating. He would amaze his audience by what could go down his throat, and astonish them even more by what came out of his rectum. The most exaggerated form of this early in the eighteenth century was the performing omnivore, who, like Harlequin or Hanswurst, wore a phallic stick in his belt, dressed as a combination of peasant and bourgeois, and had outrageous eating habits. In one depiction of him, the caption tells us that he, 'in various places in Austria and Saxony, to the great amazement of many trustworthy people, swallowed and devoured a living cat, with skin and hair, and other things no less, such as gravel, metal, raw meat, felt, hide, glass and such like, with great appetite; a whole calf suffices only to break his fast'.[4] He ate other things too, about which most readers would not want to know. Hanswurst (Jack-sausage) dressed during Carnival with a long leather sausage around his neck, and confused (or fused) to the delight of his audience the phallic and the anal. On the anal side, we learn as early as 1694 from the wife of the Elector of Hanover that sausage and shit have much in common, aside from the obvious shape similarities: 'If meat makes shit, it is also true that shit makes meat. . . . Isn't it so that on the most delicate tables shit is served in ragouts. . . . the blood puddings, the chitterlings, the sausages, are they not ragouts in shit sacks?'[5] It should come as no surprise that Germans should have chosen the name 'Hans-*Wurst*' for their favourite *commedia* character.

   The inclusion of scatology in German literature during the eighteenth century and the preceding two centuries underlines an element of protest against a sanitizing and restricting high culture and the assumption of conformity to the higher standards. A fine example of this type of protest comes from Hans Jakob Christoph von Grimmelshausen's *Der abenteuerliche Simplicissimus*, written in 1669, in which the introduction of Simplicius to court life results in a series of disasters. As a court page, he must learn the art of quiet farting, and the instruction that he should raise his left leg yields much more than the passing of wind. Encounters with high culture fail utterly to refine him; for the young Simplicius situations at court often incite panic, and panic often induces him to fill his pants. Anne Leblans puts his reactions into perspective, noting that his

> protest comes literally from below and debases everything that is high. The costly and exotic food which enters his body exits it in the form of unabashed farts. In its own language, his body tells the reader that life at the court stinks. Whereas the noblemen try to maximize social differences, the popular hero minimizes them by demonstrating that the 'high' are as low as anyone else. It is the body which pronounces this levelling truth.[6]

A writer wishing to get through to the common people might very well resort to scatological imagery, as Martin Luther does consistently, his devil possessing distinctive anal features.

   The language of Grimmelshausen was the language of Carnival, but by that point in the seventeenth century Carnival had taken distinctly high and low forms associated with the gap between social classes. Scatological language in the *Fastnachtspiel* or Carnival play of the fifteenth and sixteenth centuries in Nürnberg had an element of normality about it, as an expected and accepted transgression during Carnival time.[7] The most famous of these plays, the works of Hans Sachs (1494–1576), could ridicule any traditional figures of authority, including the nobility, the clergy or men in general, and derisive though the attacks may have been, both the targets and those suffering under their authority could share in the spirit of laughter. The language itself often dripped with scatology, adding to the laughter and placing the proceedings in a distinctly low milieu. In one such play, a farmer believes himself to be pregnant, and not understanding his condition, sends his farm hand with a sample of urine to the doctor for examination. Predictably the sample spills en route, but fortunately the donkey must urinate and the farm hand replenishes the sample. The doctor has numerous questions about the farmer's bodily functions, most of which the helper misunderstands, but when he finally grasps the questions, his descriptions embellish more vividly than the doctor anticipates. As to whether or not the farmer, Kunz Turnipfumes, can fart, the doctor learns 'my master really does rip 'em. Just this mornin' he ripped one louder than an ox cloth tearin'. That half-dead hen flew out of her roost clear over to the threshing floor.' When the farm hand finally figures out the difference between stool and school, he confirms that 'this mornin' there was a cracklin' and a shoutin' and he laid a beaut of an egg. Over there behind the fence. Big as my felt hat too. Smelled like cabbage and was larded full with a hundred folds. Boy, the old sow rubbed and rolled it around 'til you couldn't find a snout full.' When the farmer discovers from the doctor he will give birth to a colt, he retorts, 'Wife, you are to blame for this 'cuz you always want on top!' The colt turns out to be an enormous shit, which, after a purge, the farmer all but blows through the barn door; a rabbit wakened by the explosion becomes in the farmer's mind the colt. In the end the farmer tells all to enjoy Carnival, to let fun and frolic chase away sadness and misfortune.[8]

By the eighteenth century plays such as this could not have been a part of Carnival entertainments for the more elevated in society, but that did not prevent them or other types of scatological literature from being written. Even in France, where literature did not have to go through a refining process in the eighteenth century, scatological writing was not uncommon. The lawyer and legal scholar Thomas Simon Gueullette (1683–1776), for one, lived a double life, on the one hand a model citizen with an orderly existence as a public servant, and on the other, a member of a theatrical troupe of *commedia* players who wrote pieces such as *The Shit Merchant*, in which an entrepreneur sells shit to apothecaries and others on the pretence of it being honey.[9] Similarly, the smut-peddlers of Grub Street, aspiring writers who did not make it to the republic of letters, befouled the world in their writing in a way that reflected the treatment they perceived they were receiving at the hands of the establishment. 'The scatology of their pamplets', Robert Darnton writes, '– their frequent references, for example, to venereal disease passed on from the Cardinal de Rohan to the queen and all the great figures of the court during the Diamond Necklace Affair – communicates a sense of total opposition to an elite so corrupt as to deserve annihilation.'[10] Protest motivated them, in this case resulting in ranting and screaming, but nevertheless protest.

GOETHE'S INDECENCIES

While Gottsched and Gellert had fought vigorously against the vulgar abuses of *Fastnachtspiel* language and the crudity of Hanswurst, some of their bright young pupils were decidedly less prudish, indulging in these older indecencies in part as a protest against their refined, learned and sterile teachers. One of Gellert's students, Goethe, emerged as the greatest of all German writers, but that did not prevent him from occasional indulgence in the lower forms of writing. At the age of twenty-five, just a few years after his time as a student in Leipzig, Goethe wrote the beginning of a *commedia* piece 'in a spirit of high jinx', as he confessed to Eckermann half a century later, with the title

Hanswursts Hochzeit oder der Lauf der Welt (*Hanswurst's Wedding, or The Way of the World*). The dialogue, laced with scatological humour, extended only a few pages, and this preceded an absurdly long list of characters, concocted with his crony Johann Heinrich Merck. At twenty-five years of age and the graduate of a distinguished university, one might tag Goethe with the label of juvenilia in this case; certainly he enjoyed himself, but the cast of characters may have been as much in response to the sober dramas of his teachers in Leipzig. The following list gives some of the 140 names, with the brave attempt of Charles E. Passage to translate them:[11]

Ursel mit dem kalten Loch Tante	Cold-hole Ursula, aunt
Hans Arsch von Rippach	Jack Arse from Rippach
Hans Arschgen von Rippach empfindsam	Jack Arselet from Rippach, sensitive
Tölpel von Passau	Booby from Passau
Reckärschgen	Stretch-assie
Schnuckfözgen	Cuddle-pussie
Jfr Kluncke Putzmacherin	Miss Draggletassle, milliner
(Hans) Maulaff	(Jack) Monkey-mug
Peter Sauschwanz	Peter Sowstail
Rotzlöffel	Snot-spooner
Schwanz Dammerdiener	Prick, valet
Hundsfott wird extemporisiert als Gastrolle	Dogturd, to be extemporized by a guest actor
Simplizissimus kommt von der Reise um die Welt	Simplicissimus, back from his trip around the world
Quirinus Schweinigel bel esprit	Quirinus Foulmouth, *bel esprit*
Thoms Stinckloch Nichts geringes	Thomas Stinkhole, Nothing Trifling
Blackscheisser Poet	Drivelshit, poet
Fladen Candidat	Cowflop, Candidate (in Theology)
Dr Bonefurz	Dr Bonnyfart

Examples such as this in the works of Goethe may have been rare but were by no means unique. Christoph Friedrich Nicolai, who had mocked Goethe's *The Sorrows of Young Werther* with a satire titled *Die Freuden des jungen Werthers* (*The Joys of Young Werther*), earned for himself a permanent place in the Walpurgis Night scene of *Faust*, Part I, where he briefly appears as 'Proktophantasmist' (Buttocks-visionary). Goethe went much further in one of the strophes of his poem 'Nicolai at Werther's Grave':

He squatted o'er the grave a while
Depositing his little pile,

And then pronounced as up he flounced:
'Ah how could this poor lad himself so slay!
If he had shat as well as I he'd be alive today!'[12]

This poem, of course, does not belong in the literary canon, but *Götz von Berlichingen*, an early play by Goethe (1773), certainly does. The brave knight Götz finds himself surrounded by enemies and about to be captured, but he emphatically responds to a request for unconditional surrender with, 'Sag deinem Hauptmann: Vor Ihro Kayserliche Majestät hab ich, wie immer, schuldigen Respekt. Er aber, sag's ihm, kann mich – – – [im Arsch lecken]' (Tell your captain that for His Imperial Majesty, I have, as always, all due respect, but as for him, tell him he can kiss my arse!). The fame of this line has been passed down to every educated German as the 'Götz-Zitat' (the Götz quote).[13] This most famous of German insults (LMIA – 'Leck mich im Arsch'), poorly served by the English translation 'kiss', and favourite expression of Mozart, not only stands as the subject of whole books but literally dozens of proverbs, riddles, folksongs, folktales, jokes, folk poems, and, because of Mozart, musical canons. Goethe may have been the most sophisticated writer to use it in a literary work, but he was by no means the first; Grimmelshausen used it a number of times in *Simplicissimus*, including the case of a shepherd who forces a thief to lick three of his sheep, the number he tried to steal. A favourite German riddle, one of many on the theme, runs, 'Was können Sie, ich aber nicht?' (What can you do that I cannot?). 'Mich im Arsch lecken'.[14] Almost as popular as LMIA, from Grimmelshausen through the *Fastnachtspiel* to Hanswurst comedies, are the images of a poor devil filling his pants with shit, responding in panic to threatening situations or frightening more refined people away from himself because of his outrageous stink.

SCATOLOGICAL GREETINGS AMONG THE MOZARTS

We in the twentieth century have for the most part been able to claim Mozart as one of our own, but with certain limitations. He may appeal to our modern sensibilities, but much less to our olfactory sense; a bed full of shit or a load in the pants violates the propriety of a century which regards the flush-toilet as one of its most important assets. The earliest Mozart biographers, and especially Constanze Mozart's second husband Georg Nissen, also found the scatology in Mozart's letters offensive but for different reasons from ours. Constanze had a stake in the view that should be passed down to posterity of her first husband, and she (along with Nissen) simply could not present a divinely inspired genius preoccupied with bodily functions below the belt. The nineteenth century happily took Nissen's cue, since its vision of heroic achievements and spiritual elevation similarly could not include jokes about messing the bedsheets. That nineteenth-century view has by no means vanished, as studies of the transcendent Mozart abound, but the passage of time has created an almost unbridgeable gulf between ourselves and Mozart's time, forcing us to misread his scatological letters even more drastically than his other letters. Very simply, these letters embarrass us, and we have tried to suppress them, trivialize them, or explain them out of the epistolary canon with pathological excuses.

For the eighteenth century, scatology presented a problem only to those cultural and religious reformers who tried to clean up existing culture, whose sense of order depended on a humourless refinement of language and subscription to certain high principles of morality. The forces in conflict, once again a replay of Carnival and Lent, went beyond a simple identification as high and low culture. Elements of each could be present in the other, and Carnival remained the most effective mode of protest against repressive authority. The means could be subtle, as they usually are in Mozart's works, or they could be overt, especially in the safety of a private correspondence. In Mozart's letters to the 'Bäsle' his LMIA and other scatological images do not abuse or offend the addressee, but they (privately) insult the world that would prevent Mozart and his cousin from enjoying themselves. Here lay a different type of epistolary commerce (more like an epistolary compost), one that resists the high-minded republic of letters, forming a bond of subversive solidarity between the correspondents. Many have speculated on the nature of the relationship between Mozart and his cousin based on these letters, but once again we probably misread them if we attempt to turn them into biography. Readers are at liberty to draw their own conclusions if they wish to know about the relationship, but these letters, probably even more than Mozart's letters to his father, should not be taken as documents of 'a life'. These are epistolary objects, emerging from well-known patterns of written and verbal practice in the eighteenth century, a practice of opposition and defiance, not an indulgence in infantilism but a transgression into regions of unacceptability.

Some of the scatological expressions that appear in the letters of various members of the Mozart family were so commonplace that they can hardly be considered the voices of protest. Not only Mozart himself used them; when his mother wrote a good-night greeting to her husband on 26 September 1777, she did not hesitate to say, 'we lead a most charming life, up early, late to bed, and visitors the whole day; we live like princes. Addio, ben mio; keep well. Stretch your arse up to your mouth. I wish you good-night; shit in your bed with a resounding crash. It's already after one o'clock; now you can keep making rhymes yourself' (MBA ii 14). Not only did she share some of the favourite images with her son, but she also delighted in some word play – or at least a rudimentary use of rhyming when in that idiom. In English translation, of course, we lose the sense of it; the original German reads 'adio ben mio leb gesund, Reck den arsch zum mund. ich winsch ein guete nacht, scheiss ins beth das Kracht'. This appears to have been a common expression, more than likely not only in the Mozart household but much more widespread, as Mozart uses virtually the same words in a letter dated 5 November 1777 to his cousin: 'Now I wish you good-night, but first shit in your bed with a resounding crash. Sleep well, stretch your arse up to your mouth' (MBA ii 104). Only in German do we get the rhyme: 'iezt wünsch ich eine gute nacht, scheissen sie ins beet daß es kracht; schlafens gesund, reckens den arsch zum mund.'[15] Mozart had sent an Italian version of this one to his sister as early as 1770: 'addio statevi bene, e cacate nel letto che egli fà fracasso' (MBA i 369), which in translation reads 'Addio, keep well, and shit in your bed and make a big noise.'

Similar expressions appear in various greetings from the young Mozart to his mother and sister. In a postscript to one of his father's travel narratives from Rome in 1770, he concludes: 'Praise and thanks be to God for my health, and kiss Mamma's hand and also my sister's face, nose, mouth, neck, and my wretched pen and arse, if it's been wiped' (MBA i 345). In another postscript from Carnival time in Milan during the same year, he concludes, 'to you Mariandel, I rejoice straight from my arse that you have been having such a frightfully good time. . . . I kiss Mamma's hands a thousand times and you I send a hundred smooches or real smacks of kisses on your wonderful horseface' (MBA i 316). A month earlier, in the same letter written to his sister from Milan observing that Gellert's death would greatly affect the poet's productivity, his description of a ballet he and Leopold had attended included a comment in the same spirit of disrespect about a dancer, a Crudescer, 'who with each of his jumps let off a fart' (MBA i 310).

During the Carnival season of 1778, Mozart left his mother alone in Mannheim for a few days while he travelled with Aloysia and Fridolin Weber to perform for the Princess Caroline of Nassau-Weilburg at Kirchheimbolanden. On his return, he dashed off some scatological verses for his mother and sent them to her from Worms on 31 January; this is the only correspondence we have from Mozart to her aside from the few lines of greetings in much earlier letters of Leopold to his wife. Aside from the lively humour in these rhymes about defecating before and after dinner, powerful or sweet-smelling farts, and shitting in his pants, there may be implications, although unspoken, for Leopold. Mozart had told his father in December about a commission from the Dutch flutist De Jean for some chamber pieces and concertos, and Leopold had taken particular note of the 200 florins these would bring in, enough to keep Mozart going for some time in Mannheim. Leopold, who would later fly into a rage about these, when it became clear to him that his son was filling barely half the commission, would perhaps not have been surprised if he had read two lines of this poem: 'And the concerto I'll save for Paris/There I'll scrawl it down at the first shit' (MBA ii 246). Aside from the language, which Leopold no doubt hoped his son would abandon under the influence of his own sober and careful letters,[16] he would have been distressed to discover that for his son this type of commission, critical in Leopold's mind to Wolfgang's career advancement, belonged in the same category as shitting. Like Grimmelshausen's Simplicius, who believed that life at court stank, Mozart placed this type of writing in the same category (his verb for scrawl is 'schmier' or smear); not only did it smell, but one's hands were fouled doing it. These are frivolous verses, but in the light of what happened to this commission, they come closer to Mozart's attitude than meets the eye (closer, perhaps, to the nose). He also makes perfectly clear in rhymes to his mother his estimation of Herr Weber over Ramm and Wendling: 'Weber's arse is worth more than Ramm's head/And also a fungus on this arse/Is dearer to me than M. Wendling' (MBA ii 246). The language of Carnival to be sure, but in it Mozart spoke truths he would not utter to his father. The poem ends with his name spelled backwards, a gesture comparable to playing a fugue theme arseways (arschlings) or backwards (MBA ii 82). When writing to his mother, Mozart put on an epistolary mask most unlike the one worn for his father; through the letters the two parents may have had some difficulty recognizing the same son.

Leopold's preference for the language of Gottsched or Gellert did not prevent him from indulging in an occasional scatological phrase himself or enjoying it in a letter from his son. Mozart knew when it was appropriate to include the idiom in letters to his father since they shared a dislike for certain individuals or types of people in authority, and Leopold could vicariously vent some spleen in his enjoyment of Wolfgang's words. Since letters were circulated, however, one had to take care not to identify the butt of the jokes or insults too transparently. Referring to our Mufti H. C. (the Archbishop) as a Schwanz (prick) was much to Leopold's liking, but jests such as this were too dangerous and had to be stopped. On the other hand, if members of the nobility received fictitious names, like Goethe's characters in *Hanswursts Hochzeit*, no harm was likely to be done, and an equalizing of the classes that both father and son agreed on could be registered. When identifying the aristocrats present at a concert in Augsburg as Ducheße arschbömerl, die gräfin brunzgern, die fürstin riechzumtreck, and die 2 Prinzen Mußbauch vom Sauschwanz (the Duchess Smackarse, the Countess Pleasurepisser, the Princess Stinkmess, and the two Princes Potbelly von Pigtail – MBA ii 67), Mozart probably touched a comical nerve in Leopold who had left his home town under something of a cloud. The clergy of Augsburg belonged in the same category, and Mozart knew he would give his father derisive satisfaction from his story about a certain Father Emilian,

an arrogant ass and a simple-minded little wit of his profession . . . finally when he was a little drunk, which happened soon, he started on about music. He sang a canon, and said: I have never in my life heard anything more beautiful. . . . He started. I took the third voice, but I slipped in an entirely different text: 'P[ater] E: o du schwanz [prick] du, leck mich im arsch' [kiss my arse]. *Sotto voce*, to my cousin. Then we laughed together for another half hour (MBA ii 70–1).

LAUGHTER AND LMIA

Much has been written about Mozart's 'Bäsle' letters, and that ground need not be covered again here.[17] They are liberally laced with references to farts, arse licking, shit in the pants, shit on the bedsheets, and trips to the closet, but the language uses not only scatology, as sexual images also appear with frequency. Biographers have speculated on whether or not this pair had sex before Mozart left Augsburg, and little but a misguided sense of propriety prevents one from assuming that they did. These letters may tell us much about Mozart the person, but we must not forget that they are letters – letters that may be inventive in the extreme but still letters that exploit certain eighteenth-century conventions. In contrast to the more refined and sophisticated letter-writing that Leopold hoped his own letters would instill, Mozart put on the extreme opposite in epistolary masks in these letters, thumbing his nose at the Enlightenment and everything it stood for, aligning himself with the lowest forms of society, writing and entertainment, and corresponding with someone who shared his whimsical derision for the hypocrisy and affectation of high culture.

Mozart indirectly explained the spirit of these letters when he told his father the story of Padre Emilian, the conceited ecclesiastical 'prick' who inspired an LMIA part to a canon and half an hour of laughter with his cousin. Emilian was the ideal object for the derision of Mozart and his cousin: he was from the clergy – a man with airs, given to discussing the arts and music, aesthetically aspiring to notions of the beautiful, and a user of wit in his elevated discourse. At the same time, Mozart tells us, he 'was all sweetness, and wanted to fool around with my little cousin, but she made fun of him' (MBA ii 70). Here stood the perfect hypocrite, a man who feigned enlightened sophistication but really wanted more than anything else to get under Maria Anna Thekla's skirt. The half hour of laughter shared by the roguish cousins appeased the nonsense and harassment that had to be endured from persons such as this, turning the tables on those in positions of authority so as to dissipate that authority through laughter. This laughter had much in common with the laughter of Carnival so ably described by Mikhail Bakhtin, who refers to the 'comic cults which laughed and scoffed at the deity ("ritual laughter")', and myths that were comic and abusive: 'The basis of laughter which gives form to carnival rituals frees them completely from all religious and ecclesiastic dogmatism, from all mysticism and piety.'[18]

When Mozart could no longer be with his cousin in Augsburg, the Carnival laughter they shared in person had to be replaced by carnivalesque letters – letters that could howl with laughter as they hurled great clumps of shit as Hanswurst might in a *Fastnachtspiel*. Mozart made this perfectly clear when writing to her from Mannheim during Carnival time:

> So if you want to send me a reply from the town of Augsburg there, then write to me in a hurry, so that I will receive your letter, or else if I've already been

somewhat awakened [*weck*], instead of a letter I'll just get muck [*Dreck*]. Muck! – Muck! – oh, Muck! Oh sweet word! Muck! tasty! Also terrific. Muck, tasty! – muck!-lick – o charmante! muck, lick! I really like it! Muck, tasty and lick! Tasty muck, and lick muck! Now to get on to something else. During Carnival time, did you really live it up? In Augsburg one can certainly have a much better time of it than here. I really wish I were with you, so that we could hop about together and do it right (MBA ii 308).

The Carnival laughter of these letters takes various forms as they indulge in every imaginable subversion. That may be scatological, as in the passage just quoted, or sexually explicit, as the missing word in the following list teases out: 'Je vous baise vos mains, votre visage, vos genoux et votre –' (MBA ii 122–3). Sexual implications turn up elsewhere, such as these comments: 'you must choose between the two, since I have nothing in the middle to offer: beauty and chaos, straight and crooked, serious and living it up, the first three words or the last three' (MBA ii 164); 'since I left Augsburg, I have not taken off my pants, except at night before I go to bed' (MBA ii 164); or, 'I will then inspect your front and rear – I will take you all around and, if necessary, will enfold you. The only thing I regret is that I can't stay with you . . . will fondle your arse, kiss your hands, shoot off my gun in your rear, embrace you, enfold you back and front' (MBA ii 524).

These letters do not single out individuals for insolent laughter, but the clergy and religious orders may very well find themselves included in lists with the lowest of the low:

> Good heavens upon my soul, Croatians, afflictions, devils, witches, gamblers, battalions of the cross for ever, by all elements, air, water, earth and fire, Europe, Asia, Africa and America, Jesuits, Augustinians, Benedictines, Capuchins, Minorites, Franciscans, Dominicans, Carthusians and Brothers of the Holy Cross, Canons regular and irregular, and all do-nothings, villains, curs, bullies and toadies, pricks one on top of the other, asses, buffaloes, oxen, fools, fatheads and boobies (MBA ii 121–2).

Salzburg had more than its share of these orders, with Benedictines running the university and Capuchins (whose brown and white robes were the inspiration for the coffee named cappuccino) with a monastery atop the Kapuzinerberg. While treating religious figures in this way may have been only moderately subversive, introducing God transgressed far beyond the acceptable. Including God in a twisted passage, following an LMIA reference, such as 'I am, I was, I should be, I have been, I had been, I should have been, oh if I were, oh that I might be, would to God I were, I would be, if I will be, oh that I should be, I will have been, oh that I had been, would to God that I had been, what? – a stick-in-the-mud' (MBA ii 309–10), may have connotated some disrespect, but not as much as his reason for not returning to Augsburg, which was that 'the

10   Portion of a letter from Mozart to the Bäsle in Augsburg,
from Salzburg, 10 May 1779.

Imperial Abbot would not allow me to get away, and I cannot detest him for
that, because that would be against the law of God and Nature, and whoever
does not believe this is a wh--e' (MBA ii 524).

WORD PLAY

Mozart's most clever subversion of these letters came in letter writing itself, in
puns, rhymes, distortion of syntax, and nonsense passages – in short, anything
that violated the principles of good writing so dear to the Enlightenment. Since
these depend on specific workings (or nonworkings) of the German language,
they are also the most difficult to illustrate in English. Emily Anderson has tried
to translate some of the distortions with passages like 'I have received reprieved
your dear letter, telling selling me that my uncle carbuncle, my aunt can't and
you too are very well hell. Thank God, we too are in excellent health wealth.'[19]
In the same letter, Mozart rambles on nonsensically in reference to a common
friend in Munich:

And say that I beg the youngest one, Fräulein Josepha, to forgive me, why not? – Why should I not beg her to forgive me? Strange! Why should I not? Say that she must forgive me for not having yet sent her the sonata I promised her and that I shall send it as soon as possible. Why not? – What? – Why not? – Why should I not send it? – Why should I not dispatch it? – Why not? – Strange! I don't know why I shouldn't – Well then – you will do me this favor. – Why not? – Why should you not do it? – Why not? – Strange! I shall do the same for you, when you want me to. Why not? Why should I not do it for you? Strange! Why not! – I can't think why not?[20]

Wolfgang Hildesheimer clarifies the 'sense' of this passage, speculating on what happens

> if we substitute for the word 'send' (*schicken*) another that rhymes with it (*ficken* – 'fuck'). For that reason, the writer corrects himself sanctimoniously and substitutes a synonym for *schicken* (*übersenden*). . . . 'Why not?' must have occurred to the cousins often enough at the beginning of their relationship, until they came to see that there was no reason why they should not 'do it'.[21]

One can only imagine that Leopold would have been duly horrified; his worst fears were realized in the images and language of these letters. For almost two centuries Leopold's attitude prevailed. No one published these letters in their original language until the editors of *Mozart: Briefe und Aufzeichnungen* presented them in 1962; Emily Anderson's translation from the 1930s, in *The Letters of Mozart and his Family*, presents them as somewhat more innocuous than Mozart wrote them.

LOOSE CANONS

Not only in letters do we find Mozart using scatological language but in musical works as well – most notably in canons whose authentic texts only recently surfaced. Suppression in this case took a different form; unlike the letters, where Constanze's second husband, Georg Nissen, scratched words out of the originals or otherwise prevented the words in question from making it into print, music publishers issued the canons but with unobjectionable texts substituted. As in the letters, Mozart favoured the LMIA theme in these canons, but the Leipzig publisher Breitkopf & Härtel, printing Mozart's works in the Œuvres complettes as they received manuscripts from Constanze after Mozart's death, provided them with texts such as 'Lasst froh uns seyn' (Let us be joyful), 'Nichts labt mich mehr als Wein' (Nothing refreshes me more than wine), and 'Essen, Trinken, das erhält den Leib' (Eating and drinking preserve the body).[22] The actual texts show Mozart having the same subversive fun in the canons as in the 'Bäsle' letters (given here without repetitions):

Leck mir den A . . . recht schön, fein sauber lecke ihn. Das ist ein fettigs Begehren, nur gut mit Butter geschmiert, denn der Lecken der Braten mein tägliches Thun. Drei lecken mehr als Zweie, nur her, machet die Prob' und leckt. Jeder leckt sein A . . . für sich. (Lick my behind, real' well, lick it nice and clean. That is my greasy desire, well shmeared with butter or lard, since the licking of ass is my daily routine. Three can lick more than two can; come here, give it a try and lick. Each one has an ass to lick.)

Bei der Hitz im Sommer eß ich gerne Wurzl und Kräuter auch Butter und Rettig; treibt fürtreflich Wind und kühlet mich ab. Ich nehm Limonade, Mandelmilch, auch zu Zeiten Horner Bier; das im heißen Somer nur. Ich für mich in Eis gekühlts Glas Wein. Auch mein Glas gefrohrnes. (In the heat of summer I like eating beetroot and kraut, also butter and radish, making splendid wind that cools me right off. I drink lemonade and almond milk, and at times some Horner beer; only in the summer's heat. Have myself an ice-cold glass of wine, and a glass of fruit punch.)

   Leck mich im A . . . g'schwindi, g'schwindi! [repeats] (Lick my behind, hurry!)[23]

Should one probe beneath the surface of the 'Bäsle' letters, the canons or the riddles to find deeper psychological significance in reference to Mozart's relationship with his father, his mother, or women in general? Anyone who has read Freud's 'Character and Anal Erotism' with its emphasis on orderly, parsimonious and obstinate traits will be well aware of the possibilities.[24] These documents will, alas, provide Freudians (although thankfully not Freud himself) with a field day, but the results should be taken for what they are worth. Laughter of the sort found in these pieces may imply an element of protest, just as Carnival laughter does, but fantastic projections of castration, death, mutilation, decline and isolation surely belong in the mind of the beholder.

Chapter 7
Operatic Epistles

The surge in Mozart's operatic activity after returning from Paris can be seen very much in relation to his new predicament of being back in Salzburg, and the correspondence with Leopold about opera over the next few years takes some fairly unexpected turns. The spirit of revolt evident in the 1778 letters soon permeates the new operas, especially when Mozart had time to reshape the texts, as he did with *Idomeneo* and *Die Entführung aus dem Serail*. Now the subtle subversion of the letters carried into the operas, often with such subtlety that the barbs all but escape notice. Until the performance of *Die Entführung*, Mozart's letters to his father continued to be highly strategic, and the strategies point in some ways to the operas themselves. Beyond that opera his letters to Leopold gradually tailed off into oblivion, with one final revival over the incomplete and inane *L'oca del Cairo*, after which father and son wrote only sporadic and brief letters to each other.

Mozart made his grudging return to Salzburg in January 1779 after sixteen unshackled months, having been in Paris, Nancy, Mannheim, Augsburg, Munich and other parts unknown, and now there was hell to be paid. To ease the aggravation of his return to captivity, he attempted to arrange for his merry cousin Anna Maria Thekla to meet him in Munich and accompany him on the final and otherwise unbearable leg of the journey. If he had to endure the wrath of his father and the displeasure of his patron, at least he would have her with whom he could scoff, talk dirty, and no doubt much more. Reconciliation may have been slow in coming back in Salzburg, but it appears it did happen. Mozart had offended his father in every possible way in his letters; not only had he despoiled Leopold's massive epistolary project, but he had also shattered his father's credibility in Salzburg with friends, associates and employer. He also appeared not to take seriously the precarious financial position Leopold now found himself in because of this sojourn. In the reconciliation he had to account for empty pockets as well as blank manuscript paper, and if actual reconciliation did not occur, as least father and son agreed to tolerate each other. In January 1779 Mozart could see nothing but the drudgery and chains of Salzburg staring him in the face for the foreseeable future, and for the time being he would have to make the best of it. That meant coexisting with his resentful father and his detested employer.

At this point he had only one chance of escape, and that lay in opera. Two decades before the end of the eighteenth century no other type of composition carried the prestige of opera – the grandness, the sense of spectacle, the rapport with an audience, the appeal to the high and mighty. Instrumental music ranked relatively low in the eighteenth-century scheme of things, existing in the case of the symphony for specific functions of court, serving more personal or presentational purposes as the concerto did for the composer/performer, or designed for the enjoyment of amateurs and connoisseurs, as was true of most chamber music and sonatas for solo instruments. In 1779 Mozart did not neglect instrumental music entirely, writing works related to his duties in Salzburg or to be published to reach the larger outside musical market, but he did not plunge into this as he did with opera. During the sojourn of sixteen months opera had been very much on his mind, and Mozart was, after all, a very experienced opera composer by the age of twenty, having by then completed as many as nine operas. In fact, some of his dissimulating comments on opera written from Paris to keep Leopold at bay, despite the lack of librettos or anything set to music, did not preclude a genuine desire on his part to write an opera.

Success on this trip in part depended on securing a commission for an opera: Mozart knew this and his father knew it even better, producing endless advice on following the local taste in opera. Early in the sojourn Mozart could fantasize about commissions, as he did in Munich on 2 October 1777: 'I would agree to a contract with Count Seeau (as all my good friends have advised) as follows: to deliver each year four German operas, some *buffe* and *serie*; and to have a *sera* or benefit performance of each for myself, which is the custom. That alone would yield at least 500 florins for me' (MBA ii 29). This required a favourable audience with Count Seeau, and Mozart tried his best: 'At eight o'clock this morning I met with Count Seeau; I made it very brief, merely saying: I would only like, Your Excellency, to explain the strength of my case and myself. . . . I spent sixteen months in Italy, have written three operas and I am well known' (MBA ii 31). At this point the interview bore no results, but by early 1780, with the Mannheim court integrated with the one in Munich – and many good friends in that court to recommend Mozart – Seeau would in fact give Mozart his big opera-writing break.

A NONEXISTENT OPERA: *SEMIRAMIS*

Alexandre et Roxane, the nonexistent opera in Paris, identified on 5 April 1778 and much discussed by father and son, may have been part fantasy, part wishful speculation, and part dissimulation. Six months later, as he faced the inevitability of his return to Salzburg, Mozart's new nonexistent opera, *Semiramis*, while still very much in the category of dissimulation, appears at least to have had some chance of coming into being. For the moment, it gave him an excuse to cut a letter to his father short: 'Why must I be brief? Because my hands are full with things to do. Just to please Herr von Gemmingen and myself I am now writing the first act of the declaimed opera (which I was engaged to write) *for nothing*; I will bring it with me and then complete it at home.' A likely story, composing a commissioned work for nothing; the only nothing was what Mozart brought home of this work. Yet, there are reasons with this one to believe that something actually did stir in his mind. His comments continued: 'You can see how greatly I am enthused about this type of composition. Herr von Gemmingen is the poet, you understand, and the duodrama is called "Semiramis"' (MBA ii 516). During his early stay in Mannheim Mozart had seen two operas by Georg Benda, *Medea* and *Ariadne auf Naxos*, works that used an unusual technique which Mozart described with a desire to emulate: 'as you know well, there is no singing, only declamation – and the music is like an obbligato recitative accompaniment. Occasionally speaking and the music run simultaneously, which then produces the most glorious effect' (MBA ii 506). The latter technique, 'melodrama', would catch on in a strong way some time later, in Beethoven's *Fidelio* (the dungeon scene), and Weber's *Der Freischütz* (the Wolf's Glen scene), to say nothing of virtually every film after the advent of sound in cinema and television drama more recently, but in 1778 it was a genuine novelty which Mozart seriously wished to try. While *Semiramis* never materialized, he did in fact apply the technique in a work that came close to fruition, his so–called *Zaide*[1] of 1779–80, demonstrating the sincerity of his words on this to his father in 1778.

The two librettos that stimulated Mozart's imagination during the Paris sojourn and immediately afterwards sufficiently to bring one of them near to completion, *Semiramis* and *Zaide*, have something much more fundamental in common than the potential for melodrama (or spoken dialogue accompanied by instrumental music). Both texts are intimately related to dramatic works by Voltaire (*Sémiramis* and *Zaïre*), adapted by Otto Heinrich von Gemmingen and Johann Andreas Schachtner respectively. Was it mere coincidence that Voltaire, whose close friend Mme d'Épinay Mozart had boarded with in Paris and whose letters became models for Mozart's, should have been at the centre of his operatic efforts at this time? One suspects not. In Voltaire's works Mozart could see the direction for his own strategy of revolt; all the targets of Mozart's own discontent were addressed by Voltaire, including oppressive authority, paternalism, God, religion, and excessive order, and Voltaire worked these with sufficient subtlety and skill to elude the hatchets of the French censors. At the same time, the nature of this revolt, while subversively aiming at the authority of state and church, achieved its means through representations or irony that demonstrated personal conviction about an existing order that could be repaired and need not proceed to a call to arms.

If Mozart ever took Gemmingen's text for *Semiramis* any further than comments in his letters, no trace of it has survived. Voltaire's *Sémiramis*, while getting off to a rocky start – partly because of the censor Crébillon who had written his own version in 1717 – eventually emerged as one of Voltaire's most popular plays. Certain aspects of the play may have appealed to Mozart, especially the defeat of the ignominious pretender to power Assur, but the focus of the work on the potentially incestuous relationship between the queen Sémiramis and her son Arsaces (or Ninias) who had been lost as a child – with all its oedipal associations – in the end did not serve Mozart's purposes.

THAT DOG VOLTAIRE AND *ZAIDE*

The themes of *Zaïre*, on the other hand, a work regarded by many as Voltaire's finest tragedy, undoubtedly resonated much more strongly with Mozart. Set in a Turkish harem, it pits Christian against Muslim with no preference for either side, underlining Voltaire's concept of 'ethical relativity' – the notion, as he echoed Pascal in 1741, that 'what is true on this side of the Pyrenees is false on the other'.[2] Both perpetrate vicious acts, the Christians in their zeal as crusaders and the Muslims in their methods of defence. Similarly, both demonstrate tenderness and reconciliation, and Christianity, no doubt to the chagrin of Europeans, revealed no exclusive claim to morality. Zaïre, French by birth but unaware of her background because of the capture of her family during her infancy, gives her love willingly to the Sultan Osman who wishes to make her his sole wife. Chaos ensues for her when she discovers that her father's dying wish had been for her to affirm her Christian heritage. The dilemma turns to tragedy when the sultan mistakes her brother Nerestan for a lover, killing her and then himself. Christianity and filial duty prove to be her undoing; her life would have been one of glorious happiness without knowledge of her religious or family roots. One of Voltaire's favourite themes emerges here, concerning the things that go wrong in the best of all possible worlds; the evils that occur for no just cause and senseless behaviour or fate cause him to wonder 'What a wretched gamble is the game of human life!'[3]

The text prepared by Schachtner, or at least what one imagines the text to be since the original completed version is lost,[4] falls far short of the tragic depth of Voltaire's play, which had been performed in Salzburg in 1777.[5] Mozart set out working on it with no commission, taking his chances on possible performance in Salzburg or Vienna, indulging his own interest in German opera and aiming at an expanding audience for Singspiel. He completed two of three acts, taking it much further than one would expect of a work with so defective a libretto; as an opera composer he was in a transitional phase, and his search for a quick solution to his Salzburg drudgery may have caused him to suspend his judgement longer than he should have. The libretto was on the right track with its association with Voltaire, but not close enough. Here Zaide falls in love with

Gomatz,[6] an innocent prisoner doing hard labour for the sultan, and his attempt to rescue her from the harem results in capture by the sultan's men. Mozart's score ends with their pleas for mercy being rebuffed by the sultan. A successful treatment of this type of subject for Mozart would have to wait a few more years as well as for residence in an operatic centre such as Vienna: it came with *Die Entführung aus dem Serail*.

In order to score a Voltairian success, as Mozart discovered soon after *Zaide*, he did not need a specific text or an adaptation of a play by Voltaire. Just as letters could be masks worn for the benefit, amusement or deception of an addressee – a technique Voltaire had mastered and Mozart put into practice in the last fourteen years of his life – opera too could be a type of artistic mask, also benefiting, entertaining and deceiving its audience. The great operas of Mozart beginning with *Idomeneo* in a sense are masks, each achieving its ends with radically different means, setting up complex relationships between the audience and the work. If opera can be taken as a mask, there was no more appropriate time for it to be worn than during Carnival, to seduce the audience as a masquerade, and if his operas were not always produced during Carnival, that spirit usually lurks not far beneath the surface of the work. While he was writing these operas, Mozart's letters to his father continued to be highly strategic.

LETTERS ESSENTIAL BUT IRRELEVANT: LEOPOLD AND *IDOMENEO*

From January 1779, the date of Mozart's reluctant return to Salzburg, until November 1780, when he left for Munich to complete *Idomeneo* at the court which had commissioned it, Mozart's residence at home meant the correspondence with his father could be given a break. One would like, of course, to have been a fly on the wall in the Mozart house at this time, especially during the first few days or weeks when Leopold had every reason to vent his rage at his son. Mozart had all but destroyed Leopold's life in the previous sixteen months: apart from returning with empty pockets, blank manuscript paper and no prospects for employment elsewhere, he had presided – much too irresponsibly for Leopold's liking – over the death of Leopold's wife; further, his behaviour not only embarrassed Leopold but violated his religious and moral codes, he had virtually demolished Leopold's credibility at home, and he had savaged the epistolary project that by this point had preoccupied Leopold for close to two decades. Did Leopold rant and rave in person, as he had in some letters over the past few months, or did he accept defeat graciously, recognizing he had been outmanoeuvred by his son? Of two things one can be fairly certain: Leopold did not let his son off the hook easily, trying, if nothing else, to instill the strongest guilt feelings possible; also, Mozart came back a changed person, no longer prepared to take the treatment from his father he had received in the past. At least these two things can be assumed, since in the next round of letters both remained in place. Two strong wills now confronted each other, and eventually a truce had to be called; life under the same roof would likely continue for the foreseeable future, and the terms of coexistence needed to be worked out.

The break Mozart so urgently needed to get out from under that roof came from Munich in 1780, with the commission of *Idomeneo*. Fortunately for us, the poet selected to prepare the Italian libretto based on the French text of Antoine Danchet was Giambattista Varesco, the Archbishop's chaplain. While necessity required the composer to write most of the work in the city of the eventual performance where he could meet the specifications of the singers, orchestra and dance director, the librettist's presence there was much less urgent, especially since most composers did not require extensive revisions to a completed text. Mozart's need for revisions went far beyond that which composers normally demanded, not only to meet the local conditions but to make the work in musical and dramatic terms exactly what Mozart wanted it to be. With Mozart in Munich as of early November 1780 and Varesco back in Salzburg, they hit upon the happy solution of using Leopold as the intermediary between them; being able to confront Varesco directly with requests for changes would surely facilitate completion of these from a reluctant poet, to say nothing of the fact that the elder Mozart still had more clout at court and could wring these revisions more successfully from a librettist sceptical of the judgement of a composer twenty-four years of age. Mozart, understanding his father well, undoubtedly knew the risks involved, the danger that Leopold would not allow the opportunity to escape of having his own say, but the benefits appeared to outweigh the annoyances of the interference. Consequently, the process of revision and to some extent composition was recorded for posterity.

Considering what Mozart had been through since September 1777, having gained his personal and musical independence, he was not about to let Leopold shape this work in his image. Preventing that from happening but at the same time keeping Leopold happy in his role as intermediary required a fresh epistolary strategy. As the correspondence continued intensively from early November 1780 to late January of 1781, because of Varesco's objections it became increasingly necessary to marginalize the librettist's role, by printing the libretto in a form the librettist would see and could accept, but placing it in the opera itself – which, it could be safely assumed, the librettist would not hear or see in a printed form – with the alterations that met the composer's objectives. Leopold went along with this deception, simply insisting that the printed libretto should meet with Varesco's satisfaction, but Leopold did not suspect that he was receiving similar treatment. He had much advice to offer on this work, including the largest aesthetic and dramatic issues, the feasibility of the changes proposed by Mozart or agreed to by Varesco, and musical details right down to choices of instruments or expression marks. Mozart could not rebuff this advice and keep Leopold as intermediary; he had to discuss it regardless of how useless or irrelevant he might take it to be. In some cases the advice could even be right, but such triumphs could not be granted. Through a variety of epistolary means, Mozart had to make the advice appear useful even when it was not, to seem relevant when it pointed to a type of work Mozart had no intention of writing, or to make it clear that he had known it all along if the advice in fact was correct. Proof of success in this correspondence lay in creating no visible ruptures in the already tenuous relationship; Leopold and Nannerl happily packed their bags and set off on 25 January in a spirit of family unity to join Mozart in Munich for the première of *Idomeneo*.

For both Mozart and his father the terms of the new correspondence differed noticeably from the past. Technically the initiator of the epistolary commerce was now Mozart, since this correspondence served a specific purpose for him. Occasional deception continued to be part of his strategy, but now in a way very different from 1778. Leopold no longer wrote with any aspirations about publication as that had been purged from his system some two years earlier. The moralizing that had so dominated the earlier set of letters disappeared with the publication plans, although not because the moralizing was any less necessary. In fact, Mozart's behaviour of the recent past had proved the opposite to be true, but Leopold no longer had an audience for these remarks as the outside one had evaporated and he knew full well his son had become impervious. Yet, not having utterly lost his citizenship in the republic of letters, Leopold continued to write as a master letter-writer, fully expecting these letters to be circulated among the Munich circle of friends. Most of the contents concern people and events, not the composition of *Idomeneo*, and he expected circulation in the normal sense of eighteenth-century letters. A remark by Leopold on 2 December made that at least partially clear: 'Give our regards to all our friends; and always keep in mind when you get a letter from me, that I would have to add a special sheet of paper if I were to enclose all the compliments and regards which people ask me to write to you' (MBA iii 43). As these separate sheets never materialized, it followed that circulation of entire letters or at least portions of interest to friends would be in order.

Lacking the moral stiffness and Gellert-like rhetoric of much of his early writing, these new letters – free of the constrictions that he previously thought should be applied – emerge as perhaps his finest. Not only does he convey information effectively and even elegantly as well as argue persuasively, but he interjects delightfully written anecdotes, some of a personal and embarrassing nature. One of these anecdotes arose from his new status as a widower:

A proposito of compliments: on my name-day Madame Maresquelle came to congratulate me, said her compliments in French and in the process kept on tilting her right pockmarked cheek to my face. I did not give it a second thought, and did not see any monkey business going on; finally she came so near that I awoke from my stupidity and realized that I was to enjoy this favour and place a kiss, which I did with the greatest embarrassment. In an instant she also turned her left cheek, and now I had to kiss that one too. I quickly looked at myself in the mirror, for I felt as embarrassed as I did in my youth when I first gave a woman a kiss, or when after the ball in Amsterdam the women made me kiss them. I believe it would not be a bad idea to call her when I sit for the painting of my portrait, since I would then have much more vivid colour (MBA iii 46).

Mozart, unaccustomed to such admissions from his father who refrained here from treating him like a child, picked up the spirit in his reply: 'You must get yourself a little more into the habit of kissing. In the meanwhile you could practise on Madame Maresquelle. Because here whenever you go to Dorothea Wendling's (where everything is done more or less in a French style) you must embrace both mother and daughter – but of course on the chin, so that their rouge doesn't turn blue' (MBA iii 49). Mozart delighted in these stories from his father, and another one, involving the raiding of a wine cellar (MBA iii 83–4), invoked the response 'I enjoyed the burlesque very much' (MBA iii 86).

While coexistence or reconciliation appeared to be in place, resentment and rancour lurked not far beneath the surface in some of these letters, occasionally surfacing in ways reminiscent of the worst of the 1778 breakdown. With two letter writers as skilled and subtle as these, a surface reading would probably miss certain ironies or needling that had been perfected in years gone by. These ironies could even slip by the other, such as Mozart's little jab that, 'Well then, I will not write any more, since you write so little to me' (MBA iii 55). Leopold took him at his word, replying, 'You write me that my letters to you are too short, yet what new things can I dig up from here' (MBA iii 56), forgetting that a few weeks earlier Mozart had said the opposite: 'I do like it whenever you write me a lot. . . . But you must pardon me if I do not write you very much – every minute is precious' (MBA iii 28). Mozart's shot about short letters may very well have been an ironic reminder of overbearing letters from the past; he wrote this in mid-December, and some advice was now beginning to trickle into Leopold's letters, advice as unwelcome now as it had been in 1778.

Leopold had his own subtle ways of needling, and this came in various forms. One may be surprised to see Mozart giving common-sense advice to his father on things that should be self-evident, as he did on 22 November: 'In your last letter you keep repeating: Oh my poor eyes – I do not want to write myself blind – half past seven in the evening and no glasses. But why do you write in the evening? And why without glasses? That I do not comprehend' (MBA iii 27). Had Mozart actually forgotten his father's methods of making him feel guilty? Here Leopold is at it again, letting his son know how great a sacrifice his letters to his son were. In his next letter Leopold appears to have taken the advice: '[written] at half past nine in the evening with eye glasses. I have spent the whole day in the cathedral and with pupils' (MBA iii 32). At half past nine on 25 November total darkness prevails, and Leopold therefore still interjected an element of self-sacrifice, writing after dark (and ruining his eyes) because of his hectic schedule during the day.

At other times the stings are considerably less subtle. Among the delightful stories of kisses or the wine cellar burlesque Leopold included a very different type, concerning the departure of their friend Francesco Ceccarelli, an Italian castrato, from Salzburg. To be sure, Leopold had just received a letter from Ceccarelli's father requesting information about his prodigal son, but his way of presenting it to Mozart – entirely speculative on Leopold's part – bristled with reflection on past behaviour and a warning for the future: 'He [Ceccarelli] has not written to him [his father] for a long time, and has probably led him to believe that when he set out on the journey, he was leaving Salzburg for good, because he does not want to lend his poor father any assistance and loves to spend his money on all sorts of useless clothes and (as you know) on all kinds of ridiculous trifles' (MBA iii 33). With this type of indirect castigation, Mozart continued to pay for his past folly and his own urge to flee Salzburg. Matters became even nastier a few days later: 'I wrote nothing other than that your sister was ill, and surely I had to write you that. In any event, stay upright and do not worry on account of me. But should you get ill (*which God forbid*) do not be secretive about it with me, so that I can come directly and care for you. If I had been with your mother, I would like to believe, she would still be alive' (MBA iii 38). Leopold followed this with a grudging 'her hour had come', but the intent remained clear: Mozart should suffer yet again for letting his mother die.

Interesting as the news, gossip and anecdotes of these letters may be, their main purpose concerns the composition of *Idomeneo* and Leopold's involvement (or lack of role) in it. Seldom did Mozart ask for his father's opinion on these matters, although he frequently received it; his function should be to transmit information as a third party between the two principal players. As far as Leopold was concerned, and he had good evidence to back up his position, that type of epistolary part very simply did not exist: a third party created a triangle, not a dot on a straight line. Mozart found himself having to treat him as a dot for his own purposes but at the same time making him feel like the point of an equilateral triangle. On 18 November, after upbraiding Mozart for his shabby treatment of Schikaneder (who was waiting impatiently for an aria Mozart had promised him), Leopold launched into his comments on Varesco's revisions. Mozart responded to this with little other than 'don't worry about [my opera], my dearest father – I trust that everything will go just fine' (MBA iii 28), and a long anecdote about the behaviour of the singer Mara and her cellist husband. The appearance of a ghost-like *deus ex machina* voice of Neptune near the end of the work invoked considerable discussion, and here Mozart appeared to be asking Leopold's advice: 'Tell me, don't you find that the speech of the subterranean voice is too long? Consider it with care' (MBA iii 34). The question, which includes criticism of the length of the Ghost's speech in *Hamlet*, Mozart framed rhetorically; he had already made up his mind, and fortunately Leopold agreed. In the end Mozart shortened it even more than the revision agreed to by Varesco.

A more contentious matter arose when Mozart asked for a reduction of the recitative scene of recognition between the shipwrecked Idomeneo and his son Idamante, who must pay with his life for the folly of his father's vow to Neptune to sacrifice the first person he meets on shore if he and his crew survive the wrath of a storm. Leopold wrote a long objection to any trimming at this point, perhaps the most crucial juncture of the work, in the end snapping, 'do you want to make the father and son run into and recognize each another just like Harlequin and Brigella disguised as servants in a foreign country, who meet, suddenly recognize each other and embrace?' (MBA iii 68). Leopold, of course, was right, but he had not understood his son's practical reasons for wanting the elisions, which he received a few days later: 'Concerning the two scenes which should be shortened, it was not my suggestion, but only with my consent – and why was this my judgement? Because Raaff [Idomeneo] and del Prato [Idamante] sing the recitative completely without spirit or fire – dreadfully, and *such* monotonous singing. They are the most wretched actors ever to drag themselves across a stage' (MBA iii 71). They resolved the matter by keeping the full text in the libretto with the understanding that theatrical expediency would prevail.

On various points father and son could agree, but as the epistolary exchange continued, it became increasingly apparent that two fundamentally different views of opera – or art works in general – were squaring off against each other. During Mozart's stay in Paris in 1778, Leopold had bombarded him with pages of advice on opera, especially on the taste of the local audience, and the thrust of that advice now continued. In the spirit of the mid-century Enlightenment, Leopold understood perfectly well that in order to have the greatest effect on an audience, one had first to win the audience's approbation with something digestible and intelligible, a principle Joseph Haydn would demonstrate ably with his English symphonies.[7] Leopold now advised his son 'to think about not only the musical, but also *the unmusical public*. You know that for every *ten real connoisseurs* there are a *hundred illiterates*. Therefore do not forget the so-called *popular* style, which tickles *long ears*' (MBA iii 53). Mozart felt he had to draw the line somewhere, and it would not include that segment of the population: 'Concerning the so-called popular taste, do not worry about it, since there is music in my opera for all kinds of people – with the exception of long ears' (MBA iii 60). Perhaps Mozart was enjoying a little joke here, excluding *Langohren* or bunnies (nonhumans?) from the list he should appeal to. On the other hand, this could cut deeper, implying the type of audience that the likes of Gellert or Leopold Mozart after him had wished to lead by the nose to a state of enlightened and moral refinement. Leopold seemed convinced that that audience, identified earlier in the century, remained in place, but as far as Mozart was concerned, it had died with Gellert when he was thirteen years old – if not well before that.

One senses here a continued tugging on the opera by Leopold in the direction of the older notion of the Enlightenment, the one he had found so exciting in his own youth, representing good taste, virtue and an ordered view of the world which accepted the authority of fathers over children, men over women, God over mankind, and sovereigns over their subjects. Metastasio had been an important factor in Mozart's youthful operas, with two of them, *Il sogno di*

Scipione (1771) and *Il re pastore* (1775), using librettos by Metastasio, and his name resurfaced on a number of occasions in the correspondence over *Idomeneo*. Leopold continued to admire Metastasio's ordered texts, his treatment of language, his sense of virtue, and his portrayal of a world of benevolent despotism; in a variety of ways, including the formulation of language and dramaturgy, Leopold appeared to be attempting to nudge this work in that direction. Mozart, who himself had much admiration for Metastasio and would in fact set one more Metastasian text before he died, saw this work going somewhere else, in the direction in which he had started but had run aground with *Sémiramis* and *Zaide* – towards Voltaire. As a serious work it could contain appearances of an ordered world, but as Voltaire had shown in his own *Zaïre*, appearances could be deceiving and unaccountable forces could succeed in destroying a symmetrical and ordered view of a European, Christian, patriarchal monarchy. With Voltaire's serious plays which had to get by rigorous censorship, unlike his ironic poems or *Candide* which could be disseminated anonymously, he had to use a rapier instead of a bludgeon, and he did this so skilfully that the thrust of the rapier could usually not be felt. Here lay the ultimate model for Mozart.

SERIOUS PROTEST

Serious opera may seem an unlikely vehicle for protest; in the hands of anyone else that may have been true, but with Mozart one should expect the unexpected. Ivan Nagel opens his book on Mozart's operas with the claim that 'all expression in opera seria derives from the two gestures of menace and entreaty'.[8] *Opera seria*, in his view, reflects the world of monarchical absolutism, and this gave way in the late eighteenth century to comic opera and the aspirations of common people. This naive view of operatic transition at the end of the century depends on Metastasian stereotypes of the nature of serious opera, and Mozart can be seen in *Idomeneo* to be redirecting his thrust just as Voltaire had moved his serious plays away from the models of Racine and Corneille. It may or may not be significant that Mozart himself never referred to *Idomeneo* as an *opera seria*, choosing instead, as Daniel Heartz reminds us, the term 'grosse Oper'.[9] In the older serious modes a symmetry exists between sovereign and subjects (or the gods and the people) in which all-powerful authority takes appropriate measures in dealing with the transgressions of the people, including the dispensing of mercy and clemency. In the hands of Voltaire or Mozart that symmetry may appear to be in place but in fact it is a ruse, disguising the incompetence or feebleness of authority.

An event of November 1780 and the discussion of it by Mozart and his father illustrates aptly the respective attitudes of these two correspondents to the authority of absolutism. Maria Theresa, for forty years empress of the Habsburg empire, died on 29 November, and Leopold informed his son of the news with all due solemnity: 'If today were a post-day, this would be one of the first among many letters letting Munich know of the death of the Empress. The messenger came today, Saturday, the 2nd [of December], at half past three in the morning. . . . I do not know what effect it will have on the opera in Munich; here for the time being it has stopped the journey of the Archbishop' (MBA iii 42). His precision about the arrival of the courier suggests the magnitude of the news, as if to say one should remember what one was doing at that moment. In subsequent letters discussion ensues on the appropriate length of time for mourning – six weeks or three months. For Leopold the death of the monarch demanded an appropriately reverential response, but Mozart could see nothing more than a potentially annoying interference with the daily routine: 'The death of the Empress does not affect my opera in the least, since absolutely none of the theatres have been closed, and performances are going ahead as usual' (MBA iii 47). Fortunately – even in Vienna – the theatres were to open in six weeks, 'a very sensible decision, for mourning, if extended too long, does not do the dead lord or lady as much good as it does harm to many people' (MBA iii 54). Maria Theresa's death evoked from Mozart a response similar to the one he made concerning Gellert's death, as the world was now free of this tedious old woman. Even to his father he could hint at his sentiments on this matter, saying, 'next week everyone will drag about in mourning – and I, who must always be here and there, must also put on a *tearful* show' (MBA iii 47).

The fate of Idomeneo in Mozart's opera does not fare much better than his attitude towards Maria Theresa. This great warrior king of Crete, having defeated the Trojans and all other nations in his path, finds himself about to perish at sea in a storm on his return home. He strikes a deal with Neptune to save him and his army if he sacrifices the first person he sees on land, and needless to say, he meets his son, Idamante, whom he does not recognize because of his prolonged absence. His refusal brings suffering on Crete, and the decision he faces will cut his line to the throne (sacrificing his own son stops him in his tracks, but one assumes he would have fewer scruples about running through the son of a stranger). His other choice, to allow the suffering to continue, will also break his authority and force his abdication. Neptune's *deus ex machina* intervention preserves the line, but it relegates Idomeneo himself to an ignominious retirement.

The Voltairian thrust of this opera, already noted by Nicholas Till,[10] concerns God's authority as much as a sovereign's, and in this case we clearly lack a god capable of endearing himself to the people. Here we see nothing other than a cruel and angry god, demanding human sacrifices and total obedience – a god from the darkest realm of the superstitious past. The preservation of cruel and angry gods depends on priests prepared to exploit these characteristics, priests easily recognizable in eighteenth-century Austria and France, and portrayed by Mozart in *Idomeneo* in the form of the High Priest, who insists on Neptune's will being carried out.[11] The god depicted here bears strong similarity to the Christian one so repugnant to Voltaire, described in his poem *Épître à Uranie*, and already cited above in chapter 4 (p. 102), a god we are expected to love who turns out to be a hateful monster whose cruel treatment of people prevents Voltaire from recognizing 'the god I must adore'.[12] The intervention of Neptune – the subterranean voice, much discussed by the Mozarts – must, according to Leopold, 'be moving, terrifying and extraordinary; it should be a masterpiece of harmony' (MBA iii 23). For Mozart that would give far too much credit to the gods; he responded that the appearance must be short, and as for the harmony, Mozart manages nothing more than a few interlocking resolutions of fifths – hardly a masterpiece of harmony. In all of his operas, Mozart clarifies his dramatic thrust in the music itself.

Not only does Idomeneo the sovereign take a battering in this work but he takes it as a father figure as well, having to surrender power to his son well before he would have preferred. But the transfer of power represents no more than the tip of the iceberg; much has gone on before that to show Idomeneo as an insensitive and undeserving father. Not only a conqueror, Idomeneo shows himself a bigoted and intolerant one as well, angry at his son for extending human decency towards the Trojan princess Ilia. In the famous quartet from the opera, one of the most glorious of all operatic numbers, a performance of which by members of his own family caused Mozart (we are told by Constanze) to rush from the room in tears,[13] Idamante defies his father, stating his intention to wander off and seek his death. Idomeneo, now completely ineffectual, may oppose his son's suicide, but he must choose between that and doing the deed himself. If he does not opt for the latter, the god Neptune will be even angrier.[14] He can do little but cry out 'O cruel Neptune'. The family performance, with Leopold as Idomeneo and Mozart as Idamante, struck very close to home; one can only imagine that Mozart's departure from the room must have been preceded by a stinging look from Leopold. Having struck a blow to the ordered worlds of political and religious absolutism Mozart adds paternalism to his targets.

While one may not be altogether surprised by these three targets, Mozart unexpectedly introduces a fourth, which undoubtedly proves to be the most interesting of all. Father and son are caught in a death spiral, neither knowing how to cheat the gods of their sacrifice nor apparently concerned for the vacuum this will leave in the governance of Crete. Only Ilia has a solution, but unfortunately it requires a Wagnerian sacrifice on her part; like Senta from *Der fliegende Holländer*, who willingly offers her own life to release the Dutchman, she makes a similar offer to save Idamante. In contrast to Wagner's misogyny and the requisite submissive woman, Mozart's opera has another prima donna completing the quartet, a mythological character with a classical vengeance to be sure, but one who manages to turn the ordered world of fate and authority on its head. This is Electra, daughter of Agamemnon, King of Argos, and, according to Varesco in his *argomento*, 'a refugee in Crete because of the tragic events in her homeland; she was in love with Idamante, but he did not return her love'.[15] Some may wish to dismiss her as a stock character, placed schematically to provide the work with some spice in the form of rage arias that would not make sense coming from any other characters, although not really making sense from her either because of her apparently less integrated role in the drama. Such assumptions arise from imagining the eighteenth century to be an age of reason instead of an age of deception. Mozart challenges conventional order at every turn in this opera, and while he may achieve his goal through sublimation, he can bring protest to the surface with Electra. Not coincidentally, the character who disturbs the world in which matters take their ordered if tragic course is a woman. It has been suggested that Baron Grimm had a role in the choice of this opera, although Mozart's treatment of Electra owes much more to Mme d'Épinay, who undoubtedly acquainted him with the 'debate on women' in France and helped him to see how to approach it in contrast to his German contemporaries.

Like the Queen of the Night in *Die Zauberflöte*, Electra's rage seems connected with the violent disruptions of nature. The eighteenth century saw nature as something to be tamed, to be placed in gardens where in could be controlled and manicured – arranged in symmetrical patterns that bore the imprint of civilization. The wild and chaotic nature that lay beyond the walls of the garden or the boundaries of the city threatened to be menacing unless tamed by literary works such as those by Leopold Mozart's friend Solomon Gessner. Violent storms with the capacity for massive and chaotic destruction, like earthquakes, struck the most fear since their randomness placed them beyond all intervention, including prediction. Electra's rage in her first aria, 'Tutte nel cor vi sento' (Furies arise and rend me), far exceeds her reaction to rejection from Idamante; not only does she invoke furies from hell but the D minor tonality of the aria, itself a key associated with death and storms, avoids closure at the end, shifting to the new key of C minor, the key of the storm which immediately follows and threatens to shipwreck Idomeneo. Her tonally destabilizing music and the implications of this for her disruptive role in the work have been ably described by Gretchen A. Wheelock, who compares her music with that of Osmin from *Die Entführung aus dem Serail*, music which, Mozart tells us, 'forgets itself'.[16] Her final aria, 'D'Oreste, d'Ajace', cut by Mozart for the Munich performance because of time constraints, immediately follows Neptune's subterranean speech and musically overshadows Neptune in the strongest possible way. Avoiding the harmonic richness and sense of terror Leopold had recommended for Neptune, Mozart lavishes these on Electra, making her musically and dramatically the most interesting character of the work. Her protest may border on derangement, but that in no way suggests marginalization.

LETTERS OF WAR AND PEACE

'Now, the day before yesterday Stephanie junior gave me a libretto to set. . . . It has a Turkish subject and the work is called: *Belmont und Constanze*, or *Die Verführung aus dem Serail*' (MBA iii 143). With this delightful slip of the pen, writing 'seduction' instead of 'abduction', Mozart introduced his next opera to his father on 1 August 1781. Just as a set of letters had circumscribed the few months of residence in Munich for the composition of *Idomeneo*, the same holds true for his next opera, *Die Entführung aus dem Serial*, written for Joseph's National Singspiel in Vienna. Using the première of the opera as the boundary for this next set of letters, they extend from March 1781, with Mozart already in Vienna, to July 1782, when Mozart questioned Leopold's cold response to the success of the opera. This new sixteen-month period virtually matches the previous one of 1777–79 for frequency of letters and substance; fifty-seven letters from Mozart to his father have survived from this time. Perhaps more significantly, not a single letter from Leopold to his son during the entire decade that Mozart lived in Vienna was preserved. The likely reason for this, contrary to the one put forward by Wilhelm A. Bauer and Otto Erich Deutsch, editors of *Mozart: Briefe und Aufzeichnungen* (MBA vi 61), involving Constanze's possible destruction of them after Mozart's death, perhaps because of negative views in them about herself, appears to have more to do with actions taken by Mozart himself. The epistolary commerce between father and son, driven by Leopold's desire to disseminate the letters, had ended in January 1779, and Leopold's instinctive epistolary habits, formed by twenty-five year of practice, simply took over, preventing him from discarding the letters from his son. For Mozart, saving letters had been something forced on him by the commerce, and that having ended, he perhaps cheerfully tossed out the letters from his father, especially the ones aflame with criticism of himself.

Despite the absence of letters from Leopold, his side of the correspondence comes through loud and clear in many instances as Mozart responds to specific points – especially the excoriating ones. Once again this correspondence takes on a new direction with Mozart now in Vienna. Publication, of course, had ceased to be an issue, and the same held true for sharing the contents of letters among friends, as far as Mozart was concerned. Leopold no longer assumed an intermediary role as he had in the recent letters from Munich, and this active and substantial correspondence therefore did not arise from that type of necessity. Mozart was not a mean-spirited or ungrateful son, and on one level this correspondence appeared to be a genuine attempt to relate to his father as an adult. On other levels, though, strings may very well have been attached, ones that obliged Mozart to write frequently and to achieve certain ends in his letters. Strategy also played a part, arising from a need to convince Leopold on certain fundamental issues, and at times he found it necessary to employ dissimulation and evasiveness as he had done in the past. The primary issue, as in 1778, was Mozart's independence, and directly related to it stood the financial debt that Leopold made clear over and over that Mozart owed him. Leopold believed the best way for that to be repaid lay in Mozart's continued employment in Salzburg; the remuneration may have been paltry but at least it was steady and dependable. Mozart, on the other hand, believed he could make much more money in a large cosmopolitan centre such as Vienna, and much of his discussion about compositional or performance projects served the purpose of bringing Leopold around to agreement on that. The marvellous descriptions about progress made on *Die Entführung* were unlikely the result of a need for composer-to-composer shop talk; these descriptions served the much more practical function of convincing Leopold of the soundness of Mozart's present career strategy, and that had direct implications for his prospects of paying off the debt quickly.

Shortly after his arrival in Vienna two issues for Mozart held the greatest possible importance, involving critical directions in his life and works, and on both matters the need for Leopold's concurrence played a major role. He could, of course, simply plough ahead, ignoring Leopold's opinions and reactions, but Mozart's own sense of family values prevented him from taking that course. The first of these matters concerned his permanent separation from Salzburg which involved quitting the employment of the Archbishop. This had been on his mind long before we first hear about it in letters from Vienna in 1781, certainly going back to Munich if not to Paris in 1778. The question arose how most effectively and if possible painlessly to make the break, and that opportunity arose early in 1781 when the Archbishop took his entourage to Vienna to accompany him during his visit. Mozart hoped that cause would arise for him to submit his resignation, and that came quickly enough with some help from Mozart himself; in protesting his innocence to Leopold he clearly wrote for his father's benefit. The truth on this point may be blurry, but a letter to Maria Anna Thekla, dated 23 October 1781, in which he admits 'that the gossip which people so much like to circulate about me is partly true and partly false' (MBA iii 169), probably comes closer than the squeaky clean image provided to his father.

The earliest letters from Vienna, during March and April of 1781, provide Leopold with the image of the ideal son, one whose courtesy, industry, good judgement, refinement and obsequiousness all shine through – the son that Leopold in fact had hoped to cultivate in the letters of 1777–8. If Leopold bought this tone, he was surely losing his grip, since these letters seem distinctly designed to soften him up for the outrageous proposition shortly to follow. Leopold was probably too shrewd to be taken in, and in any event it did not temper his response to the proposition. Further, Leopold believed the rumours of Mozart's alleged professional and private misbehaviour reaching him from a number of sources, and he addressed these in his own letters, as we can tell from Mozart's replies, without the least amount of delicacy. Mozart assured him he was no longer the rake or the idler he had been in the past, but Leopold's own experience of the past had taught him not to believe his son on such matters.

The correspondence during April, May and June of 1781 flew back and forth frequently and intensively as Mozart attempted to prepare his father for the ensuing rupture with the Archbishop and then explain it as inoffensively as possible. Leopold himself disliked the Archbishop and resented his own mediocre position, and surely these sentiments could be played on, along with admiration Leopold should feel for his son's courageous actions. Derisive comments about Salzburg officials had always elicited guffaws in the past, and he laced these letters with sufficient raillery. Further, he solicited Leopold's advice on the matter, asking on 8 April for 'fatherly and consequently most friendly advice', professing 'that because of my love for you I renounce all my wishes and desires' (MBA iii 103–4), almost certainly having already made up his mind. Leopold, Mozart expected, would admire his courage and realize that more money could be made as a freelance musician in Vienna, and if Leopold feared his support being detected, they could play one of their old epistolary games: 'Write to me clandestinely that you are pleased, but in public tell me off in fine fashion, so that no blame can fall on you' (MBA iii 111–12).

In response Leopold not only railed but he cut his son to shreds, apparently with no cyphers to reduce the sting. As these letters continued, Mozart could no longer keep up a pretence of civility. In mid-May he could still deflect the criticism with the recognition that 'I could not have suspected anything other than that in the heat of the moment (which I already expected) you would have vented how taken aback you were, as I was actually forced to read' (MBA iii 116). Only a few days later he could no longer refrain from fighting fire with fire: 'I also do not know what to write first, my dearest father, since I cannot recover from my astonishment, and do not see how I can, if you continue to think and to write in this manner. I must tell you frankly that there is not a stroke in your letter to let me recognize my father!' (MBA iii 117–18). The acrimony became worse, as Mozart responded to Leopold's claim that he had never shown his father any affection, and ought now to show it for the first time. On the personal front the battle had been lost, and Mozart now had nothing but his honour to defend, although he knew that even here he could not move Leopold. In the end he could do nothing but describe the rupture, hoping that Leopold might feel some sympathy in response to his portrayal of the Archbishop's scurrilous actions, and take his chances on his own without Leopold's approval. Attempts to maintain a civil correspondence after this episode were all but doomed.

The other primary issue, directly related to independence, concerned Mozart's plans for marriage. Mozart finally brought the subject up in a letter dated 15 December 1781, but he had to admit in the ensuing struggle with Leopold that this plan had been conceived long ago and that Leopold should have been told much sooner. In fact, early in May 1781, instead of returning to Salzburg as was expected of him, Mozart moved into the Webers' house; one suspects that matters proceeded very quickly with Constanze. Again, rumours spread rapidly about the pair, in Vienna and abroad, and it did not help Mozart's case that Leopold already knew about it. To make things worse, the scoundrel (as Mozart called him) Peter von Winter had described Constanze to Leopold as a slut. If Leopold had been livid about the rupture with Colloredo, which after all bore directly on his own employment, he came to the end of his wits over the marriage plans. Knowing, however, that ranting and raving made little impression on his son, he adopted his own strategy of silence. This proved enormously effective, as Mozart now received a dose of his own medicine, but in the end it did not change Mozart's course in the slightest. At the end of the day, Mozart had left Salzburg, broken permanently with the Archbishop, and had married the woman he wanted to marry; he entertained a bizarre notion that all this could be accomplished with Leopold's blessing, and he dug deeply into his best epistolary resources to facilitate that goal. His revelation of the marriage plan had started with the words 'Oh how happily I would have opened my heart to you long ago' (MBA iii 180), appealing like a Richardson or a Gellert to Leopold's best literary instincts. While that appeared to work on a businessman like Puchberg a decade later, it cut no ice at all with this addressee, leaving his father cold. One day after the marriage Leopold's reluctant consent arrived.

In the context of this extraordinary correspondence and the massive wedge it drove between father and son, with Mozart invoking a staggering range of epistolary strategies involving cajoling, stroking, dissimulation, avoidance, and the style of novels, there emerges perhaps the most penetrating discussion by Mozart on any of his works – the practical and aesthetic remarks to his father on his opera *Die Entführung*. Keeping the larger correspondence in mind, should these remarks be regarded in ways different from the rest, as isolated statements providing answers to the most important questions about Mozart's compositional approaches and artistic directions – as Mozart's ultimate declaration of artistic intent? That would be a little naive. The letters in question, dated 1 August, 8 August, 29 August, 26 September (two notes, a score and a full letter that day), 6 October, and 13 October 1781, play their own distinctive role in the correspondence as a whole. Anyone who believes they form a detached picture of Mozart's aesthetics should be very concerned about their abrupt cessation – the fact that they deal with Act 1 of the opera only and avoid the much more interesting and substantial alterations made to Acts 2 and 3. These letters fall directly between the rancorous discussion of the break from Colloredo and the even more divisive exchange to come on the subject of marriage, and Mozart, anticipating the latter, may very well have provided these as a type of peace offering, hoping to excite his father's old ardour for that type of consultation. In a sense, he was paying a debt here, not only in describing what should ultimately become a financial success and help in evening the score with Leopold, but also a debt of information on a matter in which Leopold had routinely participated in the past.

This, of course, could be risky; if Leopold received information, he might very well begin to interfere – to offer advice and attempt to impose his own stamp on the project. He had tried his best to do this with *Idomeneo*, and Mozart had had no option but to listen, since Leopold played an essential role in dealing with Varesco. At this point Mozart had no use for Leopold's advice and had no obligation to maintain a pretence of being interested in it. Leopold, true to form, offered advice on the libretto, to which Mozart, not wishing to alienate his father any further than had already happened or would occur shortly concerning Constanze, responded most reasonably on 13 October. That was the last time Mozart wrote to his father about *Die Entführung*, other than to inform him of the barest details of the schedule of composition, rehearsal and performance. At no point after 13 October did he discuss any features of the work itself. The results Mozart had hoped to achieve in whetting Leopold's old appetite for his works were not forthcoming:

> Today I received your letter of the 26th, but such an indifferent, cold letter, which I could never have expected in response to my written news concerning the good reception of my opera. I believed (judging from my own feelings) that you would scarcely be able to rip open the parcel for eagerness to see your son's work, which in Vienna (while not just pleasing) is making such a sensation. . . . You alone – have not had enough time (MBA iii 216).

Even worse, Leopold upbraided his son for boasting and criticizing, for making enemies of other musicians, removing one of the last pieces of common ground between father and son.

The circumstances surrounding the descriptions of work on *Die Entführung* beg the question of whether the accounts themselves or the attitudes on composition were entirely straightforward. If Mozart intended these descriptions to convince Leopold of the soundness of his operatic enterprise – in other words, the potential for it to be a success with the audience and to make money – we must then ask if the remarks may have been somewhat skewed in the direction of what Leopold would want to hear. With the matter of leaving the Archbishop's service out on the table, Mozart had regretfully had much to say that his father would not appreciate hearing about the flood of admonitions he had been forced to endure three years ago, chiding Leopold for committing the worst of fatherly sins – of cold-blooded unfatherliness. In response to Leopold's stinging letters of reprimand, Mozart replied on 19 May 1781 that, 'I must tell you frankly that there is not a single stroke in your letter to let me recognize my father!' (MBA iii 117–18), and similarly on 9 June, 'As for the larger *motive* why I left . . . no father would be angry with his son over that; he would have been much angrier if his son *had not done it*' (MBA iii 127). And, if failure as a father were not enough, Leopold received an earful as well on his own cowardly obsequiousness with the Archbishop. Leopold, Mozart surely imagined, now wearing his Voltairian mask of compositional confidante, would be pleased to hear about not only the opera itself but the process of composition and the artistic values behind it, especially if those processes and values were ones that Leopold himself espoused.

As if to prime Leopold for the discussion on *Die Entführung* to be forthcoming in the near future, Mozart informed his father on 26 May 1781 that not only did Count Rosenberg, Director of the Court Theatre in Vienna, receive him politely, but that as a regular at Countess Thun's salons he hobnobbed with the likes of Baron Gottfried van Swieten and Joseph von Sonnenfels. Leopold, well aware of Sonnenfels's activities as a reformer of the theatre, would be delighted that his son kept company with the best minds of Vienna as well as persons of high moral standards who, in the tradition of Gottsched and Gellert, insisted on works of art serving enlightened objectives. Certain aspects of Mozart's discussion of his opera take a distinctive Sonnenfelsian turn, and one must note that the opera which finally emerged had much less of that character than these comments would lead one to believe.

Mozart was now on Sonnenfels's territory, and his first comments to Leopold on composing an opera for Vienna account directly for Sonnenfels's reforms:

> I have no concern whatever about [the opera's success], if only the libretto is good. For do you really believe that I would write an opéra comique the same way as an opera seria? In an opera seria there should be less frivolity and more erudition and sensibility, as in an opera buffa there should be less of the learned and all the more frivolity and merriment. That people also want to have comic music in an opera seria, I cannot prevent. But here [in Vienna] they correctly differentiate on this point. I definitely find in music that Hanswurst has not yet been eradicated, and in this case the French are right (MBA iii 132).

Sonnenfels disliked all comic works, putting forward Gluck's serious works as the most desirable model, but Joseph II preferred comic works. Both types were performed in Vienna, but neither should be contaminated by the presence of the other. Sonnenfels, as was noted in chapter 1, had reserved his most ardent censure for Hanswurst, and Mozart noticed quite rightly that Hanswurst managed to keep popping up in various guises because of the audience's affection for him. Leopold no doubt shared Sonnenfels's view that this was unfortunate, and Mozart invokes the taste of the French here, chiming in his agreement with Sonnenfels on the matter. These views, in the end, bore no resemblance to practice as *Die Entführung* not only exploits the greatest possible mixture between comic and serious, but sees the birth of a new form of Hanswurst, parachuted into Vienna in the form of a Turkish servant in the role of Osmin. Osmin's part, arguably the best one in the opera and certainly involving the greatest revisions from the original text by Christoph Friedrich Bretzner, did not happen by chance; Mozart had good reason to expand the role, giving the opera a subversive edge which sharply undermined his words to Leopold.

The name Gluck arises with some frequency in this correspondence, and Mozart had to be fairly careful what he said about him. No one disputed the preeminence of Gluck among all opera composers of this time; even Sonnenfels and Joseph II agreed on that. Leopold Mozart shared this view but he felt a lingering animosity towards Gluck, going all the way back to 1768 when Leopold, with his twelve-year-old son in Vienna, imagined some sort of conspiracy against them with Gluck as the leader (MBA i 270). The grudge remained alive and well a decade later when Mozart was in Paris and Leopold advised him to avoid the company of Gluck (MBA ii 272). On arrival in Vienna in 1781 Mozart had no personal reason to disparage Gluck, but he did it all the same, assuring his father that the Emperor was not taken with Gluck (MBA iii 153), giving Leopold some satisfaction for his old wound. By mid-September 1781 Mozart had some cause to be annoyed with Gluck, since the elder composer's *Iphigénie en Tauride* and *Alceste* were to bump *Die Entführung* to a much later date. The annoyance, expressed on three separate occasions, did not translate into anger, since the responsibility did not lie with Gluck, and in the long run the delay served Mozart well, allowing him to transform his opera from something fairly trivial to a substantial work. Mozart clearly appreciated the advantage the delay provided, and he did not refrain from telling Leopold that Gluck had been very complimentary about his opera, which even received an extra performance at Gluck's request (MBA iii 219). In the preface to one of the Gluck operas to be performed, *Alceste*, Gluck had included his famous dictum on the subordinate role of music to the poetry, and Mozart now contradicted that with his statement that 'in an opera the poetry must absolutely be the obedient daughter of the music' (MBA iii 167). Neither, of course, should be taken out of context and turned into a generalized aesthetic pronouncement, and Mozart surely knew well enough how pointless and potentially troublesome statements of this kind could be.[17] This one seems more for Leopold's satisfaction than his own aesthetic outlook.

The delay resulting from the choice of Gluck's works to entertain Grand Duke Paul Petrovich of Russia placed Mozart in an enviable position, something he realized only later, able to rework a lightweight piece that would have done him little credit in its original form. Mozart had launched into the opera with lightning speed, and had he continued at that pace, the work might very well have run into the same barrier that blocked the completion of *Zaide*. With time on his side, this opera could become not just a vehicle to display his music but a work with a purpose, and clearly the libretto placed in his hands by the librettist Johann Gottlieb Stephanie, only marginally adapted from the original by Bretzner, did not sustain that. Stephanie, an extremely busy man – and one with a nasty disposition besides – would have to be mobilized into action to make revisions, an almost hopeless task for a young composer from the provinces sharpening his teeth on his first mature Viennese opera. For the last round in Munich, Leopold had carried out all the dirty work, goading Varesco into making the necessary changes. Mozart had tried to head off the unwanted advice from Leopold on the libretto which brought about the end of the discussion on this opera, with remarks about his relationship with Stephanie on 26 September:

> But I cannot write any more, because the whole story is being revised – and this actually at my insistence. . . . there must be great changes, in fact a completely

new plot must be brought forward – and Stephanie is up to his ears in work. Of course we must have a little patience. Everyone hurls abuse at Stephanie – it may be that to me he is only so friendly to my face. But nevertheless he is arranging the libretto for me – and, in fact, just as I want it – to a hair – and, by God, I cannot demand more than that from him (MBA iii 163–4).

Leopold did not recognize his cue to exit here – to leave the libretto alone – and received punishment for his intrusion with silence on Acts 2 and 3.

SUBVERSION IN THE SERAGLIO

Mozart's achievement with *Die Entführung* took the work very much out of Sonnenfels's camp and put it into Voltaire's, although some of Mozart's methods would not have been condoned by the latter, just as they were belittled by Goethe.[18] Much more than the abortive *Zaide*, the text Mozart finally insisted on bore a fairly strong resemblance to Voltaire's *Zaïre* in both content and substance. A principal change from Bretzner concerned Osmin, as Mozart himself explained: 'But in the original libretto Osmin has only this single song to sing, and nothing else, except for the trio and the finale. So he has received an aria in Act I, and will also have another in Act II' (MBA iii 162). The changes were not slight, provoking a protest, although probably not written by Bretzner himself, that 'a certain man in Vienna by the name of Mozart has had the audacity to misuse my drama *Belmonte and Constanze* as an opera text. I hereby most solemnly protest against this infringement of my rights and reserve the right to take further action.'[19] The possibilities Mozart imagined for the part were undoubtedly spurred on by Ludwig Fischer, the singer chosen for the role, a man whose voice was so low that the Archbishop claimed he sang too low for a bass (and Mozart took special pleasure in building this large role for someone underrated by Colloredo), but a performer who enjoyed having 'the entire local public in support of him'. Mozart's often quoted description of 'Drum beim Barte des Propheten', in which Osmin's 'violent rage oversteps all sense of order, balance and objectivity', giving rise to music which must also 'forget itself' (MBA iii 162), illustrates how he intended the role. It suggests, along with other adjectives for Osmin such as stupid and surly, the presence of Hanswurst, in Turkish garb to be sure, but Hanswurst all the same. His abusive behaviour gives him an edge the other characters lack, not meanness that alienates him from the audience, but a delightful invective greeted with gales of laughter. Pedrillo most certainly recognizes him as Hanswurst, suspecting strong drink to be one of his indulgences, but Pedrillo underestimates his extraordinary capacity for wine; because of this misjudgement of his true Hanswurst qualities, the entire plot to rescue Constanze and Blonde fails.

Most importantly, Osmin was a man who 'oversteps all sense of order, balance and objectivity', precisely those facets of enlightened society held dear by the autocratic reformers of the Habsburg empire. The insults hurled by Osmin at almost everyone in the opera shoot beyond the confines of the proscenium, violating the sensibilities of those coming to the theatre expecting decorum to be preserved. Yet Mozart plays his insurrectionary hand with subtlety, allowing Osmin's offensiveness to be disguised by laughter, and, as he informs Leopold, presents him in a manner in which the role 'must never reach the point of expressing disgust'. As for the effect of this on the music, 'even in the most horrible situations, [the music] must never offend the ear, but must still give pleasure; it therefore must always remain music'. In 'Drum beim Barte des Propheten', that influenced the choice of key changes: 'I have not chosen a key foreign to F (the key of the aria), but one closely related to it, not the nearest, D minor, but instead the more remote A minor' (MBA iii 162).

As one would suspect in a work with an abusive character like Osmin, subversion takes other forms as well, guises so subtle as to go completely unnoticed. The issue concerning women raised in *Idomeneo* continues to be aired here – and in most of Mozart's subsequent operas as well. The plot establishes a symmetry involving two sets of lovers which on the surface appears to sustain the traditional divisions of authority of masters over servants and men over women. The young Spanish nobleman Belonte comes to rescue his beloved Constanze from the clutches of the Pasha who received her as a gift from pirates. Belmonte enlists the aid of his former servant Pedrillo – now a gardener in the service of the Pasha – whose own affections are directed to Constanze's maid Blonde. The Pasha's wish to possess Constanze and Osmin's desire for Blonde, needless to say, complicate matters. One may be surprised to find Belmonte leaving the details of something as important as the rescue of his beloved in the hands of his servant. Our century would assume incompetence on the part of the nobleman, just as we would judge Count Almaviva in Beaumarchais's *The Barber of Seville*, but Belmonte may very well consider rescues or penetration of the seraglio as the servant's province, not unlike Leopold Mozart's clarification that no young man of substance should make his own travel arrangements.

But regardless of how we consider the distribution of responsibilities, Mozart presents us with little or nothing to find admirable in Belmonte, making this especially clear in the music itself. Belmonte has three substantial arias in the opera as well as a fourth short one (the opening of Act 1), musical numbers which allow for the representation of character, and in each of these Belmonte comes forward as nothing other than a moonstruck lover – utterly lacking any sense of resolve related to the task at hand or the enemy he must face. For one of these arias, 'O wie ängstlich, o wie feurig', Mozart himself explains how he defines him musically:

Do you know how I have expressed it – and even indicated the throbbing of his love-smitten heart? – by the two violins in octaves. This is the favorite aria of all who have heard it – and mine too. I wrote it specifically for Adamberger's voice. One sees the trembling – the wavering – one sees how his swelling breast heaves – which I have expressed with a crescendo. One hears the whispering and the sighing – which I have indicated by the first violins with mutes alone with a flute playing in unison (MBA iii 162–3).

Pedrillo seems to have the edge over his master, with a diversity of representations that includes a battle cry, but his aria intended for that purpose, 'Frisch zum Zumpfe' (On to battle), exudes indecision and lack of confidence, especially with the incessant repetition of the words 'Nur ein feiger Tropf verzagt' (Only a cowardly dolt loses heart) and Mozart's musical exposure of him at these points. When captured by the Pasha, Belmonte can do no better than pull rank (class) and grovel: 'Pasha! I have never lowered myself to begging before. . . . But I lie at your feet and beg you. I am of an old Spanish family. They will pay any ransom for me.'[20]

What Belmonte lacks in resolve and courage, Constanze more than makes up for. In her three arias she presents something much richer than the one-dimensional Belmonte, demonstrating a deeper sense of sorrow in 'Ach ich liebte' and 'Traurigkeit ward mir zum Loose', and astonishing us in 'Martern aller Arten' with extraordinary strength of character. Certain musical features can be isolated in comparing Constanze and Belmonte which give the listener a sense of the character behind the music, and one of these involves the way their musical lines build to climaxes through the approach to and sustaining of high notes. Constanze builds to her climactic notes with a sense of resolve, arriving at the climax on strong beats as the logical consequence of a building process. And the climax may have an edge to it, as happens in 'Traurigkeit ward mir zum Loose', where the arrival on the word 'Herz', underpinned harmonically by a diminished seventh chord, leaves a feeling of unrest.

In contrast to Constanze, Mozart leaves Belmonte high and dry when he gives him a high note in his opening number 'Hier soll ich dich denn sehen', turning his high G into what amounts to little more than an upper pedal tone for four measures as the orchestra marginalizes him with its thematic material. In his last aria, 'Ich baue ganz auf deine Stärke', he fares even worse, relegated to a much lower B flat pedal on the final syllable of 'vereint' for five long measures as the orchestra takes over. A similar treatment for Constanze in 'Martern aller Arten' on the word 'Segen' along with the occasional large upward leap suggests a touch of hyperbole to parallel the too strident text. In spite of that, she displays strength and emotion unknown to Belmonte, and is neither the first nor the last woman in Mozart's operas to make her male counterpart seem weak-kneed in comparison.

Pasha Selim requires some comment as well, this figure of authority whose apparent Metastasian clemency at the end of the opera is regarded by virtually everyone who has written about this work as an act of enlightened high-mindedness. When Mozart evokes genuine emotion in his operas, he achieves it with music that stands out in a special way, as happens for example in the complex forgiveness of the Count ambivalently offered by the Countess at the end of *Le nozze di Figaro*. In the case of Selim, the role lacks music entirely as it was written for speaking voice only. There has, of course, been debate over whether or not the role lacked music for dramatic reasons or if it was the purely practical consideration of the unavailability of an appropriate singer/actor. Yet, if we are to be genuinely moved by the sincerity and depth of Selim's final act of clemency, it seems inconceivable that Mozart would not frame it in musical terms. A closer look at Selim's words may very well raise some questions about the benevolence of his motives.

When he discovers that Belmonte is the son of his arch-enemy, the man who destroyed his happiness, forcing him with terrorizing tactics, as he claims, to leave his native land and lose his beloved, he initially gloats, relishing the pain he can inflict on his hated rival. Selim puts the obvious question to Belmonte: 'Tell me, if you were in my place, what would you do?' The discouraged but perceptive Belmonte replies, 'My destiny would be pitiful.' Selim agrees: 'And so shall it be. As he did to me I shall do to you. Follow me, Osmin. I will give you orders for their torture.' Constanze attempts to console him with a romantic vision of death, and Belmonte, accepting the guilt of his father's sins, resigns himself to the punishment. Selim now astounds all with his clemency, but his words are worth noting carefully: 'Your people must indulge in injustices because you seem to take them so much for granted. But you're deceiving yourself. I abhor [*verabscheut*] your father too much to follow in his footsteps. Take your freedom. . . . Tell your father that you were in my power and that I set you free. Tell him it gave me far greater pleasure to reward an injustice with justice than to keep on repaying evil with evil.' Torture and execution may have satisfied Selim's need for vengeance in the short run, but his ultimate solution placed his detested enemy in his power for eternity. He does not render this act with love and forgiveness, but with contempt for a snivelling youth, a woman who refused his advances, and a man at the source of his misery. His revenge was surely the greater with the power he now held over them.

While Mozart may leave questions unanswered with the songless Selim, he brings matters into focus in the concluding vaudeville. The praises for the 'noble' Pasha seem misdirected as his benefactors misunderstand his motives. Only Osmin gets things right and stomps off in his usual rage. The work ends with a chorus of janissaries singing Selim's praises, and like the first time this C major chorus appeared in Act 1, it has a middle section in A minor, the key in which Osmin oversteps the bounds of order in 'Drum beim Barte des Propheten'. The vaudeville preceding this final allegro vivace offers Mozart's clearest commentary on the events at the end of the work. Ivan Nagel gets the ironic spirit of the vaudeville correct, but he does not find the right conclusion:

> The round sung by the liberated has the spirit and rhythm of a children's counting rhyme. The vengeful man is counted out . . . Herr Osmin has to stand in the corner until he learns what the others sing to him with gentle devotion: 'to be humane, kind, and forgive unselfishly'. . . . exultant children's voices mockingly, merrily pipe the refrain, as if the Four Boys had suddenly hidden themselves in the clothes and voices of Konstanze and Belmonte, Blonde and Pedrillo.[21]

Nagel takes Osmin to be the sole recipient of their mockery (out-goes-you in the children's game), but Mozart casts his ironic net much further than that. Just as Osmin's abusiveness went beyond the proscenium, this child-like rendering of the moral does the same, teasing an unsuspecting audience which imagined Selim had forgiven unselfishly. The apparent attack on enlightened authority and values which characterizes the work itself does not square with the vision of the work Mozart fed to his father while he remained prepared to write letters about *Die Entführung*.

A GOOSE EGG

During the years separating *Die Entführung* and *Le nozze di Figaro* the extraordinary correspondence between Mozart and his father flared up briefly, sputtered and then faded. The frequency of their letters fell off considerably during 1783, and by the middle of 1784 even Leopold, with his almost compulsive sense of epistolary commerce, gave up on saving the few scribblings from his son. From Leopold's active correspondence with his daughter during this time we know that father and son continued to exchange letters, but Mozart's were so short that Leopold defined them by their length in lines – which sometimes could be counted on the fingers of one hand. Between the premières of these two operas, a surprisingly long gap of almost four years, opera remained of the utmost importance to Mozart, and the one rekindling of the correspondence placed Leopold back in the role he had held in late 1780 as an intermediary between his son and the librettist Varesco.

The operatic conditions in Vienna changed rapidly during the early 1780s, and Mozart's hiatus reflected his not always sound efforts to adapt. Joseph II abandoned his National Singspiel in 1783, and the new emphasis on Italian comic operas placed Mozart head to head with some very tough competition from the likes of Antonio Salieri and Giovanni Paisiello, unlike the German hacks such as Ignaz Umlauf before 1783. Now married and with a child on the way, Mozart leapt ahead almost blindly to meet the challenge, and the result was two abortive schemes for comic Italian operas after the success of *Die Entführung*. One may be surprised to find Mozart expending any energy on the first of these, *L'oca del Cairo* (*The Goose of Cairo*), a decidedly harebrained libretto, but now on relatively unfamiliar operatic territory, it at least provided him with the comfort of working conditions that he knew well. With Varesco as the librettist back in Salzburg and his father more than eager to be the conduit for his constant badgering for alterations, the setup seemed entirely workable although certainly not ideal. The rub was Varesco's competence, which Mozart knew perfectly well had severe limitations, but as with the final stages of *Idomeneo*, he could simply ignore the poet and make the necessary changes himself. In case Leopold still thought Varesco capable, Mozart set him straight in no uncertain terms:

> and if it [the opera] is to be pleasing (and he [Varesco] hopes to be rewarded), he must revise and alter things as much and as often as I insist, and he must not follow his own notions, since he has not the slightest practical experience and knowledge of the theatre. You can always let it be known to him that it doesn't even make much difference if he writes the opera or not. I know the plot now; and therefore I can revise it as well as he can (MBA iii 275).

Mozart instinctively knew that something was amiss here; not only did he lack complete confidence in his librettist but the plot was so silly and improbable that it had little chance of succeeding. For the moment, though, he did not act on this instinct as he should have: 'I must tell you, incidentally, that I did not object to this goose story completely because two people capable of greater insight and consideration than myself did not decide against it, these being yourself and Varesco' (MBA iii 294). One wonders what Leopold may have written to his son to deserve this heavy-handed irony. If Leopold did not feel the full brunt of this irony he would have been a complete fool – and that he was not. Mozart had made it perfectly clear in the earlier letter that Varesco had no knowledge or understanding of the theatre, and he now parallels Leopold's 'insight and consideration' with Varesco's. Mozart finally had the sense to abandon the project, although not before almost completing the first act, writing to Leopold on 10 February 1784 that he no longer had the 'slightest intention of producing it'. The better part of a year had been lost. With the practical reason for letters gone, the correspondence tailed off into the void.

THE GHOST OF VOLTAIRE

One of the first great successes for the Viennese buffa troupe, Paisiello's previously composed *Il barbiere di Siviglia*, received its première in August 1783 and held the audience for an unprecedented four seasons. The sensation translated for Paisiello into a commission which yielded his *Il Re Teodoro in Venezia*, to a libretto by Lorenzo da Ponte's rival Giambattista Casti. Both Paisiello operas stemmed from notable literary works, Caron de Beaumarchais's play of the same name for the former and a portion of Voltaire's *Candide* for the latter. These two operas by Paisiello, with whom Mozart soon became friendly, along with their literary antecedents, had a profound effect on Mozart and a direct bearing on his next completed opera. Thanks to Leopold's letter to his daughter we at least have some secondhand knowledge of Mozart's response to these events, and in the case of *Il re Teodoro* the reaction appears actually to have been physical. In one of the last notes that Leopold saved, dated 8 May 1784, Mozart observed that Paisiello had just returned from Russia and would soon write an opera for Vienna. In September Leopold reported to his daughter what Mozart had told him, that 'at the new opera by Paisiello he perspired right through his clothes, and in the cold air had to try to find the servant who had his overcoat' (MBA iii 331). The performance in question took place in late August, and the possibility of 'cold air' in Vienna at that time seems unlikely in the extreme. Alfred Einstein suggests that this work must have struck Mozart 'like a bolt of lightning',[22] and Georg Knepler believes the 'illness' had more to do with the impact of the work than the nonexistent cold air.[23] Here Mozart encountered a libretto which, better than any opera to date, found the spirit of Voltaire.

That Voltaire continued to be a factor in Mozart's choice of Beaumarchais's *Le Mariage de Figaro* there can be little doubt. In fact, the shift now appeared to be complete: Mozart had by this time entirely rejected the old notions of the Enlightenment espoused by his father, wholeheartedly embracing the vision of 'that dog Voltaire'. After Voltaire's death, when many in France were perfectly happy to let the memory of him fade, Beaumarchais emerged as a fanatical supporter, working tirelessly to rehabilitate Voltaire's much maligned reputation (especially at the hands of the clergy), to keep Voltaire's works in strong public view, and to infuse the spirit of Voltaire's revolt in his own works. In his most spectacular and exhausting effort, he took on the task of publishing Voltaire's complete works – a daunting enterprise not only because of the staggering amount that Voltaire had written but because most of his works were banned in France. In fact, he met this mission with unflagging zeal, steering through the political minefields from the publication of the first volume in 1783 to the 162nd in 1790 (a rate of about twenty per year).[24]

More important for Mozart, though, was the inclusion of Voltairianisms in his dramatic works, *Figaro* in particular, and the potential these had to be offensive to those in authority. Lest one should miss the connections, Beaumarchais prevents that in the seventh couplet of the vaudeville which brings *Figaro* to an end, with these words spoken by Figaro himself:

> Fate is the only thing that gives a chap his start:
> One man is King, the other tends his sheep;
> Chance is the distance keeping them apart,
> But if you've got the wit, no mountain is too steep.
> Anoint me twenty kings, each with his royal mark,

Death will pluck them down from their thrones, however high:
But talent is immortal: Voltaire will never die![25]

This text, of course, did not survive Da Ponte's adaptation of the play, and
neither did Figaro's famous monologue with its biting attack on the aristocracy
in Act 5, which Ralph A. Nablow convincingly argues owes much to Voltaire's
verse satire *Le Pauvre diable*.[26]

A feature which remains central to the opera, although the source cannot be
exclusively attributed to Voltaire, is the very premise of the Count's duplicity:
le droit du seigneur. Not only had Voltaire written a play by that name, but he
dealt with the subject of a lord asserting his sexual rights over his female
subordinates in his *Essai sur les mœurs*, in *Défense de mon oncle*, as well as in
the articles *Cuissage* and *Taxe* from the *Dictionnaire philosophique*.[27] Aside
from Voltaire, there were other treatments of this subject, by Desfontaines,
Dufresny, L. de Boissy, and other anonymous writers, both in plays and philosophical works. A lively debate has sprung up as to whether or not this practice
actually took place in the Middle Ages or more recently, and it does not help to
dismiss the right, as Heartz does, as a fabrication of Beaumarchais,[28] especially
considering the vitality of the subject earlier in the eighteenth century. In this
debate anthropologists have been much more prepared than historians to claim
the existence of the practice; more relevant to the issue stands the conviction
during the eighteenth century that it existed. The attack by Voltaire, in line
with his anti-Christian sentiments in *Epître à Uranie*, seems to lament, as W. D.
Howarth points out, that '*this* is the Christendom that our crusaders were
defending'. Voltaire did not view this as a curiosity of doubtful historical
practice, but as 'the symbol of an inhuman system of power and privilege . . . of
ecclesiastical power perverted'.[29]

Even more debated than this issue of historical practice is the question of
whether or not Mozart's *Figaro* remains a politically volatile work. Da Ponte
gives the impression that he succeeded in getting it past the censors by persuading them (and Joseph himself) that all the politically offensive material had
been removed. Not only have seditious statements like Figaro's Act 5 monologue been excised but so has much of the Act 3 trial scene, in which Marceline
vents her spleen on misogyny in a decidedly feminist attack. She does not deny
her faults, but reproaches any man who would insist on dragging those forward
after thirty years of decent living, diverting his own criminal negligence: 'Any
man who passes harsh judgements on us today has very likely been the ruination
of ten such luckless women in his own lifetime! . . . Men of no compunction,
you brand us with contempt as the playthings of your passions, your victims!
You are the ones who should be punished for the errors of our youth' (193).
These passages may be missing, but that does not change the fact that the
women remain the superior people in the opera, both in the libretto and even
more strikingly in the music. Nor have we lost the representation of servants as
much more adept than their masters in virtually every facet of life.

THE MARRIAGE OF ALMAVIVA

The question in the end does not concern whether Mozart's version is politically more toothless than Beaumarchais's. The political thrust remains intact, but it would be naive to think that Mozart intended to make a political statement – although one tame enough to get by the Viennese censors. While a comparison of the play and libretto may generate this sort of debate, consideration of the music changes the discussion radically, taking the work out of the political sphere, placing Mozart's concern for primary human issues at the centre. Wye Allanbrook correctly identifies Susanna and the Countess as the principal characters, enabling some of the other characters to be touched by their humanity,[30] not, perhaps, unlike the way the French *salonnières* humanized some of the *philosophes* during the middle of the century. A cross-class friendship of the type noted by Allanbrook has its own political implications, and once again the music embraces a new sense of equality. Yet, in spite of the depth of humanity Mozart plumbs with his music, a treatment relatively absent from the high energy, hide-and-seek[31] romp of the play, in the end he employs musical irony to undermine the possible humanity to which he has introduced us earlier on. If we leave the theatre thinking that love has triumphed, we have fallen into his trap.

To set the groundwork for the humanizing character of the work (and eventually the ironic ending), Mozart had to treat the Countess in a special way, allowing her to avoid the pandemonium of Act 1 and enter with dignity at the beginning of Act 2 with 'Porgi amor qualche ristoro'.[32] The lengthy orchestral introduction to this cavatina, with a graceful pair of clarinets providing an enriching obbligato, places the listener in the right frame of mind. When her voice enters it does so with unaffected simplicity, using rising gestures and falling appoggiaturas, with rhythms that leave her slightly off balance. A solemn ascent to a climax on the word 'morir' (death) on an A flat takes unusually long to resolve. The delayed resolution represents an avoidance of the tonic E flat, and that delay finds her even more rhythmically unsettled than at the beginning. The music convinces us that her words of deep regret about lost love – the count now treating the marriage as nothing but a formality as he looks away from her for sexual diversions – are genuine. Regardless of how much she may be drawn into the intrigues as the plot unfolds, we will always remember her with dignity conditioned by our first exposure to her.

Beaumarchais's Countess gets no such special treatment as she finds herself in the fray in the first act, and similarly at the end of the play; her forgiveness of the Count – caught in the garden with his own wife disguised as Susanna – can be taken cheerfully by all concerned, including herself as she joins in the laughter. Mozart's Countess does not let the Count off the hook with that sort of geniality. Her words may not be so different from Beaumarchais's, but her music places her on an entirely different level. One cannot help but be struck in this andante section after the energized allegro molto preceding it by the similarity of the music underlying her words of forgiveness and that of her cavatina 'Porgi amor'. Melodically it begins with analogous rising figures, phrases end with descending appoggiaturas, and it also has similarly unsettled rhythmic figures. Even harmonically it has a comparable delaying of the tonic, twice going through deceptive cadences before the resolution. Also, the pairs of oboes and violins in the penultimate bar suggest the obbligato clarinets in the cavatina.

While the seriousness of her reply may show the depth of her humanity, there may be an added dimension, relating to the sentiment of 'Porgi amor'. There she sang a lament, expressing the most profound regret, and by returning to that music of lament here, she seems to realize a darker truth in her words of forgiveness. This time the Count was caught and had little choice but to repent. The next time the opportunity arises, he will probably act the same, although perhaps a little more discreetly to avoid detection. Reform seems an unlikely prospect, and her humanity has not rubbed off on him. Her most generous words exude regret as she steels herself for a future of his unfaithfulness. The contentment that the others express after her gesture, still andante, remains permeated by her lament, belying the happy text. Mozart opts for a much more Voltairian conclusion than Beaumarchais had, raising the spectre of mirage in the best of all possible worlds.

During the mid-1780s Mozart and his father no longer exchanged more than an occasional scribbled note to each other, and none of these has survived except for one letter by Mozart dated 4 April 1787. Leopold died less than two months later, a full five months before the première of *Don Giovanni* on 28 October in Prague; even if Mozart had wanted to say anything to him about the composition of this work the opportunity no longer existed. Noting the coincidence of the composition of this work and the death of Leopold Mozart, some writers, especially those favourably disposed towards psychoanalysis, have argued an autobiographical function for *Don Giovanni* involving Mozart and his father. Mozart as Don Giovanni symbolically kills his father the Commendatore, but fails to rid himself of the stern father figure who comes back later to haunt him and even to drag him to his punishment for a life of defiance.[33] For those who have read the letters between Mozart and his father as biography, this interpretation of the work has an obvious appeal.

If, on the other hand, the letters have been read as an epistolary narrative with clashing styles and conflicting strategies, they may still be seen to have a bearing on our understanding of a work such as this, but probably not in any biographical sense. Those who prefer an autobiographical reading of *Don Giovanni* should take particular note that Giovanni's father, Molière's Don Luis – a character remarkably like Leopold Mozart whom Juan took special pleasure in deceiving – has vanished from Da Ponte's text without a trace. The generation gap remains a factor here but not so baldly as to show a son dismantling his father's dignity. Mozart had devised a way of coming to terms with his father a decade earlier, and in the year of his father's death – having enjoyed complete independence from him for a number of years by that time – he could not have had the slightest reason to make a public spectacle of long-buried hatchets. That is not to say that many of the issues of contention between the two of them do not surface in this opera; to be sure they do, but in much more generalized or universal ways, involving conflict with authority at the levels of religion and state as well as family.

Chapter 8
Mozart as Harlequin

Mozart's love of Carnival, expressed with such relish to his cousin Maria Anna Thekla in 1778, remained strong in the years that followed; his Carnival-time activities in Vienna vividly confirm this. Since Leopold enjoyed Carnival as much as his son, Mozart could write to his father on this subject with enthusiasm and little or no fear of chastisement, and this he did on 22 January 1783 about his plans for the Carnival of that year:

> And now one more request, for my wife gives me no peace about it. You no doubt know that it is Carnival time, and that there is as much enthusiasm here for dancing as in Salzburg and Munich. So, I would really like to go as Harlequin (but not a soul must know about it) – because here there are so many genuine asses who attend the Redoutes. Therefore I would like you to send me your Harlequin costume. But it must arrive as soon as possible – until it does we will not appear at the Redoutes, even though they are already in full swing. We prefer balls in private homes. Last week I gave a ball in my apartment. But you understand that the chapeaux each had to pay two gulden. We got started at six o'clock in the evening and finished up at seven. – What, only an hour? – No indeed – until seven o'clock the next morning (MBA iii 251–2).

Mozart's plan went much further than merely presenting himself as Harlequin: 'I think that during the last Carnival days we will put together a company of masqueraders and perform a little pantomine, – but I beg you, do not give us away' (MBA iii 257).

THE CARNIVAL PANTOMIME OF 1783

Mozart described his masquerade plan, with a full list of the company, a month later:

> On Carnival Monday our company performed its masquerade at the Redoute. We put on a pantomime which exactly filled up the half hour when nothing else

was happening. My sister-in-law [Aloysia] played Colombine, I Harlequin, my brother-in-law [Joseph Lange] Pierrot, an old dancing master (Merk) Pantalone, and a painter (Grassi) the doctor. The plot of the pantomime and the music to it were both mine. The dancing master, Merk, was kind enough to coach us, and I can tell you that we played it with real charm. I am enclosing for you the announcement which was distributed to the masked onlookers by a mask, dressed as a hobbling postman. The verses, although nothing but simple rhyming couplets, could have been better. I had no part in writing them. The actor, [Johann Heinrich Friedrich] Müller, threw them together (MBA iii 259).

A fragment of the autograph of this *Faschingspantomime* survived (K. 446/ 416^d), and has been published in the *Neue Mozart-Ausgabe*, with the first violin part only and an outline of the characters' actions and emotions. The plot could be that of any *commedia dell'arte*, with Colombine the focus of the attention of the old doctor as well as the young Harlequin and Pierrot, all of whom clash with Pantalone. Quite possibly a playful competition between Mozart and Lange for Aloysia may have been built into the plot.

Just after requesting the Harlequin costume, Mozart informed his father of a plan for an opera, already in progress: 'Just now I am writing a German opera *for myself*. I have chosen for this Goldoni's comedy – Il servitore di due padroni – and the first act has already been completely translated' (MBA iii 255). This opera never materialized, dancing all night undoubtedly taking its toll, but this was an interesting choice of a work, as was the notion of choosing something by Goldoni for a German opera. *Il servitore di due padroni* uses an archetypal *commedia dell'arte* scenario, with a cast of characters belonging to that theatrical tradition: Truffaldino (Harlequin, the servant), Pantalone, Dr Lombardi, Brighella, Smeraldina (the maidservant), and the lovers Clarice, Silvio, Beatrice and Florindo. Truffaldino describes himself as short and thickset, having plenty of wit to his talk, and one suspects that in the German translation he would be even more thickset and have a greater appetite, making him more recognizable as Hanswurst. In attempting to juggle two masters at the same inn, he devises a crude dissimulation as he plays them off against each other, improvising his way out of awkward situations resulting from his not being able to read or mixing his masters' belongings together; while fairly successful he cannot avoid the occasional beating. One can easily understand Mozart's attraction to the play and enjoyment of this servant: Truffaldino has some of the most striking features of Harlequin, including a combination of oafishness and cleverness, a sharp tongue, an insatiable desire for food and women, a sense of his own accomplishments, an ability to improvise and deceive, and an uncanny inventiveness for lying his way out of trouble. This 'work' may belong in the category intended to convince Leopold of his productivity, but, considering Mozart's love of the scenario and the appeal of the main character, one can only regret he did not actually see this one through.

HARLEQUIN

Mozart's wish to attend the Redoute as Harlequin and his placing of himself in that role in the pantomime may very well tell us something about Mozart himself, who undoubtedly identified with this character above any others in the *commedia dell'arte*. Harlequin proved himself as diverse as the actors who recreated him generation after generation, but some characteristics can be described; because of his mixture of apparent simplicity with actual complexity, he appealed equally to common people and sophisticated viewers. With his agile and acrobatic body he can turn a backward somersault in the air while holding a glass of wine, and not spill a drop. He can wriggle out of any awkward physical situation, and his body reflects his equally supple mind which permits him to do the same verbally. Morality means nothing to him, but this does not prevent him from exhibiting little malice; even when cheated he seldom seeks revenge. With that type of temperament he rarely initiates intrigues, but his skill at extricating himself from an awkward spot defies comparison. On the surface he may seem a fool, but he still displays a quickness of mind, lacing his quips with his usual sense of fun. This sense of fun motivates his eagerness to put on a disguise, and his deceptions are more in jest than intended to do injury. He has been described as

> a mixture of ignorance, simplicity, wit, awkwardness and grace. He is not so much a fully-developed man as a great child with glimmerings of rationality and intelligence, whose mistakes and clumsy actions have a certain piquancy. The true model of his performance is the suppleness, agility, grace of a kitten, with a rough exterior which adds to the delight of his action; his role is that of patient servant, loyal, credulous, greedy, always amorous, always getting his master or himself into a scrape.[1]

HEDGING, WRIGGLING, DISSIMULATING

Identifying with Harlequin, to be sure, was nothing more than a Carnival game, but in the case of Mozart the game itself became part of a larger phenomenon, something reflective in a sporting way of his own inclinations concerning morality, a fascination with masks or presenting himself with different faces to different people – especially in letters, nimble and clever turns of phrase in speech, letters or riddles, dancing, and in extricating himself in inventive ways from difficult situations, sometimes by playing the fool or by the sheer ingenuity of thought. Mozart's morality had long been a sore spot with his father, as was noted in the correspondence in chapter 5, with Mozart protesting against Leopold's accusations with professions of innocence and assurances of his regular attendance at mass or confession. The truth of the matter appears to

11   Harlequin: engraving by Giuseppe-Maria Mitelli, late
seventeenth or early eighteenth century.

have caught up with him on his return to Salzburg in 1779, and the new strategy
in letters of the next few years was to feign having learned his lesson from
misguided behaviour of the past and to claim henceforth to be on the straight
and narrow. Correspondence on this matter intensified while Mozart was in
Vienna in 1781, still in the entourage of Colloredo, as reports filtered back to
Leopold in Salzburg of his son's unbecoming activities. Following the strategy
he had learned so well in Paris, Mozart approached the matter calmly, betraying
little or no annoyance with Leopold – in short, seeking the manner of extrica-
tion that offered the least amount of resistance. In early April, this gave rise to
the assurance that Leopold should 'think no more of my stupid actions, of
which I have repented long ago with all my heart. With misfortune comes

wisdom, and I now have very different thoughts' (MBA iii 103); these were precisely the words a moralist father would wish to hear, flattering him that his own moral instruction may have had some role in the conversion.

By 1781 Leopold knew that words of this nature were not to be believed, and besides, the rumours of Mozart's lasciviousness persisted, prompting more inquiries and admonitions. The correspondence surviving from this time goes one way only, as has been noted, with Mozart's letters intact and his father's missing. Leopold, the planner of epistolary projects, saved the letters he received by force of habit; Wolfgang, now entirely off the hook as far as the early biographical project was concerned, no longer felt any obligation to save his father's letters, and possibly discarded the excoriating ones with a sense of relief. In May the tone of response to Leopold's haranguing remained similar to that of April:

I know and recognize all my faults; but – can't a man improve himself – can't he actually have reformed already? . . . You surely must believe me that I have changed completely. . . . You certainly must have confidence in me, that I am no longer a fool. And even less should you believe that I am a godless, ungrateful son. Therefore rely entirely on my head and my good heart – and you will certainly not regret it (MBA iii 120–1).

By June not only had the rumours not evaporated but they had become more pointed, calling for responses dealing with specifics. The events of Carnival were very much at issue, and while continuing to pacify, Mozart dug deeper into the spirit of Carnival itself – or the techniques of Harlequin – in attempting to get Leopold off his case:

Do not concern yourself, my dear father, about the well-being of my soul! I am as susceptible as any young person, but for my own consolation I could wish that all were as faultless as I am. Perhaps you believe things of me which are not so. My chief fault is that *it may appear* I do not always act as I should. It is not true that I bragged about eating meat on all fast-days; but I did say that I would not make anything of it and did not consider it a sin, for I take fasting to mean to make an effort, to eat less than usual. I take in mass every Sunday and holiday, and if possible, on work days too, as you know, my father. The only encounter I had with the person of ill repute was at the ball. And I did that already long before I knew of her bad reputation – and just because I wanted to be certain of having a partner for the contredanse. Then I could not suddenly abandon her without telling her the reason – and who would say such a thing to a person's face? Did I not in the end every now and then desert her and dance with others? For that reason also I was really delighted that the Carnival had ended. By the way, no one, unless he passes for a liar, can say that I ever saw her anywhere else, or went to her house. Incidentally, you can rest assured that I genuinely hold my religion securely; and should I ever have the misfortune (God forbid) to fall into misdirected ways, I shall speak of you, my most upright father, as entirely blameless. For I alone would be the scoundrel, as I have you to thank for all good things and for both my temporal and spiritual well-being and salvation (MBA iii 129–30).

These words, of course, ring of dissimulation and wriggling. Mozart does not dispute that he had not always acted as he should; his faults, however, should be ignored or forgiven. On the matter of eating, he appears to approach the gluttonous indulgence of Hanswurst, but in the manner of Harlequin engages in a theological disputation, splitting hairs over what actually constitutes a sin. The matter of the prostitute is dicier, and Leopold, himself fond of Carnival and dancing, would surely understand the protocol of the contredanse. For Leopold Lent was a stronger force than Carnival, and therefore the ever-religious, church-attending son could find no more appropriate words than to rejoice in the victory of Lent in the battle, expressing positive delight at the end of Carnival. Lest this should not seem convincing, a final disclaimer was in order: in case he should go off the rails, Leopold, his moral mentor, need not feel responsible. These were not the words a father would want to hear, one who presumably cared more about the moral welfare of his son than his reputation as a moralist – a reputation already in tatters after the events of 1778. Mozart's hedge in this case reads more as an admission of guilt, as a warning to Leopold that he would probably hear more of the same – because it was in fact happening – and that he should finally stuff his outdated morality and leave his son in peace.

Leopold, ever the moralist and interfering father, did not get the hint to leave his son alone, to avoid relying on rumours, and to refrain from discussing his son's behaviour with other people. Mozart could take most of this in his stride, continuing in the manner of epistolary dissimulation he had mastered, but touches of annoyance nevertheless crept in. By September of 1781 the annoyance began to show:

> From the way in which you have taken my last letter I regret that you (as if I were an arch-villain or a fathead or both at once) put more stock in the gossip and scribblings of other people than in me, and that consequently you place absolutely no trust in me. But I assure you that all this makes no impression on me. . . . Now one thing I do beg of you, when you write to me about something that in your opinion I have mishandled, or which you believe might be better, and I then write my ideas about it to you, then keep it strictly as something spoken, as I would, between father and son alone, as a secret, and not as something about which anyone else should know – this I beg you . . . I have troubles and worries enough here to maintain myself; and you could certainly spare me having to read annoying letters (MBA iii 154–5).

Leopold could not free himself from a notion of epistolary commerce in which letters were to be shared, even ones dealing with private and intimate matters.

Now Mozart attempted to instruct his father in the new rules of the exchange, rules that should finally put to rest Leopold's public role as a moralist in his letter writing.

These matters came to a head over Mozart's renewed involvement with the Weber family, and information that was getting back to Leopold about his son and one of the Weber sisters. By December major damage control needed to be applied, and Mozart now framed his response in the classical epistolary context of the words 'O how much I would have liked to open my heart to you long ago', words that the well-read Leopold should have recognized as being at the core of the appeal to the reader in virtually every epistolary novel from the eighteenth century. In this case Mozart adds some measure of defence, claiming he would have opened his heart much sooner but for being 'held back by the reproaches which you might have made to me for *thinking of such a thing at an inappropriate time*'. In opening his heart, again Mozart replayed the battle between Carnival and Lent, explaining the necessity of his actions to combat his baser instincts:

> The voice of nature speaks as loud in me as in anyone else, and perhaps louder than in many a big strong oaf. I cannot possibly live as most young people do at this time. First of all, I have too much religion; secondly, I have too much love for my neighbour and too much honour and sense of decency to allow me to avail myself of a fallen woman, and third, too much horror and disgust, too much dread and fear of diseases and too much love of my health to mess around with whores. Therefore I can also swear that I have never had anything like that to do with that sort of woman. However, if it were to happen, I would not conceal it from you, because, to be sure, erring is always natural enough in a man, and to err *once* would also be mere weakness – although I would not venture to promise that I would necessarily be content with a single lapse if I had erred just once in this way (MBA iii 180).

Again, Mozart hedges, dissimulates, and indulges in some curiously convoluted sophistry about his abstinence or possible involvement with prostitutes, tempering his disavowal in Harlequin-like manner with words designed to leave his respondent confused, and he succeeds in leaving uncertainty and frustration. Also, for Leopold's benefit, Lent triumphs over Carnival: 'but with my temperament, which is more inclined to a peaceful and domesticated life than to noisy, wild living . . . I can think of nothing more necessary to me than a wife' (MBA iii 180).

Based on Mozart's virtual admissions to his father as well as the hints of a lifestyle that emerge from correspondence with others, it seems fairly certain that the impression he gave Leopold of his upright life was anything but true – that he thrived on a ribald lifestyle and had mastered the harlequinesque art of covering his tracks. The company he chose indicates that his life could not have been otherwise, as the likes of Wendling, von Jacquin, Stoll and Dittersdorf were very merry fellows. People of the theatre attracted him espe-

cially, and like Weber in Mannheim, in Vienna he found himself once again in
league with a lascivious friend from Salzburg days, Emanuel Schikaneder.
Already in Salzburg, Schikaneder had been immortalized in one of the delightfully painted Bölzlschiessen targets, as an incorrigible Don Juan, pictured
flirting with a girl on the Linz bridge over the Danube. He muses in a cartoon
caption, 'ich verspreche was ich keiner halte' (I promise what I cannot keep),
while another girl waiting for him wistfully hopes 'Er wird schon kommen' (He
will soon come to me). Schikaneder's sexual exploits, documented by his
nephew Karl Schikaneder in a biographical sketch, far exceeded the occasional
error in judgement: 'My uncle, as is well known, was always having other love
affairs'.[2] It appears that he left a trail of children across Germany and Austria to
women of various social ranks from actresses to the highest nobility. Mozart and
Schikaneder spent their time together clearly doing more than collaborating on
Die Zauberflöte; the depiction of this by Peter Shaffer and Miloš Forman in
Amadeus was probably not too far off the mark as they captured the eighteenth-
century flavour of the relationship. The suggestions of Mozart's dissolute life in
other fictional accounts, including Eduard Mörike's in *Mozart auf der Reise
nach Prag* – 'whether enjoying or creating, Mozart was equally regardless of
moderation'[3] – may have been truer than their writers suspected.

MORE EPISTOLARY MASKS

Leopold remained Mozart's primary correspondent until the mid-1780s, but
during the last decade of Mozart's life the list of other addressees grew rapidly,
and one reads these letters with delight as he put on an entirely different
epistolary mask depending on his assessment of the inclinations of the correspondent or the degree of intimacy with that person. He had learned the
techniques of disguise or masking from the French *épistoliers*, and was now
able to enjoy the approach to the fullest, showing himself to be a person (or a
multitude of persons) entirely other than the one known to Leopold. The
playfulness, cleverness, wit and mental agility, along with his shrewd reckoning
of what would amuse or stir his addressee, tell us much more about Mozart than
the actual contents of these letters. The supple approach evokes Harlequin, and
one may be surprised that even in the last years of his life, when physical
suffering must at times have been excruciating, Mozart's letters are never
lugubrious unless directed to a particular correspondent who seemed to Mozart
well disposed towards descriptions of woe.

Some of the correspondents over the last fourteen years of his life include his
sister Nannerl, his wife Constanze, Constanze's father Fridolin Weber, the
Abbé Bullinger, Baroness von Waldstädten, Sebastian Winter, Baron Gottfried
von Jacquin, the choirmaster Stoll, and Michael Puchberg. There were
numerous others as well, often with no more than one letter to the addressee in
question, and reading all of them resembles observing a *commedia dell'arte*

12 Bölzlscheibe: Schikaneder.

performance, in which the writer–performer changes masks at will, finding the one most suitable for the addressee, playing the part to the fullest. If one seeks to find the 'real' Mozart in the letters to any single person among these, one will not only be disappointed but also misguided in the exercise. The apparent contradictions contained in these letters should not be taken as personality traits or as signs of emotional instability; rather, they result from characters who communicate effectively, who recognize the inclinations or temperament of the subject and give a command performance. In these various letters, one sees Mozart as a humourist (or tease), in serious roles, as an adviser and moralist, as one who enjoys sex – even promiscuity – as a steadfast husband and as one sorry to be married, as a lover of fun, and as a chronic hypochondriac-complainer, succumbing to a hard life and physical ailments.

THE COMEDIAN

Humour in a letter indicates an intimacy with the addressee designed to suit the particular nature of the friendship. To Anton Stoll, a schoolteacher and choir-master at Baden near Vienna, Mozart plays with his name, addressing him as 'Liebster Stoll! seyens kein Schroll!' (Dear Stoll! Don't be a crackpot!) (MBA iv

reproaches to his wife Constanze, his air of seriousness appears to be genuine, and one of these incidents, just before they were married, came fairly close to derailing their nuptial plans. Unlike the sensible woman he described to his father, she shared his enjoyment of frivolous entertainments, and on occasions allowed herself to be carried away beyond the bounds of discretion. On the occasion before their marriage, he showed annoyance that she would be 'so unashamedly inconsiderate as to say to your sisters – and, note it well, in my presence, that you had allowed a Chapeau to measure the calves of your legs. No woman who cares about her honour can do something like that' (MBA iii 206). He chided her for not thinking of her marriageable status, for the fact that the company included people aside from intimate friends, and that persons from other social classes were present. If she had to play the game, surely she could tie the ribbon herself, as any self-respecting woman would do: 'I – I – myself would never in the *presence of others* – have done that to you. I would have given you the ribbon so you could put it on yourself.'

Seven years into their marriage, she was still in need of reminders about her behaviour, as was the case while she was in Baden in August 1789 for her health:

> Of course I am glad when you have some fun – most certainly – only I would like to wish that you would not sometimes make yourself so cheap. In my view you are too loose with N.N. . . . N.N., who is usually a well-behaved person and especially respectful to women, must have been led astray by you into writing in his letter the most atrocious and crudest sottises. A woman must always keep herself respectable – otherwise people will begin to prattle about her. . . . Remember that you yourself once admitted to me that you *too easily give in*. You know the consequences of that (MBA iv 96–7).

The person in question, who cannot be identified since his name was crossed out in the letter by a later hand,[5] had probably himself read novels such as Laclos's *Les Liaisons dangereuses*, and like Mozart, whose own behaviour was not always exemplary, appeared interested in gaining the favours of another woman. While Constanze was in Baden taking the cures along with, it seems, enjoying herself, and on other occasions as well, Mozart in all likelihood was not feeling starved for affection or more corporeal gratification. His moralizing tone to von Jacquin, then, may be somewhat more facetious, as it appears the two of them had on occasions enjoyed some womanizing together. Another of Mozart's descriptions to him of Prague included a ball,

> the so-called Breitfeldischen ball, where the nucleus of the Prague beauties tends to gather. This would have really been for you, my friend! I imagine I see you – running would you believe – no, limping after all those pretty girls and women! I neither danced nor cuddled with any of them, in the first place, because I was too tired, and the latter as a result of my inherent naivety (MBA iv 9–10).

Neither reason rings true, and von Jacquin would have known that. Mozart was there with his wife, under the close scrutiny of a city that could not get enough of his music, and the simple law of discretion would have determined his actions. He implies that had he and his friend been together under more convivial circumstances, they would have thoroughly enjoyed themselves.

When Mozart wrote to von Jacquin early in November 1787, on the occasion of the first performance of *Don Giovanni*, undoubtedly in response to a letter from his friend, von Jacquin received a response that was probably more practical than moral:

> you now seem to be entirely abandoning your prior somewhat *restless style of life*. No doubt you are becoming more persuaded every day of the truth of my threatening little lectures? Are the pleasures of a fickle, capricious crush not as far removed as the heavens from the blissfulness which true, decent affection provides? Undoubtedly you often thank me profusely from the bottom of your heart for my chiding? You will yet make me feel very conceited. However, joking aside, you basically do owe me a little thanks . . . (MBA iv 59).

The extent of the jesting remains open to question, as Mozart continues,

> for I certainly played no insignificant role in your reform or conversion. My great-grandfather had a habit of saying to his wife, my great-grandmother, who told her daughter, my grandmother, who passed it on to her daughter, my mother, who repeated to her daughter, my own dear sister, that it is a very great art to talk well and elegantly, but that one perhaps no less great was to shut up at the right time. So I will follow the advice of my sister, thanks to our mother, grandmother and great-grandmother, and put a stop not only to my moral digression but to my whole letter.

LOVE, SEX AND INTRIGUE

Mozart occasionally reminded Constanze in his letters to her of his love for her, his constancy, that she need not fear for his love, or the wholesomeness of their marriage. On occasions he would bolster this with sexual images of a very private nature, particularly if they had been separated for any length of time resulting from his trips or her cures:

> If I were to tell you everything that I do with your dear *portrait*, you would often have a good laugh. For example, when I take it out of its case, I then say, greetings to you, Stanzerl! – greetings, greetings – little scamp – hard shooter – horny rogue – little bagatelle – Schluck und Druck! – and when I put it away again, I let it slide in little by little, saying all the time, Stu! – Stu! – Stu! – but with the *special emphasis* which this word so full of meaning demands . . . Well, I expect I

have been writing down something very foolish (to the world at least); but to us
who love each other so intimately, it is certainly not foolish (MBA iv 81).

Mozart's reference to 'the world' here suggests an interesting possibility. At
this point in 1789 Mozart knew perfectly well that his accomplishments had
made him a highly visible public figure of interest not only to his contemporaries but posterity as well. He also knew (having learned from his father among
others) that the letters of people in his position would likely be published some
day, if not while he was alive then at some later time. As he and Constanze were
periodically separated, he appears to have established his own late epistolary
commerce with her, and perhaps designed his letters at least to some extent to
be of interest to a larger public – even involving matters of great intimacy.
Unlike his father's public letters a decade earlier, Mozart's commerce did not
serve a primary moral purpose (although some actually do); instead, they
project a diversity of images the writer may have wished to leave of himself. No
one-dimensional character comes through here, but instead a complex and even
intentionally contradictory impression of someone capable of moralizing as well
as enjoying the anticipation of sex. Aside from his words to 'the world', other
references in these letters point to their publishability. The most striking of
these, as had been true of his father many years earlier, was his itemized list
from Berlin on 23 May 1789 of the letters he and Constanze had exchanged:
'First of all I will enumerate all the letters which I wrote you, and then those I
received from you. [After an initial list he notes] and this one is now on the 23rd.
That makes eleven letters. I received your letters of [the list continues]. Therefore six letters. Between April 13th and 24th, as you can see, there is a gap'
(MBA iv 88–9). Constanze would one day have to decide what to do with these
letters, and not unlike Mozart in response to his father, she had no wish to see
them in print. If she had any second thoughts about this, her more sober second
husband, brandishing a disapprovingly deleting pen, put a firm end to that.

In the letter from Berlin containing the list, the sexual images become even
more vivid, as he could hardly wait, so he claimed, to get back:

> Prepare your dear pretty nest very neatly, for my little fellow deserves it most
> assuredly; he has really behaved himself well and wishes nothing but to possess
> your sweetest [. . .].[6] Picture that rogue to yourself; as I now write he crawls onto
> the table and [points] to me with questions. So I give him a rough bump on the
> nose – but the rascal is simply [. . .] and now the scamp burns all the more and
> can hardly be controlled. I very much hope you will drive out to the first post
> depot to meet me? (MBA iv 90).

Yet, Constanze was not the only one to receive protestations of affection from
Mozart. A fascinating woman in Mozart's life, one who clearly requires more
attention, was Martha Elizabeth, Baroness von Waldstädten, who, separated
from her husband, lived in Leopoldstadt. As an excellent pianist, she took a

strong interest in Mozart, both professionally and personally, and appears for him to have virtually jumped from the pages of Laclos's *Les Liaisons dangereuses* as the Marquise de Merteuil: a woman with experience, an appetite for intrigue, love and sex, and one with the means and intelligence to accomplish things when all conventional routes seemed futile. She held a position of respect in society, as even Leopold wrote to her on occasions on musical matters and concerning the affairs of his son. Mozart appears to have become a close friend shortly after permanently settling in Vienna, and she undoubtedly made it clear to him that he could depend on her in time of need. That time arose early in August 1782, as Frau Weber misconstrued the nature of Mozart's affection for her daughter Constanze, and a catastrophe very nearly happened. Mozart, in fact, felt more at ease discussing this matter and how to resolve it with the Baroness than he did with his future wife:

> Madame Weber's maidservant . . . has also told me something in confidence which, even though I do not believe it could happen, since it would be a prostitution for the whole family, yet seems possible when one realizes Madame Weber's stupidity, and which consequently plunges me into anxiety. Sophie broke out into tears, and when the maidservant asked her what the reason was, she then said: tell Mozart in secret he should arrange for Constanze to go home, for my mother is absolutely determined to have her picked up and returned by the police. – Are the police in Vienna allowed to keep watch on any house? Maybe it's just a trap to make her return home. But if it could happen, then I can think of no better ways and means than to marry Constanze tomorrow morning – or even today, if possible. For I would not like to expose my beloved to this scandal – and that cannot happen to my wife. . . . I entreat you, dear Baroness, to let me have your generous advice and to give us poor creatures a hand. I will remain at home all day. I kiss your hands a thousand times and am your most obliging servant (MBA iii 217–18).

A postscript follows: 'In the greatest of haste. Constanze knows *nothing* of this as yet. Has Herr von Thorwart been to see you? Is it necessary for the two of us to call on him after lunch?' Here lay a challenge of the type the Baroness loved and appeared to thrive on. She arranged the matter swiftly and in style; the marriage of Mozart and Constanze took place that very day (4 August 1782), with Thorwart, Constanze's guardian, as witness, and a wedding feast provided by the Baroness, which, according to Mozart, 'was more princely than baronial' (MBA iii 219).

Her machinations, however, were by no means purely benevolent towards the young lovers; her interest in Mozart and his in her did not diminish with the marriage, which she, like Leopold, appears not to have found suitable. Like her French counterparts well known to us from novels such as Laclos's, separated women living alone with sufficient time and money to be ingenious, she did not include self-denial of physical gratification as part of her lifestyle. In reproaching Constanze for allowing a young gallant to measure her calf with a ribbon, Mozart compared this behaviour to the Baroness's in a deprecating way he would clearly not wish to get back to his friend: 'If the Baroness actually allowed it to be done to herself, that is quite a different matter, since she is already past her prime (and cannot possibly still be alluring) – and generally, she is a connoisseur of such things. I hope, dearest friend, that you will not lead a life like hers, even if you do not wish to become my wife' (MBA iii 206). Perhaps the Baroness would have been amused if she had read this about herself, since she would have been well aware that Mozart was lying – possibly to protect the relationship he had with her. As for past her prime, she was thirty-eight at the time of this incident, hardly an aging coquette (or cocotte) throwing her unwelcomed favours to the wind.

'Cannot possibly still be alluring' indeed! Not only could she, but she had thoroughly succeeded in beguiling and ensnaring Mozart. In his letter to her of 2 October, two months after the hastily arranged marriage, his words are indecently unbecoming for a married man, especially one married for such a short time:

> I can truly say that I am a most happy and unhappy man! – unhappy since the time when I saw your Ladyship at the ball with your hair done so beautifully! – for – my whole sense of peace is lost! – Nothing but sighs and groans! The rest of the time I spent at the ball I did not dance – instead I leapt about. The meal was already ordered, but I did not eat – I crammed it in like an animal. During the night instead of slumbering peacefully and sweetly – I slept like a log and snored like a bear! – and (without deluding myself too much) I would almost wager that for your Ladyship *à proportion* things went more or less the same! You smile! – you turn red! – Ah yes – I am happy! – My luck is made! But alas! Who pats me on the shoulder? Who glances into my letter? Alas, alas, alas! – My wife! – Now, in God's name; I have taken her and must keep her! What is to be done? – I must praise her – and imagine that the praise is true! . . . All right then, courage! – I would like to ask your Ladyship that – pfui, the devil – that would be too indecent! *A propos*. Does your Ladyship not know the little song?
>
>> A woman and a jug of beer,
>> How can they hold together?
>> The woman owns her own supply
>> Of which she points an ample pair at me.
>> Then they hang together.

Didn't I bring that in very neatly? But now, *senza burle*. If your Ladyship could give me a pair this evening, you would be doing me a great service. For my wife is – is – and has urges – but only for beer prepared in the English way! Well done, little wife! I see finally that you really are good for something. My wife, who is an angel of a woman, and I, who am a fine speciman of a husband, both kiss your Ladyship's hands a thousand times and are eternally your

faithful vassals,
Mozart magnus, corpore parvus,
     et
Constantia, omnium uxorum pulcherrima
et prudentissima (MBA iii 231–5)

Once again, a masquerade ball appeared to have a subverting effect, and Mozart, knowing well the appropriate epistolary mode of response, played his part to the best of his ability. He may at this moment have seen his marriage as an obstacle to such a liaison, although that would not prevent it from occurring in letters. The Baroness, much less naive and not interested in anything permanent with a composer whose star would probably dim, would not have seen it that way. On the other hand, this may have been nothing more than a seductive epistolary game.

TO THE FATHER OF THE STRING QUARTET

Mozart's letter dedicating a set of string quartets to Joseph Haydn dated 1 September 1785 seems on the surface to be a normal if not slightly crude dedicatory letter, following the standard self-deprecating rhetoric of this type of letter.[7] When one considers the differences between Mozart's and Haydn's quartets, however, the rugged praise directed to Haydn may strike one as something less than genuine. Mark Evan Bonds points out that Mozart's modelling of Haydn here may be as much a competition as homage or flattery, as Mozart takes individual types of procedures or forms and attempts to show himself superior to the master of the string quartet. His repetitive references to Haydn as his friend in the letter may, as Bond suggests, be intended to portray himself to the public as Haydn's equal (a view his contemporaries would not have shared),[8] although the rhetorical purpose of the repetition could cut even deeper. Considering that when Mozart wrote to his father about the death of his mother, he had repeated 'God's will' over and over, lacing the repetition with irony, one wonders if the rhetorical strategy in this case may not be double-edged.

As a dedication, Mozart directed this letter to the larger public, and it was included with the first published edition of the quartets (op. 10, 1–6) which Artaria issued shortly after the letter had been written. Leopold knew about this dedication by the middle of September, referring to its high quality and good taste in a letter to Nannerl (MBA iii 413). A vestige of that good taste lay in the fact that Mozart wrote it in Italian, the language which remained the medium of high culture in Vienna, and for the purposes of cultural dignity it presumably would have been inconceivable to issue such a letter in German. Yet the language itself drew Leopold's notice; the possibility exists that Italian adds a touch of pompousness to the apparent dignity since it was after all a foreign language. If any shreds of irony were to creep into the letter, that could be achieved more effectively in the language of 'high culture', a language more given to affectation from an honest German's point of view – a language over which Sonnenfels had lost friends in his attempts to rid it from the Viennese stage.

On the surface, this letter should not arouse the slightest amount of suspicion; Mozart and Haydn had been the best of friends since their first meeting, in spite of the age gap of almost two and a half decades, with nothing but professions of admiration from each. Mozart knew Haydn's brother Michael well from Salzburg, and Michael was the butt of many a Mozart joke; both Wolfgang and Leopold knew perfectly well that Joseph stood at an entirely different level. The affable Haydn was old enough to be Mozart's father, and the dedication draws heavily on this image. The quartets themselves become Mozart's sons, sent into the world under the protection and guidance of their designated godfather, Haydn, not only a best friend but one who encouraged their birth and whose own quartets provided a working model. The most interesting words, couched in moral terms, come towards the end of the dedication: 'May it therefore please you to receive them kindly and to be their Father, Guide and Friend! From this moment I resign to you all my rights in them, begging you however to look indulgently upon the defects which the partiality of a Father's eye may have concealed from me, and in spite of them to continue in your generous Friendship for him who so greatly values it' (MDB 250). The father image may very well have been one of endearment to Haydn, who, lacking his own children, undoubtedly felt a special affection for the young Mozart, and as an outstanding composer would have understood the significance of Mozart's gesture in entrusting this 'fruit of long and laborious endeavour'. On this point Mozart spoke the truth, as string quartet writing, which required a contrapuntal working out of all four voices at once, challenged him more than any other type of composition.[9]

If there is anything troubling about this dedication, it lies in the father/son image, an experience so ambivalent for Mozart himself, so charged with the potential to be interpreted in different ways. On the one hand, this dedication could have some significance for Leopold, as it begs a type of paternal indulgence for faults that Leopold himself could not give. Be that as it may, Mozart wrote the dedication for Haydn and it surely concerns him alone. Mozart's quartets could certainly not be construed as Haydn's children; one would not mistake them for Haydn's own compositions, either in their working of specific procedures or even in a broader stylistic sense. Curiously, whereas Haydn's op. 33 quartets of 1781 are laced with touches of humour – of the Carnival spirit – Mozart chose to be more serious, and more elaborately contrapuntal. In fact, they are so different that one may even have difficulty thinking of them as stepchildren to the virtual progenitor of this genre of composition. Public letters of dedication were often written by someone other than the composer, as was true of Mozart's earlier dedications, but the complexity of this one makes that a very unlikely prospect.

Mozart's musical response to another type of composition, which Haydn had brought to a new respectability and level of sophistication, the symphony, offers another way of looking at the matter. In his Paris Symphonies, written in 1785 (especially No. 83, the probable first work of the set), Haydn had defined processes of development and intelligibility in which the dramatic interaction of opposing musical forces could be followed to a logical conclusion. The conclusion, through synthesis or coexistence of opposites, suggested enlightened principles of morality, tolerance or refinement.[10] Mozart, in complete contrast to this, in a work such as Symphony no. 39 in E flat, avoids that type of musical dialectic entirely, proceeding with something so symmetrical that one may be inclined to think of the symmetry as a ruse. Mozart appeared to reject Haydn's enlightened approach, not in defiance, but with calmness, cleverness and subtlety. If Mozart intended any irony in his dedication of the quartets, he would clearly not wish his genuinely dear friend Haydn to be conscious of that in the slightest.

OPENING HIS HEART

Different masks proved useful for other purposes, and that included obtaining money. His need during the last few years of his life became fairly urgent, as his sources for financial stability during the mid-1780s had more or less dried up. The rumour spreading in Vienna immediately after his death that his debts amounted to 30,000 florins, though, appears to have been exaggerated tenfold.[11] Michael Puchberg turned out to be as willing a source for providing money as the Baroness had been in providing for other needs, and Mozart had no difficulty perfecting the epistolary style that would most effectively keep it flowing. In fact, borrowing money from Puchberg proved to be very much an epistolary exercise; most of the letters sent to this fellow freemason were written in Vienna and sent within Vienna, often shortly before or after the two had met for lunch where they could have discussed such matters but apparently did not. Puchberg was not the only freemason able to provide loans to the sometimes strapped composer, and a letter to Franz Hofdemel dated March 1789 demonstrated how Mozart would request a loan in a normal way, with minimal embellishment:

> I am taking the liberty without standing on formality to ask a favour of you. I would be very much bound to you if you could or would lend me a hundred florins until the 20th of next month. On the 20th I receive the quarterly installment of my salary, and would then pay back the debt with thanks. I have depended too much on the hundred ducats (which I expect to receive from abroad). . . . I have left my cash supply too depleted, so that *at the moment* I have

an urgent necessity for some money and have therefore placed my trust in you, for I am completely convinced of your friendship (MBA iv 77–8).

Mozart could ask for a loan in a straightforward manner and be successful, as proved true in this case.

On about twenty occasions, beginning in June 1788, Mozart wrote to Michael Puchberg begging for money, ranging from a few florins up to as much as two thousand, and on most attempts he succeeded – although not in receiving the huge sums that would have amounted to a year's salary. In one of these letters, dated 12 July 1789, Mozart actually clarified the epistolary nature of these requests:

> Just recently when I was with you I was longing to unburden my heart to you, although I did not have the courage! – and I would still not have – and I tremble as I dare to write you – and I would not even dare to write, were I not certain that you know me, that you are aware of my circumstances, and are entirely convinced of my *innocence* regarding my unfortunate and most sorry situation (MBA iv 92).

This relationship worked very much on two tiers: on one level, they met for lunch, chamber music, or other social activities, and on the other, they communicated more intimately through letters in which Mozart felt he could 'unburden his heart' to his friend. 'Unburden his heart' stands as the operative phrase in these letters, repeated often by Mozart in them, followed by all the sordid details of his 'wretched condition', his illnesses, his headaches, his toothaches, his insomnia, as well as the details of Constanze's health and sleeping habits, and the expensive cures for both of them. Mozart did not divulge these details to anyone else in his letters, and clearly none of his other letters from this time wallow in such a lugubrious way, suggesting he presented these details very much for Puchberg's benefit. Puchberg, an obviously successful man of business, also had a sentimental streak – sympathy for the downtrodden – and a fascination with tales of woe, with details of suffering and sadness; he may very well have been an avid reader of the epistolary novels of Richardson or Gellert. Mozart recognized what moved him, that he was deeply touched by these matters – perhaps moved by sympathy and perhaps made uncomfortable by the embarrassment of his own riches – and could be stirred into giving to relieve his own sense of guilt or embarrassment. For Puchberg, Mozart acted a role he played for no one else, becoming for him a real-life sentimental *épistolier*, a familiar character emerging from the pages of a recognizable literary genre to touch his subject's heart (and, in this case, purse).

Assessing the actual level of misery in the descriptions Mozart penned for Puchberg has proved difficult in the light of Mozart's cheerful letters to other people at the same time. Perhaps he wrote to Puchberg only on bad days, and we should not doubt that he had many. Starting a letter with 'I am very sorry that I cannot go out and speak with you myself, but my toothache and headache are still too great and in general I still feel devoid of strength' (MBA iv 106) sets a distinctive tone for what follows. Similarly, words such as 'for some time you will have noticed my perpetual sadness' (MBA iv 104) seem somewhat calculated considering the side of Mozart that Stoll or von Jacquin enjoyed during these years. Along with the invocation of opening his heart, Mozart's postscript to one of the Puchberg letters also helps to place his epistolary mode in perspective: 'My wife was wretchedly ill again yesterday. Today leeches were attached to her and, thank God, she improves. I am truly most unfortunate, forever suspended between fear and hope!' (MBA iv 95). Readers will, of course, remember Mozart's words to his father on the night of his mother's death: 'My dear mother is very ill – she has been bled, as has become the routine. . . . For a long time now I have been suspended day and night between fear and hope – but now I have submitted myself completely to the will of God. . . . Let us dispel these melancholy thoughts; we must hope, but not too much' (MBA ii 387–8). In that case his mother's lifeless body lay in the same room in which he wrote these words, and 'hope' was intended to divert his father's attention from the grim truth. Now he used the same technique (virtually the same words), but since Constanze surely was nowhere near death's door, 'hope' probably had more to do with a forgivable loan than her health. Linking these letters with reality has proved to be a very risky business; we have here a calculated strategy – the wearing of a highly distinctive literary mask – with no more connection to the actual events of his life than the letters to his father had offered.

POSTSCRIPT

Mozart's letters to his various correspondents show him to be a harlequinesque masquerader, selecting the appropriate mask not only for the benefit of his addressee but for his own purposes which could be serious or light-hearted. No unified Mozart presents himself here; instead, he emits diverse and often contradictory signals as sinner and reformer or scamp and confidante, appearing obedient and recalcitrant or sophisticated and crude, and appealing above the shoulders as well as below the waist. To some he writes as a novelist, giving the illusion of opening his heart and occupying the moral high ground, while to others he belongs with the lowest of the Grub Street hacks, little more than a smutty pamphleteer. This diversity has caused some to doubt a connection between Mozart the correspondent and Mozart the composer; for them the letters represent the all-too-human Mozart whereas the compositions occupy a superhuman domain of genius, untouched by the sweat, the pockmarks or the occasional pleasures of reality.

Mozart's genius cannot be doubted – that, after all, accounts for the unabated fascination after two centuries – but must that genius exist in some untouchable and inscrutable realm of the mind unrelated to the person it resides in? There are, of course, risks in answering no to that question, such as opening the floodgate to ventures which use the letters as raw material for personality analysis. Wearing masks in letters, it must be concluded, obscures the person more than reveals him, making the letters unreliable documents for the formulation of a composite character sketch. Yet, the letters of Mozart can play a crucial role in the ways we understand him as a composer, and that role depends on how we read the letters. They most certainly tell us much about his times, and in part that emerges in the orbit of what eighteenth-century letter writers wished to accomplish strategically in evoking responses from readers. They tell us much about the person as well, although less in a taming biographical way than in the type of insight one can gain into the person who achieves such virtuosity in letter-writing strategies.

Notes

Introduction

1. Robert L. Marshall, *Mozart Speaks: Views on Music, Musicians, and the World* (New York, 1991), p. xviii.
2. Maynard Solomon, *Mozart: A Life* (New York, 1995), 351 and 349.
3. An Associated Press article which appeared in numerous newspapers, including the Halifax *Mail Star*, 26 December 1992.
4. An excellent start has been made on the subject of the Mozart letters by Josef Mančal, although his articles are unavailable to the English reader. Even those prepared to brave the German will be daunted by the obscurity of some of the journals in which his pieces appear. These articles include 'Briefe–nur "Briefe"?', *Acta Mozartiana* 40 (1993): 50–73; 'Zum Verhältnis Leopold Mozarts zu Wolfgang "Amadé" Mozart: Prolegomena zur Strukturbestimmung einer personalen Beziehung und der Wirklichkeitsorganisation im Zeitalter des Absolutismus und der Aufklärung', *Zeitschrift des Historischen Vereins für Schwaben* 84 (1991): 191–245, and part 2 of the same in 85 (1992): 233–71.
5. See Eric A. Blackall, *The Emergence of German as a Literary Language, 1700–1775* (Cambridge, 1959), 198–204.
6. Emily Anderson, *The Letters of Mozart and his Family*, 3rd ed. (London, 1985), 281.
7. Quoted in Ian Watt, *The Rise of the Novel: Studies in Defoe, Richardson and Fielding* (Berkeley, 1957), 191.
8. Quoted in Dena Goodman, *The Republic of Letters: A Cultural History of the French Enlightenment* (Ithaca, 1994), 143.
9. Goodman, *The Republic of Letters*, 144.
10. Quoted *ibid.*, 147.
11. Goodman, 140.
12. See Robert Darnton, *Mesmerism and the End of the Enlightenment in France* (Cambridge, MA, 1968), 161–7.
13. See Neal Zaslaw, 'Mozart's Paris Symphonies', *Musical Times* 119 (1978): 753–7, and Alan Tyson, 'Mozart's Truthfulness', *Musical Times* 119 (1978): 938–9.
14. 'An Essay on the Freedom of Wit and Humour', *Characteristics of Men, Manners, Opinions, Times*, 4th ed., vol. 1 (London, 1727), 50.
15. *English Literature in the Age of Disguise*, ed. Maximillian E. Novak (Berkeley, 1977).
16. Quoted *ibid.*, 1–2.
17. Bruce Redford, *The Converse of the Pen: Acts of Intimacy in the Eighteenth-Century Familiar Letter* (Chicago, 1986), 14.
18. See Terry Castle, 'Eros and Liberty at the English Masquerade, 1710–90', *Eighteenth-Century Studies* 17 (1983–4): 156.
19. *Ibid.*, 160.
20. *Ibid.*, 168.

Chapter 1. The Battle between Carnival and Lent

1. Quoted in T. C. W. Blanning, *Joseph II and Enlightened Despotism* (London, 1970), 95.
2. See Joseph Mack, *Die Reform- und Aufklärungsbestrebungen im Erzstift Salzburg unter Erzbischof Hieronymous von Colloredo* (Munich, 1912).
3. Charles H. O'Brien, *Ideas of Religious Toleration at the Time of Joseph II: A Study of the Enlightenment among Catholics in Austria* (Philadelphia, 1969), 40.
4. See Ernst Wangermann, 'Reform Catholicism and Political Radicalism in the Austrian Enlightenment', in *The Enlightenment in National Context*, ed. Roy Porter and Mikuláš Teich (Cambridge, 1981), 127–40.
5. 'Vorerinnerung über die Veranlassung, den Zweck, und die eigentliche Bestimmung dieses Journals', *Journal für Freymaurer* 1, no. 1 (1784): 9–10.
6. Quoted in Katharine Thomson, *The Masonic Thread in Mozart* (London, 1977), 102.
7. Robert A. Kann, *A Study in Austrian Intellectual History* (New York, 1960), 185–6.
8. *Ibid.*, 189.
9. These translations borrow from *The Great Operas of Mozart*, trans. W. H. Auden, Chester Kallman, Ruth and Thomas Martin, and John Bloch (New York, 1964).
10. Jacques Chailley, *The Magic Flute Unveiled: Esoteric Symbolism in Mozart's Masonic Opera* (Rochester, VT, 1992), 152–3.
11. *Ibid.*, 152.
12. Wolfgang Stechow, *Pieter Bruegel the Elder* (London, 1970), 57–8.
13. J. W. Goethe, *Italian Journey* [1786–1788], trans. W. H. Auden and Elizabeth Mayer (London, 1970), 446–69.
14. Johann Pezzl, *Skizze von Wien*, excerpts trans. by H. C. Robbins Landon in *Mozart and Vienna* (New York, 1991), 140.
15. Michael Kelly, *Reminiscences*, ed. R. Fiske (London, 1975), 102.
16. Landon, *Mozart and Vienna*, 141.
17. *The Autobiography of Karl von Dittersdorf*, trans. A. D. Coleridge (London, 1896), 154–5.
18. Giacomo Casanova, *History of My Life*, trans. Willard R. Trask, vol. 4 (London, 1967), 80–91.
19. Wangermann, *The Austrian Achievement, 1700–1800* (London, 1973), 52–3.
20. Kurt Honolka, *Papageno: Emanuel Schikaneder, Man of the Theater in Mozart's Time*, trans. Jane Mary Wild (Portland, 1990), 21.
21. See Eric A. Blackall, *The Emergence of German as a Literary Language* (Cambridge, 1959), 153–60, 171–7 and 181–7. This will be discussed further in chapter 2.
22. Robert A. Kann, *A Study in Austrian Intellectual History* (New York, 1960), 211.
23. *Ibid.*, 218.
24. *Ibid.*, 213.
25. Paul P. Bernard, *Joseph II* (New York, 1968), 125–6.
26. Kann, *A Study in Austrian Intellectual History*, 224.
27. See Peter Branscombe, *W. A. Mozart: Die Zauberflöte* (Cambridge, 1991), 43.
28. See Linda L. Carroll, 'Carnival Rites as Vehicles for Protest in Renaissance Venice', *The Sixteenth-Century Journal* 16 (1985): 490, as well as her *Language and Dialect in Ruzante and Goldoni* (Ravenna, 1981).
29. Tom Cheesman, 'Gluttony Artists: Carnival, Enlightenment and Consumerism in Germany on the Threshold of Modernity', *Deutsche Vierteljahrsschrift für Literaturwissenschaft und Geistesgeschichte* (Tübingen, 1992), 643.
30. Cheesman, 'Gluttony Artists', 659, in reference to Peter Stallybrass and Allon White, *The Politics of Transgression* (Ithaca, 1986), 2–6.
31. Cheesman, 'Gluttony Artists', 662.
32. Richard Sheppard, 'Upstairs-Downstairs – Some Reflections on German Literature in the Light of Bakhtin's Theory of Carnival', in *New*

Ways in Gemanistik, ed. Richard Sheppard (New York, 1990), 283.

33. Heinz Riedt, *Carlo Goldoni*, trans. Ursale Molinaro (New York, 1974), 32–3. Studies on Goldoni and Carnival include Franca Angelini, 'Le strutture del carnevale in Goldoni', in *L'interpretazione goldoniana Critica e Messinscena*, ed. Nino Borsellino (Rome, 1982), 68–78, and Jacques Joly, 'Le feste nelle commedie goldoniane di chiusura del carnevale', *Studi Goldoniani* 1 (1979): 28–61.

34. Molière, *The Imaginary Invalid*, in *The Misanthrope and Other Plays*, trans. John Wood (London, 1959), 280.

35. Edith Kern, *The Absolute Comic* (New York, 1980), 6–7. Another study of Molière and Carnival is Thérèse Malachy, *Molière: les métamorphoses du carnival* (Paris, 1987).

36. Larry W. Riggs, *Resistance to Culture in Molière, Laclos, Flaubert, and Camus: A Post-Modern Approach* (Lewiston, 1992), 68.

37. Daniel Heartz has recognized the Carnival character in the dance numbers of *Don Giovanni* in his *Mozart's Operas*, edited, with contributing essays, by Thomas Bauman (Berkeley, 1990), 179–80, while Nicholas Till acknowledges it in a more general way in *Mozart and the Enlightenment* (London, 1992), 203 and 227.

38. See Edith Kern, *The Absolute Comic*, 199.

39. Lawrence Lipkin, 'Donna Abbandonata', in *Don Giovanni: Myths of Seduction and Betrayal*, ed. Jonathan Miller (New York, 1990), 46.

Chapter 2. Leopold Mozart and the Republic of Letters

1. Quoted in Erich Schenk, *Mozart and His Times*, trans. Richard and Clara Winston (London, 1960), 12.

2. For descriptions of these, see Magnus Sattler, *Collectaneen-Blätter zur Geschichte der ehemaligen Benedictiner-Universität Salzburg* (Kempten, 1889), 304–30.

3. Virgil Redlich, 'Die Salzburger Benediktiner-Universität als Kulturerscheinung', in *Benediktinisches Mönchtum in Österreich*, ed. Hildebert Tausch (Vienna, 1949), 95.

4. Lawrence Marsden Price, *The Reception of English Literature in Germany* (Berkeley, 1932), 96.

5. Dena Goodman, *The Republic of Letters: A Cultural History of the French Enlightenment* (Ithaca, 1994), 8.

6. Leopold Mozart, *A Treatise on the Fundamental Principles of Violin Playing*, 2nd ed., trans. Editha Knocker (Oxford, 1985), p. xxv.

7. Albi Rosenthal, 'Leopold Mozart's *Violinschule* Annotated by the Author', in *Mozart Studies*, ed. Cliff Eisen (Oxford, 1991), 85.

8. Mozart, *A Treatise*, p. xxviii.

9. Eric A. Blackall, *The Emergence of German as a Literary Language, 1700–1775* (Cambridge, 1959), 88–9.

10. *Ibid.*, 171.

11. *Ibid.*, 486.

12. Mozart, *A Treatise*, 7.

13. Howard Serwer, 'Leopold Mozart', in *New Grove Dictionary of Music and Musicians*.

14. Quoted in Hans Lenneberg, 'Johann Mattheson on Affect and Rhetoric in Music', *Journal of Music Theory* 2 (1958): 51.

15. See Josef Mančal, 'Zum Verhältnis Leopold Mozart zu Wolfgang "Amadé" Mozart', *Zeitschrift des Historischen Vereins für Schwaben* 84 (1991): 208–26.

16. Mozart, *A Treatise*, 7–8.

17. Blackall, 140, 202.

18. Quoted in Mozart, *A Treatise*, p. xxix.

19. *C. F. Gellerts Briefwechsel*, ed. John F. Reynolds, vol. 1 (Berlin, 1983), 194–5.

20. Blackall, 201–2.

21. Adolf von Knigge, *Über den Umgang mit Menschen*, trans. P. Will as *Practical Philosophy of Social Life*, vol. 1 (London, 1799), 24.

22. Blackall, 206.

23. Quoted in Robert Spaethling, 'Christian Fürchtegott Gellert', in *Dictionary*

of Literary Biography, vol. 97: German Writers from the Enlightenment to Sturm und Drang, 1720–1764 (Detroit, 1990), 45–6.

24. Géza Rech, The Salzburg Mozart Book, trans. Gail Schamberger (Salzburg, 1991), 36. See illustration 9.
25. Quoted in Arthur Wilson, Diderot (New York, 1972), 276.

Chapter 3. Leopold Mozart's Biography of His 'Miraculous' Son

1. H. C. Robbins Landon, Haydn: Chronicle and Works, vol. 4 (Bloomington, 1978), 256.
2. C. F. Gellerts Briefwechsel, ed. John F. Reynolds, vol. 1 (Berlin, 1983), pp. 194–5.
3. Quoted in Donald A. Stauffer, The Art of Biography in Eighteenth Century England (New York, 1941, 1970), 312.
4. Quoted ibid., 312.
5. See Lawrence Marsden Price, The Reception of English Literature in Germany (Berkeley, 1932).
6. Quoted in The Mozart Compendium, ed. H. C. Robbins Landon (New York, 1990), 166.
7. Georg Nikolaus von Nissen, Biographie W. A. Mozarts (Vienna, 1828), 61.
8. See the description of the shooting parties (Bölzlschiessen) in chapter 2, 56–7.
9. Quoted by William M. Sale, Jr, in the 'Introduction', Pamela (New York, 1958), p. vii.
10. 'Instructions from a Father to his Son', in The Life of Professor Gellert, trans. Mrs Douglas, vol. 1 (London, 1805), 5–6.
11. See Ruth Halliwell, The Mozart Family: Four Lives in a Social Context (Oxford, 1998), 233. Halliwell, though, disagrees strongly with Maynard Solomon's contention that Leopold cried poor in the 1777–9 correspondence to implant feelings of guilt in Wolfgang and strengthen his hold over him. Halliwell gives a much more thorough and accurate view of the Mozarts' finances than any previous biographer.

Chapter 4. The Road to Dissolution

1. Erich Schenk, Mozart and his Times, trans. Richard and Clara Winston (London, 1960), 214–15.
2. Adolf von Knigge, Über den Umgang mit Menschen, trans. P. Will as Practical Philosophy of Social Life, vol. 1 (London, 1799), 179–80.
3. Ibid., 185–91.
4. Ibid., 185.
5. W. D. Howarth, Molière: A Playwright and his Audience (Cambridge, 1982), 208.
6. W. G. Moore, Molière: A New Criticism (Oxford, 1964), 56, 95.
7. These translations appear in Molière, Don Juan, in The Miser and Other Plays, trans. John Wood (Harmondsworth, UK, 1962).
8. See Anthony Levi, Guide to French Literature: Beginnings to 1789, vol. 1 (Detroit, 1994), 335.
9. Eagle in a Gauze Cage: Louise d'Épinay Femme de Lettres (New York, 1993).
10. Ruth Plaut Weinreb, 'Madame d'Épinay's Contributions to the Correspondance Littéraire', Studies in Eighteenth-Century Culture 18 (1988): 389.
11. The Memoirs and Correspondence of Madame D'Épinay, vol. 3 (Paris, n.d.), 237.
12. Weinreb, Eagle in a Gauze Cage, 52.
13. Ibid., 53.
14. Quoted ibid., 136.
15. Ibid., 16.
16. Ibid., 105.
17. Ibid., 107–8.
18. Norman L. Torrey, 'Duplicity and Protective Lying', in Voltaire: A Collection of Critical Essays, ed. William F. Bottiglia (Englewood Cliffs, NJ, 1968), 18.
19. Ibid.
20. Quoted ibid., 20.
21. Quoted in Geoffrey Bremner, Order and Chance: The Patterns of Diderot's Thought (New York, 1983), 111.
22. Harold Nicolson, The Age of Reason (1700–1789) (London, 1960), 256.

23. Paraphrased in Theodore Besterman, *Voltaire* (New York, 1969), 89.
24. Besterman, *Voltaire*, 352–4.
25. Thomas M. Kavanagh, 'Language as Deception: Diderot's *Les Bijoux indiscrets*', *Diderot Studies* 23 (1988): 105.
26. *Ibid.*
27. Rosalina de la Carrera, *Success in Circuit Lies: Diderot's Communication Practice* (Stanford, 1991), 11–12.
28. *Ibid.*, 33.

Chapter 5. The Virtuosity of Deceit

1. See Eric Blackall, *The Emergence of German as a Literary Language* (Cambridge, 1959), 297, 478 and 505.
2. Samuel S. B. Taylor, 'Voltaire Letter-Writer', *Forum for Modern Language Studies* 21 (1985): 345.
3. D. N. Leeson and R. D. Levin, 'On the Authenticity of K. Anh. C 14.01 (297b), a Symphonia Concertante for Four Winds and Orchestra', *Mozart Jahrbuch* (1976–7): 70–96.
4. Neal Zaslaw, 'Mozart's Paris Symphonies', *The Musical Times* 119 (1978): 756.
5. Alan Tyson, 'Mozart's Truthfulness', *The Musical Times* 119 (1978): 938.
6. Wolfgang Plath, 'Beiträge zur Mozart-Autographie II: Schriftchronologie 1770–1780', *Mozart-Jahrbuch* (1976–7): 171.

Chapter 6. Scatology and the 'Bäsle' Letters

1. Quoted in Wolfgang Hildesheimer, *Mozart*, trans. Marion Faber (New York, 1983), 109.
2. Maynard Solomon, *Mozart: A Life* (New York, 1995), 171.
3. Mel Gordon, *Lazzi: The Comic Routines of the Commedia dell'Arte* (New York, 1983), 32–4.
4. Quoted in Tom Cheesman, 'Performing Omnivores in Germany *circa* 1700', in *Studies in the Commedia dell'Arte*, ed. David J. George and Christopher J. Gossip (Cardiff, 1993), 58.
5. Quoted in Alan Dundes, *Life is Like a Chicken Coop Ladder* (Detroit, 1989), 110.
6. Anne Leblans, 'Grimmelshausen and the Carnivalesque: The Polarization of Courtly and Popular Carnival in *Der abenteuerliche Simplicissimus*', *Modern Language Notes* 105 (1990): 500.
7. See Johannes Müller, *Schwert und Scheide: Der sexuelle und skatologische Wortschatz im Nürnberger Fastnachtspiel des 15. Jahrhunderts* (Bern, 1988).
8. Hans Sachs, *Nine Carnival Plays*, trans. Randall W. Listerman (Ottawa, 1990), 91–4.
9. *Gallant and Libertine: Eighteenth-Century French Divertissements and Parades*, trans. Daniel Gerould (New York, 1983), 22–3, 104.
10. Robert Darnton, *The Literary Underground of the Old Regime* (Cambridge, MA, 1982), 36.
11. *Goethe's Plays*, trans. Charles E. Passage (New York, 1980), 394–5.
12. Quoted in Dundes, *Life is Like a Chicken Coop Ladder*, 74–5.
13. Dundes, 44.
14. *Ibid.*, 44–6.
15. Dundes notes this parallel, p. 66, and devotes a number of pages to Mozart's scatology (65–72, 77 and 105–6), stating, 'Indeed, I believe, his indulgence in fecal imagery may be virtually unmatched', p. 65. Dundes's thesis that preoccupation with faeces is a German character trait has not been without controversy.
16. Hildesheimer, *Mozart*, 73.
17. These include Hildesheimer, 105–24, Solomon, 161–6, Dundes, 65–72, and Joseph Heinz Eibl, 'Zur Überlieferungsgeschichte der Bäsle-Briefe', *Mitteilungen der Internationalen Stiftung Mozarteum* 27 (1979): 9–17.
18. Mikhail Bakhtin, *Rabelais and His World*, trans. Hélène Iswolsky (Bloomington, 1984), 6–7.
19. Emily Anderson, *The Letters of Mozart and His Family*, 3rd ed. (London, 1985), 358.

20. Marion Faber's translation, in Hildesheimer, 107.

21. Hildesheimer, 107.

22. Michael Ochs, '"L.m.i.a." Mozart's Suppressed Canon Texts', *Mozart-Jahrbuch* (1991): 254.

23. *Ibid.*, 259–60. Translation by Ochs.

24. Sigmund Freud, 'Character and Anal Erotism', in *Collected Papers*, vol. 2 (London, 1924), 45–50.

Chapter 7. Operatic Epistles

1. Mozart did not give a name to this incomplete work. The publisher Johann Anton André bought the manuscript from Mozart's widow and published it in 1838 as *Zaide*, naming it after the principal female character. See Carolyn Gianturco, *Mozart's Early Operas* (London, 1981), 201–2.

2. Quoted in Theodore Besterman, *Voltaire* (New York, 1969), 218.

3. Quoted *ibid.*, 352.

4. According to Alfred Einstein in *Mozart: His Character, His Work*, trans. Arthur Mendel and Nathan Broder (New York, 1945), 453, the source was Franz Joseph Sebastiani's lightweight Singspiel *Das Serail, oder: Die unvermutete Zusammenkunft in der Sclaverei zwischen Vater, Tochter und Sohn* (*The Seraglio, or: The unexpected Encounter in Slavery of Father, Daughter, and Son*), set to music by Joseph von Friebert.

5. Gianturco, *Mozart's Early Operas*, 200.

6. Nicolas Till, in *Mozart and the Enlightenment* (London, 1992), 58, argues that Gomatz was an anagram for Mozart's own name and that this character was Mozart. While Mozart could no doubt identify with Gomatz's bondage, this character is hardly of the stuff that would yield an autobiographical representation.

7. I discuss this in my *Haydn and the Enlightenment* (Oxford, 1990), 158–60.

8. Ivan Nagel, *Autonomy and Mercy: Reflections on Mozart's Operas*, trans. Marion Faber and Ivan Nagel (Cambridge, MA, 1991), 3.

9. Daniel Heartz, 'Mozart, his father and "Idomeneo"', *Musical Times* 119 (1978): 228.

10. Till, *Mozart and the Enlightenment*, 60–82.

11. *Ibid.*, 64.

12. Quoted in Besterman, *Voltaire*, 89.

13. Vincent and Mary Novello, *A Mozart Pilgrimage*, ed. Rosemary Hughes (London, 1955), 115.

14. See Heartz, 'Mozart, his father and "Idomeneo"', 231.

15. Quoted in Julian Rushton, *W. A. Mozart: Idomeneo* (Cambridge, 1993), 4.

16. Gretchen A. Wheelock, '*Schwarze Gredel* and the Engendered Minor Mode in Mozart's Operas', in *Musicology and Difference: Gender and Sexuality in Music Scholarship*, ed. Ruth A. Solie (Berkeley, 1993), 217.

17. Thomas Bauman has useful views on this in 'Coming of Age in Vienna: *Die Entführung aus dem Serail*', in Daniel Heartz, *Mozart's Operas*, edited, with contributing essay, by Thomas Bauman (Berkeley, 1990), 70.

18. Thomas Bauman quotes Goethe's opinion in *W. A. Mozart: Die Entführung aus dem Serail* (Cambridge, 1987), 107.

19. Quoted in Bauman, *W. A. Mozart: Die Entführung*, 106. Bauman argues convincingly that the document is spurious.

20. The translation here, as elsewhere in this chapter, borrows from *The Great Operas of Mozart*, trans. W. H. Auden, Chester Kallman, Ruth and Thomas Martin, and John Bloch (New York, 1964).

21. Nagel, *Autonomy and Mercy*, 149.

22. Einstein, *Mozart*, 427.

23. Georg Knepler, *Wolfgang Amadé Mozart*, trans. J. Bradford Robinson (Cambridge, 1994), 110–11.

24. Frédéric Grendel, *Beaumarchais*, trans. Roger Greaves (New York, 1977), 207–10.

25. Beaumarchais, *The Barber of Seville, The Marriage of Figaro, The Guilty Mother*, trans. Graham Anderson (Bristol, 1993), 253.

26. Ralph A. Nablow, 'Beaumarchais, Figaro's Monologue, and Voltaire's *Pauvre Diable*', *Romantic Notes* 28 (1987): 109–14.

27. W. D. Howarth, 'The Theme of the "Droit du Seigneur" in the Eighteenth-Century Theatre', *French Studies* 15 (1961): 230–1.

28. Heartz, *Mozart's Operas*, 108.

29. Howarth, 'The Theme of the "Droit du Seigneur"', 229–30.

30. Wye Jamison Allanbrook, *Rhythmic Gesture in Mozart: Le nozze di Figaro and Don Giovanni* (Chicago, 1983), 74.

31. See Walter E. Rex, 'Figaro's Games', *Publications of the Modern Language Association* 89 (1974): 524–9.

32. Tim Carter recognizes her special treatment by Mozart in *W. A. Mozart: Le nozze di Figaro* (Cambridge, 1987), 45–6.

33. Peter Gay for one follows this scenario in 'The Father's Revenge', in *Don Giovanni: Myths of Seduction and Betrayal*, ed. Jonathan Miller (New York, 1990), 70–80.

Chapter 8. Mozart as Harlequin

1. J. F. Marmontel, quoted in Allardyce Nicoll, *The World of Harlequin: A Critical Study of the Commedia dell'arte* (Cambridge, 1963), 73–4.

2. Quoted in Kurt Honolka, *Papageno: Emanuel Schikaneder, Man of the Theater in Mozart's Time*, trans. Jane Mary Wilde (Portland, OR, 1984), 39.

3. *Mozart on the Way to Prague*, trans. Walter and Catherine Alison Phillips (New York, 1947), 24.

4. Larry Wolff's unpublished paper 'Mozart's Eastern Europe: Bohemians, Albanians, Wallachians, and Turks',
read at the Mozart Symposium held at the University of Nevada, Las Vegas, on 30 November 1991, suggested this possibility.

5. When Constanze's second husband Georg Nissen inked over names in the original letters, he substituted 'N.N.' above or beside them, suggesting any one of *nomen nescio, nomen nominandum*, or *non nominato*. Not wishing the person to be identifiable, by this he implies 'Mr X'. See John Arthur's 'N.N. Revisited', *The Musical Times* 136 (1995): 475.

6. Each series of dots represents a word which has been blotted out in the autograph. Solomon speculates that these intimacies were intended to reassure Constanze of his affection for her in the light of indiscretions he may have been committing while on the Berlin sojourn as well as before leaving. She would have had good reason to doubt him. See *Mozart: A Life*, 446–50.

7. Mark Evan Bonds, 'The Sincerest Form of Flattery? Mozart's "Haydn" Quartets and the Question of Influence', *Studi Musicali* 22 (1993): 368.

8. *Ibid.*, 378.

9. Marius Flothuis, 'A Close Reading of the Autograph of Mozart's Ten Late Quartets', in *The String Quartets of Haydn, Mozart and Beethoven: Studies of the Autograph Manuscripts*, ed. Christoph Wolff (Cambridge, MA, 1980), 154–60.

10. See David Schroeder, *Haydn and the Enlightenment* (Oxford, 1990), 83–8.

11. Julia Moore, 'Mozart in the Marketplace', *Journal of the Royal Musical Association*, 114, no. 1 (1989): 18. For the rumour itself, see Franz Xavier Niemetschek, *Lebensbeschreibung des k. k. Kapellmeisters Wolfgang Amadeus Mozart aus Originalquellen*, 2nd ed. (Prague, 1808), 57.

Index